THE SLAVES

THE SLAVES

SUSANNE EVERETT

G.P. PUTNAM'S SONS, NEW YORK

A BISON BOOK

G. P. Putnam's Sons
200 Madison Avenue
New York
N.Y. 10016
U.S.A.

Produced by
Bison Books Limited
4 Cromwell Place
London SW7

Published simultaneously in
Canada by:
Longman Canada Limited
Toronto

ISBN 399-12180-3

Library of Congress Catalog Card
Number 78-52985

Printed in Hong Kong

Editor:
John Man

Design:
Laurence Bradbury
Roy Williams

Picture research:
UK Karen Pearce
Sue Goldblatt
US Jane Sugden

Editorial co-ordinator:
Fleur Walsh

THE SLAVES

CONTENTS

INTRODUCTION

by PROFESSOR ROGER ANSTEY,
Professor of Modern History, University of Kent, Canterbury, author of *The Atlantic Slave Trade and British Abolition, 1760–1810.*

A decade ago one would almost have apologized for a book on slavery. For blacks it would have revived memories of their humiliation; for whites it would have brought a recollection of veiled or acknowledged sin. In recent years, however, interest in the subject has revived at all levels, and this is surely right, for slavery is a major phenomenon of human history. It has underpinned major civilizations; and, in its most recent manifestations, it swept up millions of individuals in a massive transfer of population that established the political, social and economic realities of much of the New World. In the shanty towns of Rio and in New York's Harlem, the legacy of slavery endures, and relations between developed and developing nations are permeated by the historic imbalance of white and black, masters and slaves.

The Ancient World, as *The Slaves* begins by demonstrating, mostly accepted slavery. Although there were exceptions, such as the Stoics, the essential 'text' was Aristotle's: 'From the hour of their birth, some are marked out for subjection, others for rule.' Medieval Christendom was influenced both by the classical tradition in which Aristotle featured prominently and also by St Paul's acceptance of the institution of slavery in the Epistle to Philemon. Yet that same epistle, by its accompanying request to Philemon, the owner of the slave Onesimus, to liberate him or at least treat him kindly revealed an incipient anti-slavery message in early Christianity. The compromise of the medieval Church was in effect to accept the institution but to urge good treatment of slaves and, on occasion, the liberation of captives, especially those of one's own skin color.

There has been considerable debate on the relationship between slavery and serfdom in medieval Europe, a debate upon which we cannot enter here. Quite unambiguous, however, was the slavery which existed in parts of the Mediterranean basin in the Middle Ages and which was principally fed by the Islamic merchants' trade route across the Sahara from the interior of West Africa. Although the slaves traversing this desert route probably never numbered more than 10,000 a year, and may usually have been many less, such a figure indicates the significance of the institution of medieval slavery.

At the end of the medieval period of European history in the late 15th century, Europe therefore was accustomed to enslavement, especially of blacks and Moors. At this time Europe – and it is significant that Portugal and Spain, who were in the van, had a small population of dark-skinned slaves – began their expansion into Africa, Asia and the Americas. Within a very short time, the decimation of the indigenous peoples of the New World, mainly through European-borne diseases to which they had no immunity, led to a labor crisis in the mines and plantations developed by the Europeans.

The fatal connection – the importation of Africans as slave labor – was soon made, and although the plantation economies of the New World did not demand really large importations of Africans until the mid-17th century, the Atlantic slave trade had begun. Until recently, the volume of this trade had been the subject of what was little more than a guess, but Professor Philip D Curtin's recent pioneering work, as modified by the upward pointing amendments of other historians, suggests a total of between 8,000,000 and 11,500,000 slaves imported over three and a half centuries. Additionally, between 10 percent and 20 percent of those exported died between embarkation and landing, and a large number in the so-called 'seasoning' period, the first year after arrival. One cannot quantify the number who died as a consequence of the internal African wars which were one source of the slaves.

The slave trade had implications for Africa and the Americas (and, less so, for Europe). Africa had known slavery and slave trading before the coming of the Europeans, but the scale and finality of an export trade across the Atlantic was something new. The individual suffering the traffic caused is not quantifiable, though it can be hauntingly sensed through the record of slaves like Equiano (see pp. 56–57); but it is clear that many African states powerful enough to become middlemen or suppliers in the new trade grew in strength and that weaker societies suffered severely by it. Backward population projections, related to the convincing estimates of volume of slave exports which we have, suggest that, in the two main slave supply areas, West Africa and West Central Africa, the trade did no more than prevent a population growth in the former, but had severe demographic effects in the latter.

For the Americas, and especially Brazil, the Southern United States and the West Indies, the trade made possible plantation economies which for periods, at least, produced considerable wealth, though not necessarily for the planters themselves. All the political, social and psychological effects of slave society necessarily followed. To take the last alone, the whites, though apparently supreme, were in practice vulnerable, having to make innumerable compromises to straddle the illogicality of regarding fellow-men both as humans and as mere beasts of burden. The slave meanwhile aspired to the power, prestige, wealth and many of the values and religious beliefs of the white man and yet hated his status and the society which enslaved him. Interestingly, one dimension of a paradoxical relationship between slave and master in the Southern states, as Professor Genovese emphasizes in *Roll, Jordan, Roll*, was that the slave appropriated the white man's mainly Evangelistical Christianity. But while Southern whites had killed the early resolve of the Methodists and Baptists to prohibit slavery to their members, a modified Evangelical piety both gave strength to the slave to bear his enslavement and was an ingredient of his emerging self-consciousness and yearning for emancipation.

Emancipation came at different times, the essential beginning being in 1833 in the British West Indian slave emancipation and the conclusion with the final liberation of the Cuban slaves in 1886 and Brazilian slaves in 1888. United States emancipation came of course in the measures of 1863 and 1865. In every case, however, the ending by the several nations of their slave carrying trade preceded emancipation measures, and the anti-slavery movements have to be considered as a whole. The various natural divisions of that movement constitute a fascinating study in motivation. Probably it is correct to say that explanations straightforwardly stressing humanitarianism or economic forces are at a discount. Interpretation may still stress the one or the other as the dynamic factor, but in the context of a complex political and cultural background. Certainly the whole subject of the slave trade and slavery, of abolition and emancipation has attracted much more than its fair share of distinguished and highly readable scholarship over the last decade.

It is perhaps surprising that there have been few studies of the field for the general reader, and fewer still that draw on the wealth of available illustrations, as this book does. Some will wish to use it to broaden their knowledge of slavery and its rise and fall because of an interest in residual slavery or systems of para-slavery in the present-day world. Others may wish to explore their cultural inheritance and perhaps, from opposite perspectives, to conquer shame. Others may wish to study the slave trade and slavery simply as economic phenomena – yet they would do well to reflect on the sombre truth that so horrendous an institution could be regarded as morally acceptable by most people for a very long time. Still others may be fascinated by the process of abolition because of the interplay of the political, economic and (in my view usually the most significant) religious forces. Whatever the angle of interest, *The Slaves* is an excellent introduction, whilst at the same time it is a helpful synthesis written at a time when few have been courageous enough to attempt such an overall view.

CHAPTER I

THE ROOTS OF EVIL

SLAVERY IN THE ANCIENT WORLD

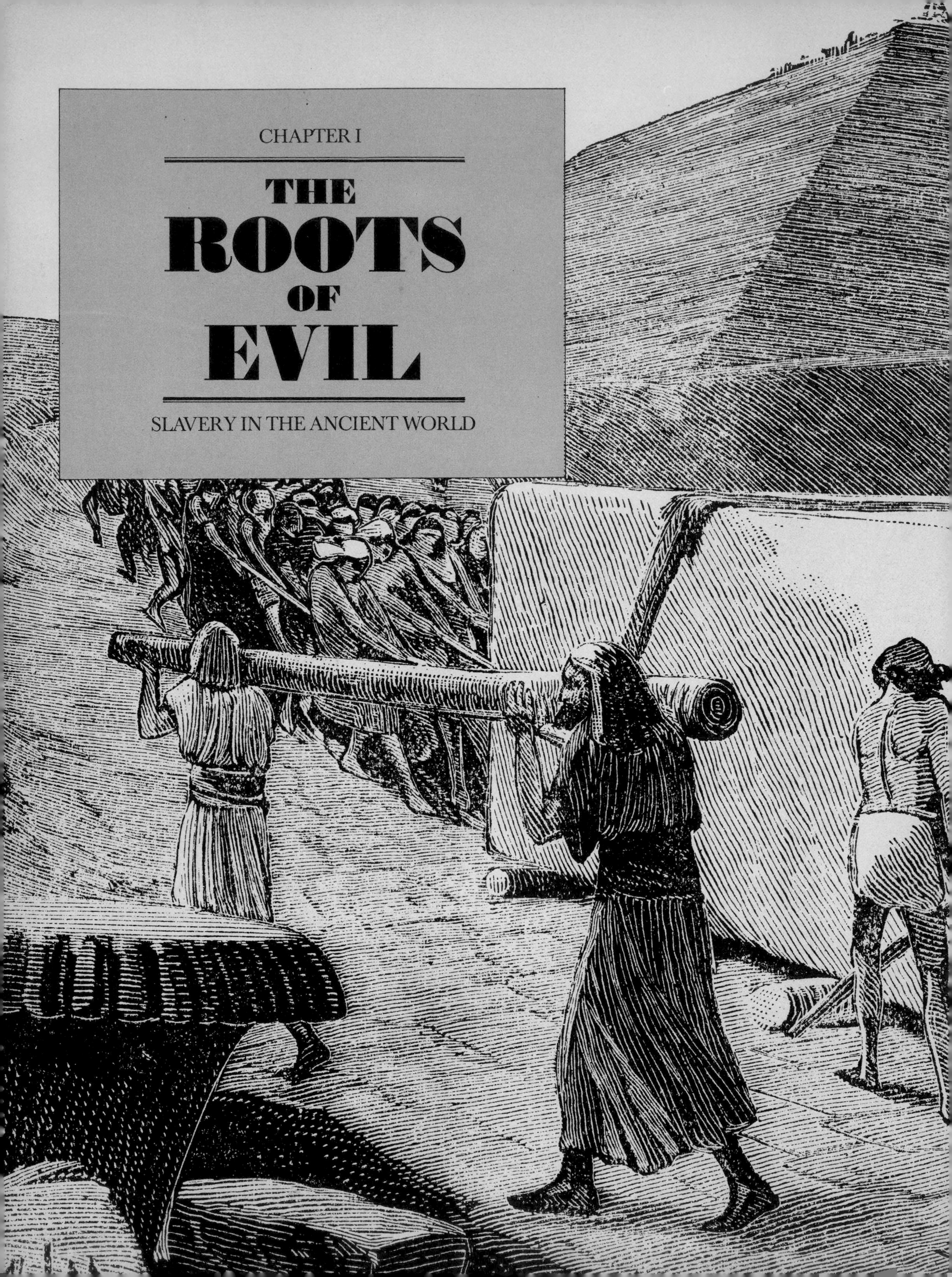

Building a pyramid in Ancient Egypt: though the pyramids were probably built by forced labor, the workers were, for most of the time, peasant farmers on whose products the economy of the country depended.

Slaves underpinned scores of cultures in the Ancient World – in Mesopotamia, Egypt, Greece, Rome, North Africa and south of the Sahara. The Bible records two prime examples: the Egyptian Pharaoh Seti I enslaved the Hebrews to achieve his grandiose dreams of bigger and better cities; and Solomon realized his vision of industrial expansion by forcing the Canaanites, Moabites, Edomites and Ammonites to construct foundries and smelteries at Ezion-geber on the edge of the Red Sea. But the dependence of all these societies on slavery varied greatly.

In both Mesopotamia and Egypt, civilization developed along fertile river valleys. But Mesopotamia, divided into waring city-states, was mainly an urban civilization, while Egypt, clinging as it did to the banks of the Nile and protected from attack by flanking deserts, remained an essentially rural and static society. Such dissimilarities led to differences in political and social organization.

A Saxon version of the building of the Tower of Babel: the Biblical legend, according to which the Lord confused the builders' tongues for their presumption in challenging Heaven, may have been based on fact – the Babylonians built a number of huge staged temples known as ziggurats, probably using slave labor to do so.

From the arrival of the Sumerians in the Tigris-Euphrates valley in about 3500 BC to the fall of Babylon under Nabodinas (successor to Nebuchadnezzar) in 539 BC, the city-states of Mesopotamia used slave labor. Slaves, at the time of the great Babylonian King Hammurabi, about 1800 BC, were divided into two grades: native and foreign, the native slaves having more often than not lost their freedom through crime or indebtedness, the foreign ones being prisoners of war or destitutes, often from no further afield than a neighboring city. All worked for the temple or the palace – the two dominant institutions of the city – and, in a few cases, for the richer citizens. All were the property of their masters, without full human status and could be sold, as Jacquetta Hawkes wrote, 'for the price of a good donkey.' Their heads were shaved, they were shackled and their flesh branded with their master's mark. However, for a native-born slave, enslavement for debt was only temporary – one of Hammurabi's laws stated that 'three years shall they work in the house of their buyer and in the fourth year he shall fix their liberty.' (Possibly this indicated a reluctance to submit a fellow countryman to bondage – it compares with the Hebrew law in Exodus 21: 'If thou buy a Hebrew servant, six years shall he serve: and in the seventh he shall go out free for nothing.')

In Egypt, it was not until the New Kingdom (c 1550–c 1175 BC) – over 1500 years after the emergence of Egyptian civilization – that slavery was established. Even then, it appeared only on a minor scale. Foreign slaves, brought back after successful campaigns, were forced to put their skills as weavers, tailors and cooks to good use in the Palace of the Pharaoh, or in the houses of the great. Many worked for the temple estates, living under terrible conditions. But on the whole the Egyptian slave led a life little different from that of the serf. Although technically a human chattel, it is thought he had some legal rights and, during the Late Period (1000–300 BC), there were slaves who rose to high office in the service of the king. Slaves never became an important ingredient of Egyptian civilization. The large subject population and enforceable *corvée* system – by which serfs had to work temporarily as slaves – made a permanent force of slaves unnecessary. Egypt could, as

Under the threat of an overseer's lash, Babylonian slaves – some native-born debtors, others prisoners-of-war – toil to build a ziggurat.

Jacquetta Hawkes said, 'have been created and maintained without them.'

Slavery remained an accepted institution in the many kingdoms that rose and fell in the Middle East in the 1st millennium BC. From the beginning, it was part of Greek civilization, perhaps the greatest of all the ancient cultures. In Homer's *Odyssey*, the swineherd, Eumaeus, tells of his childhood capture by Phoenician sailors, 'greedy rogues, with a whole cargo of gew-gaws in their black ship.' His nurse, herself a Phoenician, offered him in exchange for her passage home. 'His price,' she promised them, 'would be I know not what in sale abroad.' He was, he relates, bought by Laertes, Odysseus's father. Odysseus too, in one of his disguises, mentioned a 'rascally Phoenician, a thieving knave,' from whom he narrowly escaped being sold into slavery. But, if the evidence supplied by the *Odyssey* and the *Iliad* is anything to go by, the institution was a comparatively mild one. Odysseus himself said Eumaeus had had a good life – 'you had the luck to come into a kind man's service.'

It has been suggested that women slaves, employed in domestic work or household manufacture, were 'in a more pitiable condition' than their male counterparts but, unless they were turning the hand mills which ground the household flour, this was probably not altogether true. Certainly

A Grisly Fate for Faithless Slaves

Slaves in Ancient Greece were often loved members of a family, and the master-slave relationship seems to have been one of mutual dependence and trust. But they were none the less the absolute chattels of their masters, as this extract from *The Odyssey* testifies. Odysseus has returned home after 20 years of wandering and with his son, Telemachus, slain the local nobles who, seeking the hand of his wife Penelope, had taken up permanent residence in his palace. This extract describes the fate of those slave-girls who had betrayed Odysseus's trust by allowing themselves to be seduced by the suitors. Eurycleia is Odysseus's old nurse, a slave herself, but one who has kept faith.

'Said the great soldier then: "Rejoice
inwardly. No crowing aloud, old woman . . .
Your part is now to tell me of the women,
those who dishonored me, and the innocent."
His own old nurse Eurycleia said:
"I will, then.
Child, you know you'll have the truth from me.
Fifty all told they are, your female slaves,
trained by your lady and myself in service,
wool carding and the rest of it, and taught
to be submissive. Twelve went bad,
flouting me, flouting Penelope, too.
Telemachus being barely grown, his mother
would never let him rule the serving women –
but you must let me go to her lighted rooms
and tell her. Some god sent her a drift of sleep."
But in reply the great tactician said:
"Not yet. Do not awake her. Tell those women
who were the suitors' harlots to come here."
She went back on this mission through his hall.
Then he called Telemachus to his side
and the two herdsmen. Sharply Odysseus said:
"These dead must be disposed of first of all.
Direct the women. Tables and chairs will be
scrubbed with sponges, rinsed and rinsed again.
When our great room is fresh and put in order,
take them outside, these women,
between the roundhouse and the palisade,
and hack them with your swordblades till you cut
the life out of them, and every thought of sweet
Aphrodite under the rutting suitors,
when they lay down in secret."
As he spoke
here came the women in a bunch, all wailing
soft tears on their cheeks. They fell to work
to lug the corpses out into the courtyard
under the gateway, propping one
against another as Odysseus ordered,
for he himself stood over them. In fear
these women bore the cold weight of the dead.
The next thing was to scrub off chairs and tables
and rinse them down. Telemachus and the herdsman
scraped the packed earth floor with hoes, but made
the women carry out all blood and mire.
When the great room was cleaned up once again,
at swordpoint they forced them out, between
the roundhouse and the palisade, pell-mell
to huddle in that dead end without exit.
Telemachus, who knew his mind, said curtly:
"I would not give the clean death of a beast
to trulls who made a mockery of my mother
and of me too – you sluts, who lay with suitors."
He tied one end of a hawser to a pillar
and passed the other about the roundhouse top,
taking the slack up, so that no one's toes
could touch the ground. They would be hung like doves
or larks in springes triggered in a thicket,
where the birds think to rest – a cruel nesting.
So now in turn each woman thrust her head
into a noose and swung, yanked high in air,
to perish there most piteously.
Their feet danced for a little, but not long.'

Slave girls in a Babylonian market: an auctioneer proclaims the virtue of his wares and a scribe notes down the prices. The girls would have become the property of their owners but would also have had an established place in society, with their rights and those of their children established by law.

Eurycleia, Odysseus's old nurse (for whom his father, Laertes, had given 20 oxen) spoke to him in terms which would have been familiar to any Victorian nanny: 'Nurse,' says Odysseus, when finally recognized by the old woman on his return to his palace, 'do you wish to ruin me, you who reared me at your own breast?'

'My child,' replies Eurycleia sharply, 'no need to talk like that to me.'

Later comes a dramatic reminder of the dependent status of slaves – the 12 women who had 'taken to vicious ways' in Odysseus's absence are personally hanged by his son, Telemachus.

Not that slaves were singled out for callous treatment. Any servant, whether free or slave, could be treated harshly. The goatherd, Melanthius, who supplied the perfidious suitors with weapons and armor from Odysseus's storeroom, had his ears, nose, hands, feet and 'privy parts' cut off as a punishment. This example, although highly-colored, indicates that distinctions between freemen and slaves were, in Homeric times, blurred. As Professor Anthony Andrews points out, 'The gulf between princes and the rest is far deeper than any gulf between the different classes that serve them.'

From the 8th century onwards, further Greek colonization in and around the Mediterranean, the introduction of coined money as a means of exchange and the growth of the handicraft industry contributed to the increased demand for slave labor. Although a slave's condition was still as variable as his master's nature and position, the gap between slave and freeman widened and they became a class apart. The reasons for falling into the state of slavery remained constant. They included being an insolvent debtor, the sale of children by their free parents (except in Attica), hereditary slavery, kidnapping and piracy. Slave-dealing became an established practice – the main sources of supply being Syria, Pontus, Lydia, Galatia and Thrace (the latter supplying large numbers of children for slave export). The principal slave markets were those of Chias, Samos, Ephesus, Cyprus and Athens, at which Greeks were greatly sought after for foreign sale and Asiatics much prized by Greek buyers as 'being most amenable to command.' Public slave sales were conducted in the *agora* (market place) and Athenian law demanded 'that any concealed sickness such as epilepsy be declared beforehand by the vendor, with right of prosecution if such a sickness should later appear.'

Slavery was not only an established element in Greek society, but was accepted as vital for the preservation of freedom as the Greeks saw it. Aristotle described liberty as the 'first principle of democracy.' Democracy for the Greeks meant direct participation by every citizen in all the functions of civil and military life. But then the Greeks' conceptions of liberty, democracy and citizenship were in no way equivalent to modern ones. Their outlook was wholly aristocratic. To

Spartacus: Freedom Fighter Extraordinary

Spartacus is the only Ancient World slave to become a modern hero. His revolt of 73–71 BC has been the subject of two novels and an epic movie. Although never a real threat to the Roman Empire, he has been adopted as a cult hero by many revolutionaries, most notably the German Communists, the Spartacists, crushed in 1919. In the following extract, from Plutarch's account of the revolt, Spartacus appears as a brilliant and inspiring leader.

'A certain Lentulus Batiatus had a school of gladiators at Capua, most of whom were Gauls and Thracians. Through no misconduct of theirs, but owing to the injustice of their owner, they were kept in close confinement and reserved for gladiatorial combats. Two hundred of these planned to make their escape, and when information was laid against them, those who got wind of it and succeeded in getting away, 78 in number, seized cleavers and spits from some kitchen and sallied out. On the road they fell in with wagons conveying gladiators' weapons to another city; these they plundered and armed themselves. Then they took up a strong position and elected three leaders. The first of these was Spartacus, a Thracian of Nomadic stock, possessed not only of great courage and strength, but also in sagacity and culture superior to his fortune. . . .

To begin with, the gladiators repulsed the soldiers who came against them from Capua, and getting hold of many arms of real warfare, they gladly took these in exchange for their own, casting away their gladiatorial weapons as dishonorable and barbarous. Then Clodius the praetor was sent out from Rome against them with 3000 soldiers, and laid siege to them on a hill which had but one ascent, and that a narrow and difficult one, which Clodius closely watched; everywhere else there were smooth and precipitous cliffs. But the top of the hill was covered with a wild vine of abundant growth, from which the besieged cut off the serviceable branches, and wove these into strong ladders of such strength and length that when they fastened at the top they reached along the face of the cliff to the plain below. On these they descended safely. . . .

[Spartacus then fought his way northwards, intending to disperse his troops to their homes beyond the Alps. They refused to leave, and the army headed back to the tip of Italy, planning to cross over to Sicily. They failed to find ships, and Licinius Crassus moved against them.]

Spartacus retired to the mountains of Petelia, followed closely by Quintus, one of the officers of Crassus, and by Scrophas, the quaestor, who hung upon the enemy's rear. But when Spartacus faced about, there was a great rout of the Romans, and they barely managed to drag the quaestor, who had been wounded, away into safety. This success was the ruin of Spartacus, for it filled his slaves with over-confidence. They would no longer consent to avoid battle. . . . . Spartacus saw the necessity that was upon him and drew up his whole army in order of battle.

In the first place, when his horse was brought to him, he drew his sword, and saying that if he won the day he would have many fine horses of the enemy's but if he lost it he did not want any, he slew his horse. Then pushing his way towards Crassus himself through flying weapons and wounded men, he did not indeed reach him, but slew two centurions who fell upon him together. Finally after his companions had taken to flight, he stood alone, surrounded by a multitude of foes, and was still defending himself when he was cut down.'

[Later, in what was perhaps the most appalling atrocity in Roman history, 6000 slave prisoners were crucified by Licinius Crassus along Rome's Appian Way as a reprisal for the rebellion.]

The death of Spartacus: a 19th-century view.

allow the ruling class to devote itself exclusively to the performance of its public duties, it was essential to have, as Aristotle put it, 'members of the state . . . who are necessary as its servants, but no part of it.' In this category he listed 'mechanics, traders and husbandmen,' who had no political rights, and 'warriors, rulers and priests,' whom he regarded as eligible for full citizenship. (Plato, too, in his ideal state, saw every citizen as a landowner forbidden to engage in trade, and excluded the 'productive class' from all political rights.) Even lower down the scale, and separated from freemen by their exclusion from every social, as well as political, right, lay a section of the community upon which the continuance of a leisured class depended absolutely – the slaves.

Although the circumstances of individual slaves in Ancient Greece varied considerably and many, particularly those employed in princely households, enjoyed a life little different from any well-loved family dependent, the harsh fact remained that a master had almost complete control over a slave's life and limb. Aristotle, indeed, thought of a slave as 'a part of the master, a living but separated part of his bodily frame' and W W Buckland, the standard authority on slave law, concluded drily that, 'of the slave's civil position it may almost be said that he had none.'

It is an uncomfortable fact that the Greeks, from whom we derive so many of our intellectual and political ideals, were utterly dependent on slavery. The abolition of slavery in Greece would have disrupted the whole fabric of its society. From the 6th century BC in Athens and other Greek cities, slavery effectively replaced other forms of dependent labor. For the Greeks of the classical period (480–338 BC), it was unthinkable that society should be organized in any other way. Plato's *Republic* was firmly based on slave labor, although he drew the line, in war, at enslaving his fellow Greeks – he advised soldiers to 'keep their hands off one another and turn their energies against foreigners.'

Aristotle, like most Athenians of his age, believed that the state was the 'highest form of community' and aimed at 'the highest good.' In pursuit of the highest good it was necessary to have both rulers and the ruled – indeed, as he went on to explain, '. . . that some should rule and others be ruled is a thing, not only necessary, but expedient; from the hour of their birth, some are marked out for subjection, others for rule.' Those that were 'by nature slaves' and 'whose business is to use their body and who can do nothing better' should 'be under the rule of a master.' This severe categorization formed part of the classical Greek view of ideal society, which should balance the whole at the expense – if necessary – of some constituent parts. Equality between different classes was, therefore, unimportant.

Even Aristotle, however, came up against the unpalatable fact that not all slaves were fitted for their condition 'by nature'; in cases of slavery by capture in war he was bound to acknowledge that sometimes it was possible for the 'natural' master to become a slave and the 'natural' slave his master. But only a handful of Greek writers, notably the playwright Euripides and the comic poet Philemon, denied that slavery was preordained. 'No man,' wrote Philemon, 'was ever born a slave by nature. Fortune only has put men in that position.' On the whole, Greece, aristocratic, militant and directly organized for war, found it necessary to exaggerate rather than diminish distinctions between individuals in order to preserve the harmony of the state.

It is almost impossible to make an accurate assessment of the exact number of slaves in Greece in the classical period. Sources have been proved unreliable and interpretations by modern scholars tend to make of these sources what they will. Professor Andrews suggests that the slave population of Attica in the mid-5th century was about 80–100,000 or 'about one in four of the entire population' (Attica having, apart from Chios, the largest number of slaves of any other Greek city-state).

Many citizens owned no slaves at all. In one case, a cripple defending an action for the restitution of state dole claimed that he could not afford to keep a slave to help him in his work. There are many other cases, mostly records of inheritance, in which ownership of slaves is not mentioned.

Often, however, a man was dependent on his slaves for his wealth. Plato said that 50 or more slaves represented the possessions of a wealthy man. If so, the orator, Demosthenes, who inherited 53 slaves from his father, was prosperous and the metic (alien resident) Cephalus, who employed 120 slaves in the manufacture of shields, a rich man. Lower down the scale, an Athenian, Timarchus, inherited 12 slaves – including ten leather workers, a woman linen weaver and a leather embroiderer. Some citizens rented their slaves out. There is the description of a man journeying a considerable distance to collect the hiring money for a single slave. Another way of making income from slaves was to set up a slave in business, make him responsible for his keep, and to take a substantial share of the profits. Some owners did very well out of this arrangement – one Athenian slave, Pasion, managed a banking enterprise and was eventually given both his freedom and Athenian citizenship in recognition of his extraordinary abilities.

The Greeks divided their slaves into three categories: public, temple and private. Public slaves performed duties as diverse as exploiting the state-owned silver mines of Laurium, acting as clerks to various officials, assisting the police, performing service under street commissioners, guarding the prisons and carrying out executions.

Temple slaves cleaned the sacred building and, in Corinth, undertook to supply sacred prostitution – as Professor W L Westermann delicately put it: 'the thousand temple courtesans assigned to the Corinthian Aphrodite . . . may not be excessive and may be ascribed to the special position of Corinth as a harbor town, constantly visited by travelers and sailors.'

Privately, slaves were employed in domestic service, and in agricultural or urban work. In nearly every field (except in the household and down the mines), slaves worked side by side with freemen and in many cases – in smallholdings and small businesses, for instance – alongside their masters. The public accounts for the building of the temple on the Acropolis at the end of the 5th century BC included, of the 86 workmen whose status is known, 24 citizens, 12 metics and 20 slaves. The comparatively small-scale level at which the Greek economy operated ensured that slave labor never undercut the free – profit margins were seldom high enough and the slave remained a safe but rarely spectacular investment (even though he could be bought cheaply – often for no more than his upkeep for one year).

At the discretion of his master a slave could, occasionally, obtain his freedom. If he could find a capital sum, his owner was obliged, but by no means compelled, to manumit him. In Athens by the mid-4th century, it has been claimed that 50 per year were being released in this way. Also, under

Job: The First Abolitionist?

In the Near East for 2000 years before the birth of Christ, slavery was taken for granted. The hundreds of thousands of business documents from Babylonia, the mass of economic and legal data from the Old Testament provide overwhelming evidence that the institution of slavery was an unquestioned fact of everyday life. Slaves, used primarily in domestic service, were chattels who could be bought, sold, leased, exchanged, branded and tattooed. Legal documents record the sale of children and even of whole families. Debtors could even sell themselves into servitude.

The code of the great 18th century BC Babylonian King, Hammurabi, contained numerous clauses concerning the treatment and status of slaves, who were not considered as human beings before the law but as 'heads' as animals were. The Old Testament justifies the perpetual servitude of the Canaanites and although the Laws make it plain that a master could not kill his slave with impunity – thus recognizing the humanity of the slave – nowhere is there any indication that the institution of slavery itself is wrong.

Perhaps the only hint that there were even then men who considered slavery to be inhuman occurs in the book by the philosopher Job. Clearly speaking of domestic slavery, he recognizes the inherent brotherhood of man and thereby, by implication, condemns the inequality that separates master and slave:

'If I did despise the cause of my manservant or of my maidservant, when they contended with me; What then shall I do when God riseth up? and when he visiteth, what shall I answer him? Did not he that made me in the womb make him? and did not one fashion us in the womb?'

the Greek system of *paramone*, which was a form of indentured service, he could raise himself from slave status to that of a technically, but by no means wholly, free man.

However similar slaves and freemen seemed in practice, the two conditions differed radically under the law, which allowed an owner the freedom to punish his slave in any way he thought fit, short of actually killing him. A slave could seek asylum from intolerable cruelties in the temple, where he came under the arbitration of a priest, but if caught absconding he was liable to be branded. Sometimes, slaves were even obliged to undergo torture on their master's behalf, as in the case of a certain Andocides, accused of mutilating the busts of Hermes in Athens in 415 BC. He reported: 'I then handed over my slave to undergo examination under torture to prove the truth of my contention that I was ill and had not got up from my bed.' He was eventually cleared of the offense, but there is no word of what happened to his slave.

There was one form of service, however, for which a Greek slave was not eligible, except under the most exceptional circumstances – that of combat duty within either the army or the navy. Slaves were used as oarsmen during the Peloponnesian war, and the Athenians were reduced to calling them up as soldiers to fight against Alexander in the mid-4th century, but normally their role was purely a supportive one and they performed the same duties as in civilian life.

In neighboring Sparta, however, slaves served in the army alongside freemen. But

A reconstruction of a Roman slave market: a boy, a young man and five girls await sale with their histories and prices on labels round their necks.

these slaves (or helots), the original inhabitants of Laconia, had been conquered and ruthlessly suppressed by their elitist and militaristic masters, who subjected them to a particularly harsh system of collective bondage. Their notoriously brutal treatment masked constant fears of insurrection – Sparta's citizen population, heavily outnumbered by helots, dwindled from 8000 in the mid-5th century to under 1000 just over a hundred years' later.

By that time Alexander the Great was extending his authority throughout Greece and beyond, spreading Greek influence south into Egypt and east as far as the Oxus and the Punjab. After his death in 323 BC the dominion of Egypt came under the rule of Alexander's favorite general, Ptolemy. The subsequent influx of Greek administrative officials saw the reproduction throughout the country of the Greek household, within which domestic slaves played their customary roles.

By 146 BC, the Romans were the undisputed masters of the civilized world. With power came responsibilities, which included producing food for the occupying armies, rebuilding cities that had suffered at their hands and satisfying local landowners that they were not going to lose by the upheaval. All of these required instant, cheap labor,

Gregory's Captive 'Angels'

Before the 18th century suggestions that Christians should also be anti-slavers were rare. One man who did seem to be aware of this implication of the Christian message was Pope Gregory I (c540–604), who founded the mission to the Anglo-Saxons headed by St Augustine. This followed an incident – shown in two 19th century drawings below – once

and none came cheaper than slaves. As Professor Westermann put it: 'A great increase in the numbers of the slaves introduced into Italy and . . . Sicily must be ascribed to the capture of enemy troops and the looting of cities and towns in the Roman wars of expansion of the second century BC.'

Slavery now reached dimensions at which Homer would have stretched his eyes. On vast agricultural estates (*latifundia*), slaves worked in fields shackled together. In mines and quarries, men and women worked in grim conditions 'half naked . . . in chains, under the lash and guarded by soldiers.' But it was also under the Romans that a freedman could say, in the *Satyricon* of Petronius: 'thank heaven for slavery, it made me what you see me now,' and Pliny the Younger could write of his 'willingness to give them [his slaves] their freedom.' Between these opposite poles lay a tangled web of exploitation and repression.

The brutality with which slaves were treated on the *latifundia*, particularly in Sicily and Italy, combined with their large numbers (they outnumbered freemen by three to one between 222 and 146 BC), led to insurrections. One of the most serious occurred in Sicily in 135 BC, when 6000 slaves, starved, branded and 'insulted by unjustified beatings' rose against their exploiters. In 104–101, a second uprising required a

known to generations of schoolboys: One day in a Roman market, Gregory spotted some slave boys from Britain. Struck by their blond good looks, he asked where they came from. When told they were Angles, he punned: '*Non Angli sed Angeli*' ('Not Angles but Angels'). In fact the words paraphrase Bede's original – and less obvious – Anglo-Saxon, which translates: 'Again he asked what the people was called from which they came; they answered that they were called English. He said, 'That may well be; for their look is peerless, and also it is fit that they should be joint-heirs with the angels in heaven.'

Slaves in Roman mines: whether digging for coal (*as here*) or silver, the slaves in mines were subjected to the harshest conditions known in the ancient world. They were chained together and often worked to death.

Roman army of 17,000 to suppress it. But the most famous agitator of them all was the slave Spartacus, a Thracian by birth, who in 73 BC escaped from a training school for gladiators at Capua and, together with other fugitives, overcame two forces of the Roman army. Within two years his band of runaway slaves numbered 90,000 and controlled most of southern Italy. But, after successfully fighting their way to the Alps, his followers refused to march across the mountains and, during the retreat southwards Spartacus, his army divided, was killed and the revolt ended.

In all these uprisings, the price of insurgency was high. Owners, ever fearful of slave revolts, felt that they should be punished, as Livy put it, 'not solely in that spirit which we use toward other enemies.' To impose suitable degradation and pain, crucifixion became the form of death especially reserved for slaves. After Spartacus's uprising, 6000 rebels were crucified along the Appian Way.

Slaves lived under the continuous threat of such harsh treatment. Under Roman law, a slave came under the absolute power of his master – he could not possess property, enter into any form of contract with his owner, or establish a permanent relationship with a member of the opposite sex (cohabitation was to be tolerated or terminated at his master's whim). Entering military service was punishable by death, examination as a witness was always accompanied by torture and, if an owner died a violent death within his house, all his slaves could be put to death on the grounds that they could have prevented it. (In one case, after the murder of a certain Pedanius Secundus, 400 of his slaves were killed.)

Nevertheless, slaves were recognized as valuable investments and numerous manuals were drawn up specifying the best way to feed and equip them at the minimum of expense. Substantial rewards were offered for the return of runaways. Cato, writing about 170 BC, recognized the need for enough bread, wine, windfall olives, oil and salt to be distributed among the chain gangs who cultivated his estate, but he also said, 'issue them sparingly to make them last as long as possible.' On the subject of clothing he was similarly economical: 'A tunic three and a half feet long and a blanket-cloak every other year. When you issue a tunic or cloak, take in the old one to make rough clothes,' and he added, 'You ought to give them a good pair of clogs every other year.'

As in classical Greece, the Romans employed both public and private slaves – public slaves performing much the same duties as in Greece, except that road construction and other public works were carried out exclusively by slave labor. Privately owned slaves worked either in the country or in the town. In the country, if the estate was a large one, it was administered entirely by slaves, from the bailiff to the special group assigned to sit in judgment on their fellows and, if necessary, commit them to the slave prison (*ergastulum*).

In a large town, household slaves were, among other things, employed as domestic servants, physicians, librarians, accountants, dancers and singers. To cater for the demand for such educated slaves, the rich ran schools and the less well off paid for them to be apprenticed to an instructor. An enterprising and intelligent slave granted a *peculium* (set up in business) by his master could – as had been possible in Greece – make enough money to buy his freedom – and could acquire Roman citizenship (Greek freedmen could never achieve citizenship). So many slaves, in fact, achieved freedom in this way that in AD 3 the Emperor Augustus, fearful of the social instability it might cause, forbade all manumission by masters under 20 and of slaves under 30; and a second law passed four years later restricted the number of manumissions on any estate to 100.

Partly due to the growing influence of Christianity, conditions of slavery in the Roman Empire were made somewhat less harsh. Christian opinion, however, was by no means liberal; it favored resignation rather than abolition – St Paul, in his *Exhortation to the Ephesians,* wrote 'slaves, be obedient to the men who are called your masters in this world,' a sentiment which he repeated many times. The Emperor Hadrian abolished a master's right to life or death over his slave, and manumission was made easier. The Christian Emperor Justinian allowed slaves who were admitted to holy orders or who entered a monastery to become freemen, and he made the crime of rape against a slave-woman punishable by death.

Roman expansion ended by AD 14. Thereafter, for 400 years, emperor after emperor struggled to preserve stability despite internal dissent – in particular from the powerful army – and against the threat from the barbarian border tribes.

The end of expansion brought the beginnings of a slow, but significant change to the institution of slavery: for one thing, there were fewer new captives to act as slaves; for another, society became more static. In the late 3rd century, under Diocletian, who did much to resuscitate the dying empire, personal freedom was sacrificed to the good of the state and occupations and professions became hereditary (a system similar to the caste-structure of India). Men needed for their own support the jobs previously done by slaves. In addition, huge taxes were levied on landowners and manufacturers to pay for the support of the army. Slaves – even when available – became luxuries few could afford.

On the labor intensive agricultural estates, another form of servile labor arose – the order of *coloni*. The Roman *colonus* was a tied tenant, often bound to his master by debt through rent arrears, who gave his labor and a proportion of his produce in recompense. The condition was hereditary: a *colonus* was not allowed to leave his holding, and he could be chained and chastised if found attempting to escape. However, a *colonus* could, if able to afford it, own property and he had some legal redress against unjust demands or beatings from his master. Slaves still worked on the part of the estate cultivated by the owner, but were often allowed to manage, but not own, small farms, which they operated under much the same conditions as the *coloni*. Known as *quasi coloni,* these slaves intermarried with *coloni* and the two classes gradually became indistinguishable from one another.

When Rome finally collapsed in the face of the barbarians early in the 5th century, slavery in Europe declined. Although it revived occasionally, there were few equivalent opportunities for a dominant military power to seize and enslave defeated enemies. One revival of particular significance occurred in the 8th–10th centuries, when the Germans captured hordes of Slavs. The equation of nationality and status in Germanic languages gave us the very word 'slave.'

The next great revival in the institution of slavery resulted from the spread of Islam in Africa. By the middle of the 7th century the crusading followers of the Prophet Mahomet, who had 'submitted themselves to the will of Allah' were marching from Arabia to conquer Syria, Palestine and Egypt. From there they looked across the western desert to the fertile lands of Tunisia, Libya and Morocco. The Arab conquest of North Africa was, however, a long and tortuous affair, fiercely resisted at every step by the independent Berber tribesmen. Although the Berbers finally succumbed to the faith of Islam and, in fact, joined with the Arabs in the conquest of Spain during the 8th century, they never lost their separate identity.

The Berbers of the Tunisian plains and the coastal belt of Algeria and Morocco had already tapped the greatest future source of slaves: West Africa. Riding on camels and their large Barbary horses, the Berbers had traded ivory, feathers and skins with the Carthaginians, and supplied wild animals for the circuses of imperial Rome. They had driven their horsedrawn chariots southward beyond the Mauretanian steppe (as the rock drawings of the western Sahara testify) as far as ancient Ghana, in search of gold, salt and slaves.

Beyond the Sahara lay the vast savannah belt that the Arabs called the Sudan, or 'the country of the Black People,' stretching from the Atlantic to the Red Sea. By the 9th century, great merchant camel caravans were traveling from Tripoli and Ghadames to the oases of Fezzan and even further south, beyond Lake Chad into the kingdom of Kanem, carrying back black slaves for the households of the Arab palace city of Qairwan, on the Mediterranean. 'I have been informed,' wrote the Arab geographer, Al-Yaqubi, in the late 9th century, 'that the kings of the blacks sell their own people without justification or in consequence of war.'

The kingdom of Kanem grew from the desert peoples of the central Sahara and achieved stability in the 11th century under the Magumi prince Humai, the first of his line to become a Muslim (his successor, apparently, made the pilgrimage to Mecca three times). Of the pastoral people on the fringes of the Sahara, the Kawar and Tibesti supplied wives for the Magumi and (most important to the expansion of Kanem) the sedentary Sao, south of the savannah belt, provided the slaves, who were captured in annual raids by the Magumi cavalry. These unfortunates were destined for the palace of the ruler, the households of the Queen Mother and the Queen Sister, the courts of the princely military commanders, or the slave markets of North Africa, Egypt and the Middle East.

The need to find slaves to exchange for salt, swords, horses, books or chain mail – essential for the attraction of outside skilled labor – forced the frontiers of Kanem ever southward. By the 15th century, the center of the kingdom had shifted to Bornu, west of Lake Chad (in the northeast of modern Nigeria). It was still a slave-based society in the 19th century, its rural or domestic systems of slavery comparable to those of the Homeric world. Basil Davidson points to the three social groups 'beneath the noble families' in 19th-century Bornu – the Kambe 'freemen drawn from the ranks of free slaves'; the Kalia, 'slaves, whether foreigners or men and women captured in war'; and the Zuzanna, 'the descendants of slaves, who were also the rank and file footsloggers of the army of Bornu.' He draws the conclusion that the differences between these three groups 'were undoubtedly less important . . . than the

Tortures supposedly inflicted on Christian slaves by Muslims in the Middle Ages: from the time of the Crusades on, Christians and Muslims enslaved each other without compunction. The tortures shown here, in full (*far right*) and in detail (*right*), reflect a 17th century Christian fear of enslavement rather than the realities of Muslim treatment. In the Muslim world, slaves were mainly used in domestic service and the only widely practised cruelty was emasculation to provide eunuchs for harems.

IIII
V
VI
X
XI
XII
XVI
XVII
XVIII
XXI
XXII

differences between all these three on one hand and the nobles on the other.' This view corresponds with Professor Andrews' observation about 'the gulf between Homeric princes and the rest being far deeper than any gulf between the different classes that serve them.'

Other slave-based societies rose and fell in sub-Saharan Africa between the 9th and 16th centuries. As elsewhere, the systems of slavery were as variable as the societies of which it was a part. In Ashanti, as R S Rattray has said, 'a slave might marry; own property; himself own a slave; swear an oath; be a competent witness and ultimately become heir to his master.' In the city states of central Hausaland, such as Kano, Daura, Gobir, Katsina and Zaria, slaves lived in a circle of villages beyond the walls, existing only to produce food for the populace within. In the 'Middle Belt' states, such as Nupe, Borgu and Mamprussi, a caste of feudal knights propped up their might with 'bureaucracies of eunuchs and palace slaves,' while forcing the peasantry to produce their food and 'servile castes to forge and weave and build and wait.'

One of the greatest of the kingdoms was the Mandingo Empire of what is now Mali. It reached its peak in the early 14th century under the great Mansa Musa, who expanded his frontiers southward and ruled over a brilliant culture centered on Timbuktu. So wealthy was he that when passing through Cairo on a state pilgrimage to Mecca, he upset the Egyptian currency market with the lavish presents of gold which he distributed. As with other empires, Mandingo enslaved its defeated enemies, as this description by the Arab traveler, Ibn Battuta, of Mansa Sylayman, Mansa Musa's brother and successor, shows: 'The Sultan's usual dress is a velvety red tunic . . . he is preceded by his musicians, who carry gold and silver guitars, and behind him come three hundred armed slaves. He walks in a leisurely fashion affecting a very slow movement, and even stops from time to time.' Though impressed by the political system of his hosts, Ibn Battuta found other things of which he disapproved, above all, as Professor Roland Oliver has said, 'the freedom given to women who went about unveiled and chose whom they would as their companions.' Worse still, the female slaves of the king's court 'and at those of his provincial chiefs . . . appeared without a stitch of clothing.'

By the end of the 15th century, Mandingo declined and Songhay to the east rose, eventually absorbing much of the previous Mandingo empire. Both were to take advantage of their own traditions of slavery to trade with the Europeans.

Toward the coast lay the states of the Guinea Forest – the kingdoms of Oyo, Benin, Dahomey and Ashanti, whose lands were to be so savagely plundered during the period of the Atlantic slave trade. These kingdoms, separated as they were by dense forest from the trade routes of the Sahara, looked, with the coming of European traders, toward the sea rather than toward the desert for their prosperity.

It was from the sea, early in the 15th century, that the Portuguese, the first European country to import Moorish slaves, approached the coast of Africa, on voyages of exploration organized by Dom Henrique (popularly known as Prince Henry the Navigator), son of the Portuguese King Joao I. Arab geographers had shown the existence of a fertile land south of the barren Moroccan coastline and Prince Henry, intent on pursuing the crusade against the Moors, aimed at claiming a dominion for Portugal on the Gulf of Guinea, with a view to establishing a link with Christian Abyssinia to the east, and so presenting a combined front to his enemies from a new, southern, vantage point.

To finance this venture he instructed his explorers to bring back any items of value. In 1441 two of his captains captured 12 men, women and children from the neighborhood of the Rio de Oro. This coup delighted Prince Henry, who sent a special embassy to the Pope, outlining his plans for further conquest. The Pope was equally enthusiastic and immediately granted 'to all of those who shall be engaged in the said war, complete forgiveness of all their sins.'

In 1448, by the time the Portuguese had arrived in the Senegal and the Gambia, the Arab monopoly of the trans-Saharan traffic in slaves, which had existed for so long, had finally been broken, and nearly 1000 slaves were exchanged for the horses, silk or silver so desirable to rulers such as those of Mali and Songhay. In 1481 the Portuguese applied for and were granted permission to build a fort at Elmina on the Gold Coast. This was the foundation stone of a great and terrible edifice: the Atlantic slave trade.

THE HOUSEHOLD SLAVES OF ANCIENT GREECE

In Ancient Greece, the position of slaves varied from state to state. In some they were mere serfs, the descendants of an aboriginal population reduced by invaders and bound to the soil and their masters.

In Sparta, the slaves, or helots as they were known, who far outnumbered their masters, made up a servile force that allowed the Spartans to devote themselves to military and administrative duties.

But in industrial states, like Athens for instance, the position of slaves was very different. A few belonged to the community; they were employed in the police force, or in the mint, or in other official positions, sometimes of considerable responsibility. One Athenian slave had custody of the state archives.

The vast majority of Athenian slaves, however, belonged to individual owners. Strangely, the slaves were not set to perform specifically servile work. Most Athenian citizens were peasants or craftsmen and felt no shame in manual labor. It was, however, intolerable to them to be subject to others; hence the need for slaves. They were bought for domestic service in the slave market, which was stocked with prisoners of war, the victims of slave raids, criminals and perhaps a few foundlings. Slaves were everywhere used for domestic service, assisting the mistress of the house in her tasks of cooking, cloth-making, nursing and looking after children. The number of household slaves in a modest establishment varied from three to a dozen, though a wealthy family could have 50 or more.

Few were employed in agriculture, but artists and artisans usually had one slave or more working under his direction. These were regarded as apprentices, and their task was to remove from their master the burden of routine. The slave often engaged in the same work as his master, however, and was even expected, when trained, to exercise his creative faculties. Some slaves, for instance, were armorers; others made furniture; others almost certainly, were vase painters. Slaves may therefore have produced the vases from which these images of slave life are taken.

In this statuette only an inch high, a black slave boy – probably brought from the Upper Nile – leans back against his *amphora*.

There was one vital element in Greek slavery that injected some humanity into the institution: slaves could earn their emancipation. Although they could be bought and sold, it was customary for slaves to be given an income which they were allowed to save. With this they could eventually buy their freedom. Sometimes, too, slaves were given their freedom as a reward for loyalty and good service. With a trade and some savings behind him, any Greek slave, whether native-born or foreign, could hope to win for himself a substantial place in Greek society.

A slave relaxes bowling a hoop.

A slave trained as an armorer practises his trade.

A domestic slave carts a bed.

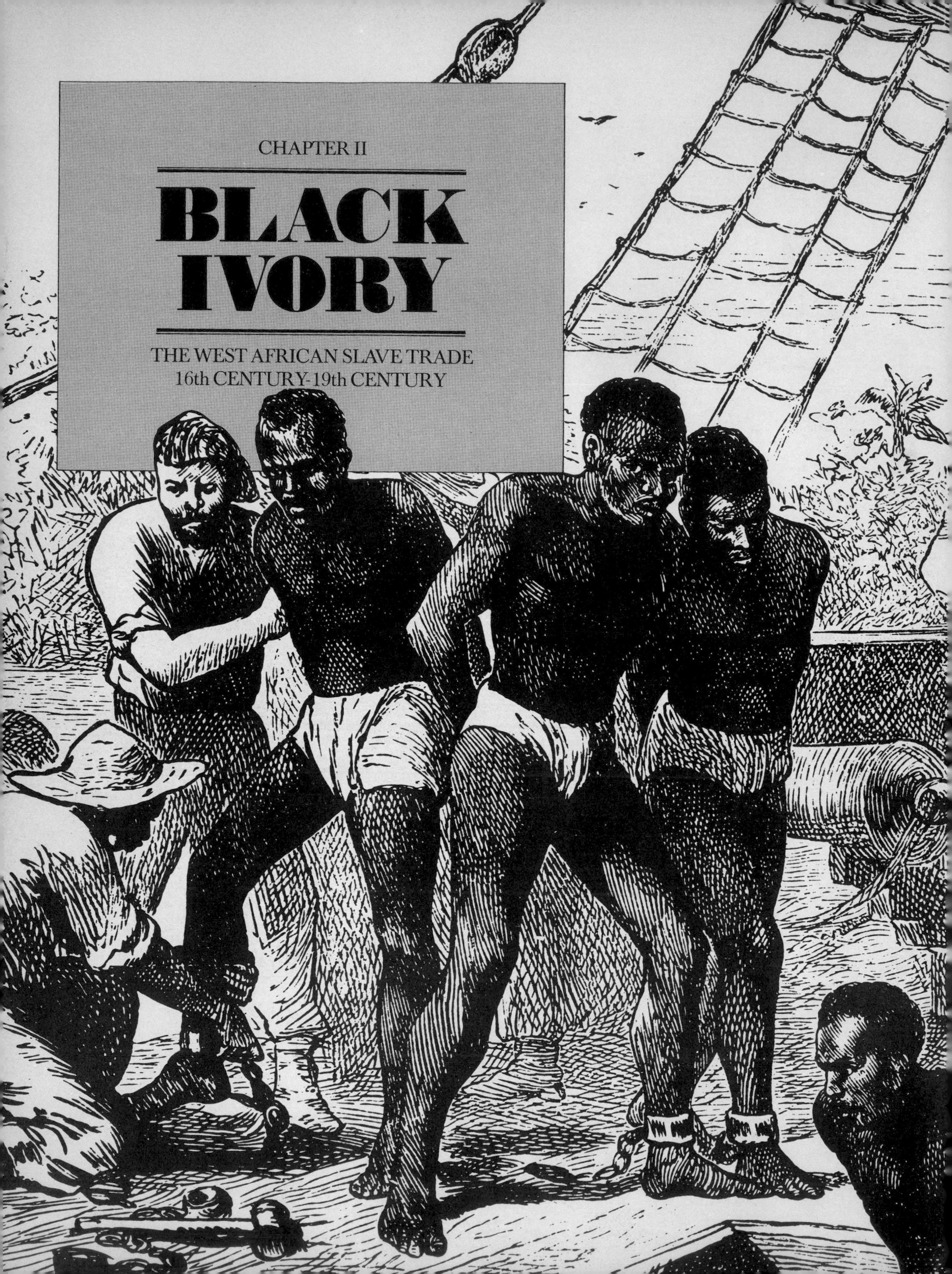

CHAPTER II

BLACK IVORY

THE WEST AFRICAN SLAVE TRADE 16th CENTURY-19th CENTURY

Prelude to suffering: fettered blacks are loaded on the West African coast prior to the trans-Atlantic voyage to the slave markets of the Americas.

With hindsight, there seems a terrible inevitability about the emergence of the Atlantic slave trade, and the beginning of slavery in the New World. Its roots were embedded in antiquity and its branches already stretched from the western Mediterranean to China. Slavery was a fact of life that needed little justification from its protagonists, who were quite ready to embrace any source of wealth, political power or social advancement.

Given such attitudes, it is perhaps surprising that the trade did not get under way sooner. Black servants were, after all, a common enough sight in Europe. A Venetian named Gonzaga bought black boys 'for the amusement of their court' and in Castile black household slaves were mentioned as being 'well fed on kitchen leftovers.' By 1492, when Columbus set foot in the West Indies, black slaves were being imported into Europe at the rate of 1000 a year.

But blacks were, more often than not, merely exotic additions to households which contained more white slaves than black. Indeed, in the 15th and 16th centuries, the permutations of enslaved colors and religions were extensive: Muslims and Christians manned Tuscan, Neapolitan and Sicilian galleys. Barbary pirates enslaved Venetians with such success that a Venetian consul was appointed in Algiers to look after their interests as best he could; and in 1551 12,000 Christian Spaniards, after an abortive attempt to expel the Turks from Algiers, fell into the hands of their conquerors as domestic slaves. In Turkey, the Sultan recruited his crack troops, the Janizary Corps (the standing army of the Ottoman Empire), by rounding up Christian boys from the western Balkan villages.

Slavery of a sort began almost as soon as Columbus discovered the New World. The impetus for it was an extraordinary arrangement arrived at by Spain and Portugal. In 1493, the Pope responded to an appeal for arbitration between the two principal contenders for colonial possessions, Spain and Portugal. Eager to see the world safely divided between Catholic powers whose influence would save heathen souls, he allocated the eastern territories of the world outside Europe to Portugal and the western ones to Spain. The line of demarcation ran down the Atlantic. The Portuguese, however, were dissatisfied with a decision which denied them Brazil. A year later, they managed to obtain an amendment through the Treaty of Tordesillas which moved the demarcation line west to intersect the mouth of the Amazon, thus granting them full territorial rights in much of Brazil.

The compulsion to convert the heathen was as strong an impulse for the Spanish and the Portuguese as the economic motive. Columbus wrote in his journal on 27 November 1492: 'After they understand the advantages, I shall labor to make all these people Christians'; and, a year later, in a speech to the King and Queen of Spain, he said: 'God has reserved for the Spanish monarch, not only all the treasures of the New World, but a still greater treasure of inestimable value, in the infinite number of souls destined to be brought over into the bosom of the Christian Church.' Later, before a slave ship could leave the Gold Coast for Brazil its cargo was baptized *en masse,* and inside the Portuguese fort of Elmina on the coast of Guinea was a chapel dedicated to St George, 'for the use of those Portuguese and their slaves who lived in the actual town.' Neither the Spanish nor the Portuguese would contemplate the introduction into their colonies of any slave 'of the race of Moors, Jews or Mulattos' – these being considered subversive elements in what were to be countries worked by grateful and obedient converts, saved by the true faith from the dark and savage practices of their own heathen lands.

For the first few years after the Treaty of Tordesillas, however, the trade in black slaves remained essentially a Mediterranean one. The early colonists in South America preferred to make use of the seemingly inexhaustible supply of willing Indian labor they found so readily available. The Indians, however, proved constitutionally unfitted for the heavy and exacting work imposed on them by their new masters. Enslaved by the Spaniards on the slimmest of pretexts – for resorting to 'unnatural sexual practices,' or for failing to conform to the authority of the Spanish crown (after having had the Christian faith explained to them in Spanish) – they were put to work looking for gold or cultivating the land.

They did not submit entirely without a struggle. Only three years after Columbus arrived in Hispaniola (now Haiti and the Dominican Republic), 100,000 Indians attempted to eliminate the small Spanish settlement of Isabella. Despite their large numbers they were no match for the Spaniards, 220 of whom combined to massacre their flimsily-clad and lightly-armed opponents, cutting them down with swords, shooting at them with crossbows and arquebuses and setting savage bloodhounds on them which, according to Bartolome de Las Casas, Bishop of Chiapas, 'when released . . . in one hour each tore a hundred Indians to pieces.' As the Bishop later drily observed, 'It is a fact that ten men in the Indies (unless in the high mountains) are enough to destroy and to dispatch with their lances 100,000 men massed against the Christians.'

Chattel slavery in the Spanish colonies virtually disappeared by the end of the 15th century, but the substitute system of *repartiamiento*, or forced labor, was no less vigorously imposed and the abuses it aroused from the *conquistadores* no less vicious. The Indians died from overwork, grief and the previously unencountered European diseases of smallpox and measles. In 1518 Judge Alonso de Zuzao wrote: 'When Hispaniola was discovered it contained 1,130,000 Indians; today their number does not exceed 11,000.' Between 1518 and 1585, according to two modern students, the Indian population of central Mexico was reduced by slave trading among the islands of the Caribbean and by death, from 6.3 million to 1.9 million.

Sickened by the plight of the aboriginal population, Las Casas returned to Spain in 1537 to petition Charles V on their behalf. He suggested supplementing their unsatisfactory labor with what had already been found to be a more durable substitute – the African Negro – and asked that a license be granted to import 12 of these for each colonist. The

Spanish barbarities in South America: Spanish *conquistadores* meet out harsh treatment to enslaved Aztecs during their 16th-century imperial expansion in Latin America.

Emperor, who was young, serious and deeply religious, and as much concerned for the souls of his newly converted Christian subjects as for the future prosperity of his colonies, agreed. He granted to one of his favorite courtiers, Lorenzo de Gomenot, then Governor of Bresa, the right to ship 4000 blacks a year to Hispaniola, Cuba, Jamaica and Puerto Rico. Gomenot, presumably unaware of the potential value of this document, first of the famous *Asientos* (or 'contracts,' meaning the exclusive license to supply the Spanish colonies with slaves), sold it for 25,000 ducats to a Genoese syndicate, which henceforth conducted a profitable trade with the Portuguese slave traders monopolizing the Guinea coast.

The Portuguese, meanwhile, had already been slave trading for some years in a small way. Secure in their new fortress at Elmina, they had sailed down the west coast of Africa as far as the river Congo where they met the local ruler, Nizinga Nkuwu, who received them warmly and offered them gifts of palm cloth and ivory. This king converted to Christianity, died in 1506 and was succeeded, after a civil war between pro- and anti-Portuguese factions, by the pro-Portuguese Nizinga Mvemba (or Afonso I as he was later baptized). The honeymoon which followed his installation was brief. Emissaries were exchanged and Afonso corresponded regularly with his 'brother' King Manuel of Portugal. He hopefully requested priests, schoolteachers, carpenters and boatbuilders.

But it soon became apparent to Afonso that his 'brother' was not to be relied upon for foreign aid. Portugal, with other more remunerative imperial possessions across the Atlantic, saw no tangible profits to be obtained from helping Afonso. With the Spanish needing black slaves to take over from the dwindling Indian population in their colonies, and corresponding labor shortages in Brazil, Portuguese traders began to fill their ships with Congolese and Angolan slaves rather than with palm cloth and ivory.

Afonso, disillusioned, but practical, at first undertook to provide slaves for this market himself, leading military expeditions against the populous Mbundu tribe on the southern border and exporting the captives from Mpinda at the mouth of the Congo river. But later, in 1526, he complained to the King of Portugal of 'the excessive freedom given by your factors and officials to the men and merchants who are allowed to come to this Kingdom, saying that they 'daily seize our subjects, sons of the land and sons of our noblemen and vassals and our relatives . . . They grab them and cause them to be sold: and so great, Sir, is their corruption and licentiousness that our country is being utterly depopulated.'

This was, in fact, less a cry for humanity than a complaint about his rapidly fading power and status. Afonso should, perhaps, have dealt with the Portuguese like his northern counterparts, the awesome Oba of Benin, who, according to James Pope-Hennessy, was 'a theocratic ruler . . . so heavily sheathed in polished gold that when he rose to his feet he had to be propped up by two slaves.' This monarch resisted all attempts to convert him to Christianity, as did the King of Whydah, on the Slave Coast, who, having once attended Mass, announced that it was 'very fine but that he preferred to stick to his own fetish.'

The treasures of the New World were not for long to remain the sole prerogative of the Spanish and the Portuguese. During the Eighty Years War (1568–1648) between Spain and the Netherlands, Portugal, her crown joined to Spain's in 1580, was forced to defend her imperial possessions against the onslaught of the Dutch.

The Dutch West India Company, formed in 1621, took 15,430 slaves to Brazil by 1623 and, in 1646 the first black slaves were landed in the earliest Dutch settlement in America, New Amsterdam, on the tip of Manhattan. (Some efforts had been made to enslave the aboriginal inhabitants of the area, but the Manhattan Indians proved intractable. A wall was built across the lower end of Manhattan island, where Wall Street now runs, 'to keep red lovers of liberty from driving the Dutch slave catchers . . . into the bay.') In 1630, the Dutch seized a sizeable portion of northern Brazil (which they were to retain until 1662, when Portugal, once more independent, reclaimed it in exchange for Dutch control of the Guinea slave trade). And by the 1640s, the Dutch had also won a commanding position on the Gold Coast, having driven the Portuguese from all their strongholds – Elmina fell in 1637 and Fort St Anthony at Axim to the west, in 1642.

Spurred on by the sight of Dutch intrusions into what had been considered an impreg-

The Dutch: One Slaving Nation among Many

The Dutch, fiercely independent and aggressive traders, had a long, if erratic, involvement with slavery. In 1572 the Netherlands revolted against Spanish rule. In retaliation Spain closed Iberian ports to Dutch ships. As a counter-measure, the Dutch began to challenge the Iberian monopoly of world trade.

It did not take them long to establish themselves internationally. By 1610, the Dutch had secured complete mastery in the East and had established several posts on the coasts of Guinea and the Caribbean. Dutch capitalists had organized the Netherlands East Indies Company. Seeking a north-west passage, Henry Hudson, working for the company, had sailed his *Half Moon* up the river that now bears his name. In 1621 the Dutch West India Company was founded. In 1626 Fort Amsterdam was established on the tip of Manhattan, a wall built (along present-day Wall St) to keep the Indians at bay, and numerous *bouweries* (farms) acquired outside it. And in 1630, a large part of Brazil, too, fell to the Dutch.

Slave trading started almost immediately. In 1646 the first cargo of blacks to be sold as slaves arrived in New Amsterdam from Brazil. But imperial expansion was a precarious activity. In the 1660s, a roistering British captain, Robin Holmes, temporarily captured all the Dutch posts in West Africa, except for Elmina – an act met promptly by Michiel de Ruyter, who seized or recaptured every post held by the English, except Cape Coast Castle. In 1664, the English captured New Amsterdam, and renamed it New York. These incidents were two direct causes of the Dutch–English War of 1665–67. When peace came, Holland ceded New York and acquired the then British outpost of Surinam (now Dutch Guiana) in its place. This was to remain the major Dutch colony in the new world.

Surinam acquired a particularly bad record for inhumanity. Slave revolts were endemic and Surinam planters and their overseers never seemed to draw the obvious conclusion that, as one of the rebel slave leaders observed in 1760, 'the whites were cutting their noses to spite their faces by so mistreating their valuable field hands that they forced them to seek refuge in the forest.' The runaway slaves or 'bush-Negroes' as they were called, formed settlements in jungle clearings which were periodically attacked by Dutch punitive columns.

Society in 18th century Surinam was similar in structure to the plantations and slave societies that characterized the sugar colonies of the other European powers in the West Indies. At the top, were the white planters. Then came the white overseers, clerks and merchants. Next the colored freedmen, the offspring of white fathers and colored mothers and a small number of free blacks. At the bottom were the black slaves.

Masters and slavers in Surinam had even less in common than they had in the French and English West Indies since the language was a curious cross of African dialects and English – a relic of the English origins of the colony.

New York's first slaves: a Dutch slave auction in New Amsterdam, the future New York.

nable Portuguese monopoly, other European nations vied with one another for key positions on the Guinea Coast. Their efforts were at first directed toward supplying slaves to Spanish possessions in the Caribbean, and to Brazil. But with the founding, during the first half of the 17th century, of European settlements in the West Indies and along the east coast of North America, it became an increasingly urgent matter to supply these new colonies with the cheap labor they needed to work their rapidly growing sugar and tobacco plantations.

The French, established along the St Lawrence river and in Nova Scotia and on the West Indian islands of Guadeloupe and Martinique, built a fort at St Louis on the Senegal river; the Danes (who later acquired four Caribbean islands) established themselves at Christiansborg (Accra); the Swedes, briefly at Takoradi; and the Germans at Great Fredericksburg (Axim).

The English had made an early start with the buccaneering enterprises of Sir John Hawkins in the 1560s, but did not take an active part in the slave trade until after 1650. Then, with increasing demand for the sugar produced on their West Indian islands (Barbados, St Christopher, the Bermudas and Jamaica) they attempted to break the foreign monopoly of the lucrative traffic in African slaves. In 1663, The Company of Royal Adventurers of England Trading to Africa was chartered, under the patronage of the Duke of York, and a new coin, the guinea, was struck in its honor.

The Company's fortunes were, however, short-lived. All but one of the forts established in its name on the Gold Coast were taken over by the Dutch just before the Second Dutch War of 1664–65 and the unlucky investors, among them Charles II himself, lost every penny of the £120,000 they had contributed. Although under the peace treaty of 1667 the Dutch retained their conquests, the English, undeterred, began building more forts and in 1672 founded the Royal African Company with once again the King as a major stockholder. It was guaranteed a monopoly of all trade in exchange for garrisoning and maintaining its new strongholds.

The Company, despite successfully beating the Dutch in the race to supply slaves to British colonies, faced fierce and prolonged competition from its own countrymen; as one writer put it: 'Interlopers from Bristol and other outposts carried more slaves than the monopolies did.' But in 1697, after pressure from planters complaining at the Company's high prices, the trade was opened up to include 'all English merchants who would pay a 10 percent tax for the benefit of the company,' with the proviso that the boat carrying the slaves should be English. And 16 years later, with the signing of the Treaty of Utrecht in 1713, Marlborough's victories during the War of the Spanish Succession secured for England the most coveted prize of all – the *Asiento* – giving the English the right to introduce 144,000 black slaves into the Spanish colonies over a period of 30 years.

Throughout the 17th century, the African slave trade was not the only means of supplying labor for the American colonies. There was another, equally callously treated class of forced immigrant, that of the white indentured servants (or *engagés*, as the French called them), who, in return for their passage across the Atlantic, undertook to serve their sponsors for between three and five years. At the end of this period a servant could expect his freedom together with a grant of land of between three and five acres from his master.

The system, in theory a reasonably fair arrangement, led in practice to violent abuses. Less valuable a commodity than the black, who was a slave for life (and whose status descended to his children) there was little or no incentive for a master to keep his servant alive for longer than absolutely necessary. As one 17th century French historian wrote: 'There were masters so cruel that they were forbidden to purchase any more; and I knew one at Guadeloupe who had buried more than 50 upon his plantation, whom he had killed by hard work, and neglect when they were sick. The cruelty proceeded from their having them for three years only, which made them spare the Negro rather than these poor creatures!' A brisk trade developed in kidnapping, particularly in England, where Bristol became dangerous ground for the young and gullible. Transportation of convicts was another means of supplying extra hands for the sugar plantations. And the rigid Protestant rule (1649–60) of Oliver Cromwell saw the forcible deportation of many Nonconformists, Irish or Scots, or any other persons considered by Cromwell likely to cause a 'religious or political disturbance.'

Abused and exploited though he was, the

BASES FOR BRITISH SLAVERS

John Atkins, an 18th century naval surgeon turned author, offers tips to slave-traders in West Africa, providing details of British bases – the chief of which was Cape Coast (*below*) – bargaining practices, a list of goods exchanged for slaves, and a callous assessment of the comparative value of different blacks:

❛ In the Windward Coast, Gambia, Sierraleon, and Sherbro Rivers may be reckoned chief; the African Company having Factors and Settlements there. Less noted, but more frequented by private Ships in this part of Guinea, are Cape Mount, and Montzerado, Sesthos River, Capes Palmas, Apollonia, and Tres Puntas. A number of others intervene, of more or less Trade; which it is their Custom to signify at the sight of any Ship by a Smoke, and is always looked on as an Invitation to Trade; but as each is alterable among them from the Chance of War, the Omission shews they decline it, or are out of Stock.

This Change of Circumstance found on different Voyages, proceeds from weak and bad Governments among themselves, every Town having their own Cabiceers or ruling Men, (or it may be three or four in Confederacy) all so jealous of the others Panyarring, that they never care to walk even a mile or two from home without Fire-Arms; each knows it is their Villanies and Robberies upon one another that enables them to carry on a Slave-trade with Europeans....

Cape Coast: The Factory consists of Merchants, Factors, Writers, Miners, Artificers and Soldiers; and excepting the first Rank, who are the Council for managing Affairs, are all of them together a Company of white Negroes, who are entirely resigned to the Governour's Commands, according to the strictest Rules of Discipline and Subjection; are punished (Garison fashion) on several Defaults with Mulcts, Confinement, the Dungeon, Drubbing, or the Wooden Horse .. . tho' the Salaries sound tolerably in Leadenhall-Street (50 to 90 £ per Ann a Factor; 50 an Artificer) yet in the Country here, the General (for the Company's good) pays them in Crackra, a false Money which is only current upon the spot....

In the Area of this Quadrangle [of Cape Coast Castle] are large Vaults, with an iron Grate at the Surface to let in Light and Air on those poor Wretches, the Slaves who are chained and confined there till a Demand comes. They are all marked with a burning Iron, ... DY, Duke of York....

Within the Castle is a Smith's Shop, a Cooperage, Store-houses, a Chappel, and Houses for the Officers and Servants. The General's Lodging communicates with the Chappel; a capacious Hall, which serves to preach and dine in, pray or drink, serve God or debate or Trade; hence they can overlook what the Company's Servants are doing....

First, on the Timing of a Cargo: This depends at several places much on Chance,

Cape Coast Castle: the principal English base on the Gold Coast (present day Ghana).

from the fanciful and various Humours of the Negroes, who make great demands one Voyage for a Commodity, that perhaps they reject next. . . .

Secondly, Of the Sorting, this may be observed in general; That the Windward and Leeward Parts of the Coast are as opposite in their Demands, as is their distance. Iron Bars, which are not asked for to Leeward, are a substantial Part of Windward Cargoes. Crystals, Orangos, Corals, and Brass-mounted Cutlasses are almost peculiar to the Windward Coast; as are brass Pans from Rio Sesthos to Apollonia: Cowreys (or Bouges) at Whydah. Copper and Iron Bars at Callabar; but Arms, Gun-powder, Tallow, old Sheets, Cottons of all the various Denominations, and English Spirits are everywhere called for. . . .

The Sale of Goods
At Sierraleon

	Gold Bars
1 Piece of Planes	10
7 77lb Kettles	26
3 Pieces of Chintz	12
1 Piece of Handkerchief Stuff	2
The Price of a Woman Slave	50
7 50lb Kettles	20
5 Pieces of Brawls	10
1 Piece of Ramal	4
1 Bar of Iron	1
The Price of a Boy Slave	35

. . . *Slaves*: Slaves differ in their Goodness; those from the Gold Coast are accounted best, being cleanest limbed, and more docible by our Settlements than others; but then they are, for that very reason, more prompt to Revenge, and murder the Instruments of their Slavery, and also apter in the means to compass it.

To Windward they approach in Goodness as is the distance from the Gold Coast; so, as at Gambia, or Sierraleon, to be much better, than at any of the interjacent places.

To Leeward from thence, they alter gradually for the worse; an Angolan Negro is a Proverb for worthlessness; and they mend . . . till you come to the Hottentots. . . .

I have observed how our Trading is managed for Slaves, when obliged to be carried on aboard the Ship. Where there are Factories . . . we are more at large; they are sold in open Market on shore, and examined by us in like manner, as our Brother Trade do Beasts in Smithfield, the Countenance, and Stature, a good Set of Teeth, Pliancy in their Limbs, and Joints, and being free of Veneral Taint, are the things inspected, and governs our choice in buying. . . .

Whydah Slaves are more subject to Small-Pox and sore Eyes; other parts to a sleepy Distemper, and to Windward, Exomphalos's. There are few instances of Deformity any where; even their Nobles know nothing of chronical Distempers, nor their Ladies, of the Vapours. Their flattish Noses are owing to a continued grubbing in their Infancy against their Mother's Backs. ❜

Cape Coast Castle: the interior from the East.

Cape Coast Castle from the northwest.

Dixcove Fort, near Cape Coast, showing gardens.

Winneba Fort, near Accra.

James Fort, Accra.

indentured servant was still more expensive to keep than the black. Eric Williams, in his *History of the Caribbean* pointed out that 'a white servant's services for ten years amounted to the price of a Negro slave. Three Negroes worked better than and cost as much as one white man.' Colonial planters of all nationalities clamored for more black labor (although in Cuba the Spaniards continued to use white labor in the tobacco industry – it was the sugar plantations which were a black slave industry).

It was the unprecedented demand for cane sugar – a crop originally brought from India via Egypt, to Cyprus in the 10th century, and from there to Madeira, the Azores, the Cape Verde Islands and finally to the Americas – that drove the slave ships on their hazardous journeys across the Atlantic. And it was the Africans – by the mid-18th century pouring into the West Indies and America at the rate of 100,000 a year – who were forced to pay the irredeemable price of their liberty in order to sustain the prosperity of the New World.

European slave captains sailed to Africa with cargoes of woollen or cotton goods (often from India), rum, brandy, iron bars and glass beads. These they persuaded African traders to take in exchange for slaves, the slaves then being transported to the West Indies, or to Newport, Boston or Charleston, themselves to be exchanged for cash, or a draft on a European bank. (The Spaniards, who lagged behind in sugar production, paid in gold.) The ships were then loaded up with sugar, tobacco, cotton or coffee and headed for home.

This 'Triangular' or 'Circuit' trade was also undertaken by the comparatively small number of American slavers (by 1758 about 20 ships a year), who crossed the Atlantic with cargoes of rum, returning to America via the West Indies to off-load their slaves and stock up with molasses to take home and make into more rum. These boats, smaller than those from Europe, were known as 'rum

On the slave coast: slaves await transportation secured in the barracoons or slave barracks. These drawings were made on the Congo coast in the 1880s, but they exemplify conditions along the west coast of Africa over the previous three centuries.

boats,' their cargo being widely used to intoxicate potential African traders, and as barter for slaves: James Pope-Hennessy pointed out that, in 1756, the accounts of two Newport ships, the *Titt Bitt* and the *Cassada Garden,* showed that 'African men are recorded as fetching one hundred and fifteen gallons of rum each, and African women ninety-five gallons apiece.'

Profit was thus of paramount importance, and the Guinea coast an area to be plundered, not developed. As a British official, writing in 1853, commented: 'It may be safely affirmed that from our first settlement on the coast until the abolition of the slave trade in 1807, we did not confer one lasting benefit on the people.' The same should be said of other European nations.

Moreover, the long string of European forts, stretching from the Cape Verde Islands to the Bight of Biafra, were locked in an unholy alliance with the kingdoms on whose territories they stood.

Each factor, or company agent, was out to dupe each native king, and each native king was eager to obtain the maximum amount of goods in exchange for the slaves or gold dust he had for sale. And between the agents and the kings lay tangled webs of African traders and caboceers (officials) and many minor European employees intent on personal gain at the company's expense. The Europeans offered cheap brassware, faulty iron bars, cottons, aged flintlocks that frequently blew up on use, gunpowder and cowrie shells (a form of currency all along the African coast). The Africans in their turn mixed copper or brass filings with the gold dust they traded – 'the dexterity of the Blacks,' wrote the 17th century French agent-general, Jean Barbot, 'in sophisticating their gold, was scarce imaginable.'

Factors were not always of a very high caliber – Jean Barbot declaring them to be mainly 'men of no education or principles, void of foresight, careless, prodigal, addicted to strong liquors . . . and . . . overfond of the black women whose natural hot and leud

In transit to the coast: fettered in a coffle – from the Arabic *cafila*, a caravan – a slave gang makes its way from the African interior to the coast.

temper soon wastes their bodies and consumes what little substance they have.'

A remarkable exception was William Bosman, chief factor of the Dutch West India Company, who, miraculously surviving the fevers that killed so many of his colleagues, lived for 14 years at Elmina towards the end of the 17th century. In his *New and Accurate Descriptions of the Coast of Guinea,* published in 1704, he left an account of his dealings with the King of Whydah in Dahomey, ('the most civil and generous negro that I have ever met'), the King of Little Acron ('an extraordinary goodnatured man, with whom I have often been merry'), and the magnificent Oba of Benin (who 'did not deign to trade directly, but delegated this distasteful but necessary duty to his wives and slaves'). The slaves supplied by the King of Whydah were, Bosman assured his readers, 'prisoners of war, which are sold by the victors as booty.' A license to trade was granted only after the European had agreed to buy all the King's slaves at a price 'which is commonly one-third or one-fourth higher than ordinary.'

The majority of factors operated on a far smaller scale than William Bosman. Often the sole representatives of one private merchant, they generally lived alone in one of the many 'factories' dotted along the coast – ramshackle buildings, built to accommodate the notorious 'barracoon' or slave pen and defended, if at all, by a handful of inadequately-armed black mercenaries.

Nicholas Owen, one such 18th century Irish factor, having himself been captured by some Africans, sold as a slave to a neighboring tribe and finally ransomed by the merchant for whom he then became factor, found the worst of his many sufferings to be homesickness: 'O how I long for the produce of Europe such as milk, sallit and a hundred other things that's good for a sick man,' he prayed. Owen died of fever. Others, such as a Mr James Ellis, 'died a Martyr to Rum,' as did a Mr Robert Forbes, who collapsed, 'after a short Illness contracted by hard Drinking.' Two years was the average life-expectancy of a white man on the Guinea Coast, and many died within days of their arrival.

The problems of keeping alive were not confined to the factors. Anchored offshore slaveship crews were liable to be decimated by fever and the 'flux' or dysentery. A current slaver's jingle ran:

Beware and take care of the Bight of Benin,
Few come out though many go in.

A slave captain's success or failure therefore depended on his ship being 'slaved' as quickly as possible, and he was not too particular where and how they were obtained. The more conventional means of enslavement, the taking of prisoners of war, criminals, debtors, or sale of slaves or family members in time of famine, gave way to kidnapping and capture by tribes in 'wars' which were little more than armed raids on neighboring villages.

Francis Moore, an English factor living at James Fort at the mouth of the Gambia in 1730, described his dealings with the King of Barsally – who, when he felt the 'insatiable Thirst . . . after his Brandy' (which apparently came over him frequently), sent a messenger to the fort, asking the Governor to

The agony of the march: weak slaves abandoned by their captors await their death.

supply 'a Sloop there with a Cargo.' In anticipation of its arrival the King plundered 'some of his enemy Towns, seizing the People and selling them for such Commodities as he is in want of . . . Brandy or Rum, Gunpowder, Ball, Pistols and Cutlasses . . . . In case he is not at War with any neighboring King, he falls on one of his own Towns . . . and uses them in the very same Manner.' Indeed, the King did not hesitate to burn down as much of these towns as he thought expedient, 'to seize the People that run out of the Fire,' and then to sell them. Ottobah Cugoano, a freed Fanti slave who published his memoirs in 1787, was kidnapped as a child, and sold 'at a European fort for one gun, one piece of cloth and a small quantity of lead.' He was, as he said 'first kidnapped and betrayed by my own complexion, who were the first cause of my exile and slavery,' but he added the moralistic rider that 'if there were no buyers there would be no sellers.'

In 1768 the English were carrying slaves across the Atlantic at the rate of 53,000 a year, the French at 23,000, the Dutch at 11,000, captains from New England at 6300 and the Danes at 1250, with the Portuguese doing a steady trade from Angola at an annual rate of 8700.

Despite some 18th century accounts of slaves traveling enormous distances to the coast from the interior, it now seems certain that the majority came from much nearer home. As Melville J Herskovits points out in his book, *The Myth of the Negro Past*, the coastal tribe, the Fanti, who acted as middlemen for tribes further north, did not, on the evidence of Ashanti-Akan-Fanti names and names of deities, obtain slaves from further afield than the Gold Coast's (modern Ghana's) present boundaries. He thus dispels the myth of what he refers to as 'thousand-mile-journeys to the sea' – perpetuated by, among others, the Scottish explorer, Mungo Park, first chronicler of the progress of a slave 'coffle' (or string of bound slaves), by pointing out that the distance from Kamalia, where the slaves were captured, to the Gambia, where they were sold, did not exceed 500 miles. Herskovits is equally abrasive on the subject of the depopulation of the coastal belt as a result of the slave trade, feeling that 'the numerous villages, and the presence of cities of considerable size all through the area, suggest that the conception of an Africa depopulated by the slave trade, without the numbers necessary to support a drain that is to be figured in the millions, stands in need of drastic revision.'

Nevertheless, although it may not have been entirely stripped bare, the 3000 mile coastline from Senegal to Angola supplied

The Impact of An Evil Commerce

It is sometimes assumed in the West that European slavers forced the slave trade upon west Africa, thus corrupting primitive, noble, tribal communities and decimating the local populations. But slavery as a result of warfare was common in sub-Saharan Africa long before European slavers arrived. Indeed, in another sense, the only wholly free men were the rulers. Beneath every king – whether he ruled an empire or a village – lay interlinking pyramids of authority based on kinship. All were joined by a variety of obligations. But all – except for prisoners of war – were protected by established law and tradition, and they were not treated as chattels but as individuals with limited rights.

The development of the European slave trade, imposed on West African societies the concept of an economic value for labor. Gradually the more powerful members of the community came to see their dependents and prisoners of war not only in terms of their class but in terms of their worth.

The impact of the trade has been extremely hard to estimate. The total number of slaves shipped across to the Americas is now thought to have been around ten million. At its peak in the late 18th century, the trade averaged about 80,000 slaves a year. About 55–60 percent of these came from West Africa. This is a monumental figure, but it should be seen in the context of sub-Saharan West Africa's total population: perhaps 25 million in the 18th century. West Africa's loss of manpower therefore was probably more or less equivalent to the natural increase of population. Though horrific in individual terms, therefore, economically and socially the trade was not as crippling as it appears.

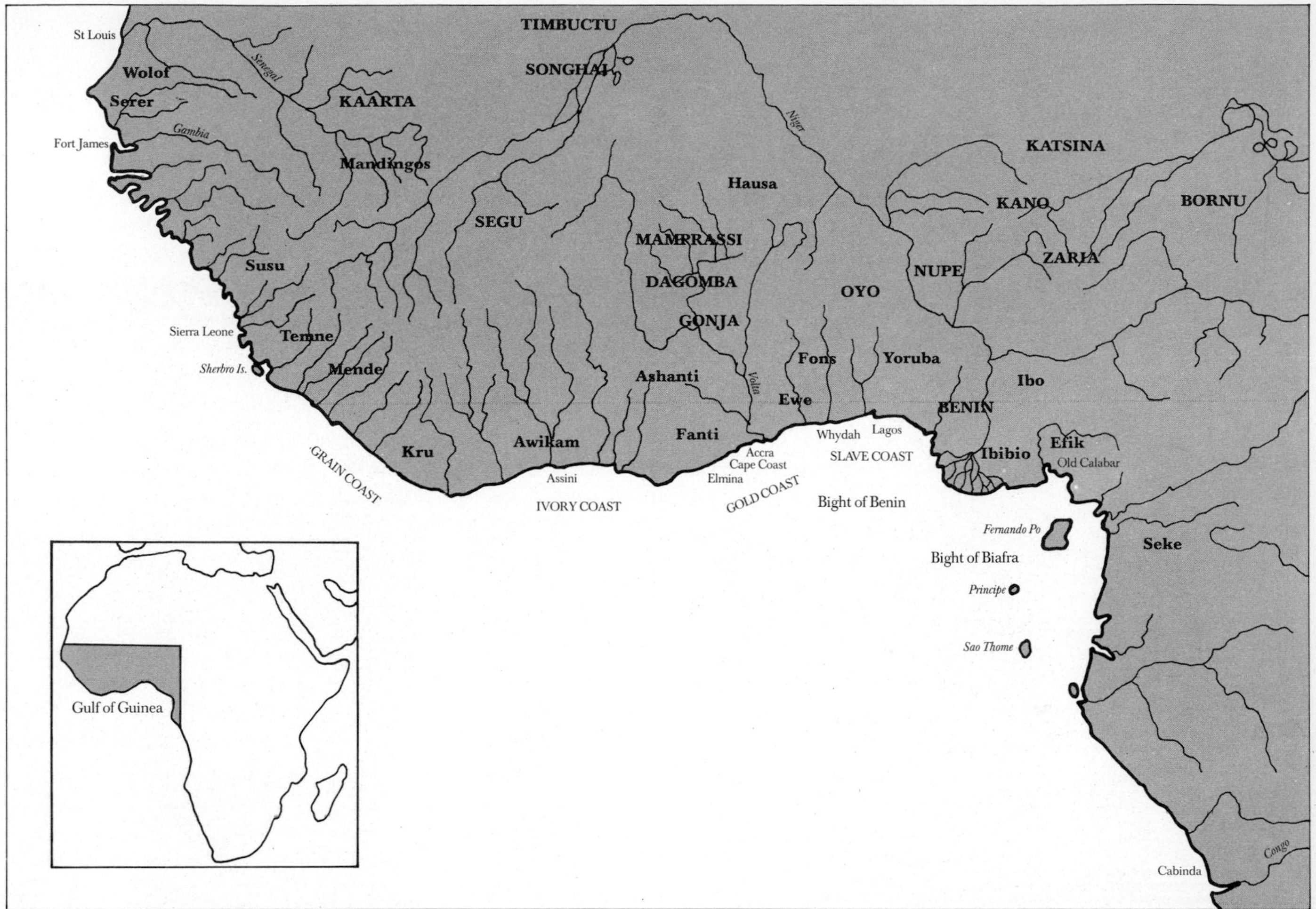

West Africa at the beginning of the European slave trade: The interior of Africa in the 17th century was a mass of tribes, kingdoms and empires, most slave-holding, continuously changing in power and extent. The time of the Mandingos' Mali empire was over. Islamic Bornu now dominated sub-Saharan Africa. Round the coast there already lay the European outposts that would be used to buy and ship enslaved Africans for the next two hundred years.

labor for the New World from almost every tribe inhabiting its shores and hinterland. Each had their own reputation amongst European traders: the Mandingos from Senegambia, described by Jean Barbot as being 'the cleanest and fittest for house servants being very handy and intelligent,' the Baga and Susu of French Guinea, the Chamba of Sierra Leone, and the Coromantees (a mixture of Gold Coast tribes, said to be either Fanti or Ashanti).

The Coromantees were much liked by the English, although of 'a haughty, ferocious, and stubborn' temperament, often involved in mutinies and uprisings and renowned for the dislike of any form of chastisement. As one of the more conscientious slave captains, William Snelgrave, wrote in 1734, 'many of the Coromantine Negroes . . . on their being any ways hardly dealt with twenty or more have hang'd themselves at a time.' The people of western Nigeria, the Yoruba, enslaved the Nupe and traded them in the markets of Calabar, and the Yoruba in their turn were captured by the Fon from Dahomey. The Dahomans, used as they were to cultivating the soil, fetched high prices, whereas the Ibibio and Efik tribes from eastern Nigeria were gentle, but prone to melancholy, often resorting to suicide when things became too much for them.

Given the fate that awaited a slave after falling into the hands of his captors, it was not surprising that some preferred death to life. Ottobah Cugoano described being taken in a boat to a ship off Cape Coast Castle: 'There was nothing to be heard but the rattling of chains, smacking of whips, and the groans and cries of our fellow-men. Some would not stir from the ground, when they were lashed and beat in the most horrible manner . . . . And when we found ourselves at last taken away, death was more preferable than life, and a plan was concerted amongst us that we might burn and blow up the ship and to perish altogether in the flames; but we were betrayed by one of our own countrymen.' And Captain Phillips, of the slave ship *Hannibal,* recorded that 'the Negroes are so wilful and loth to leave their own country,

Ready for shipment: French dealers drive their property, suitably branded and fettered, into canoes to take them to the slave ships riding at anchor in deeper water.

that they have often leap'd out of the canoos, boat and ship, into the sea, and kept under water till they were drowned, to avoid being taken up and saved by our boats.'

These ships, known as guineamen or slavers, were about 80–90 feet long, 25 feet wide, and had an average tonnage of between 120–150. They often lay for over three months at anchor, while their captains, resorting to every trick of the trade, assembled the 300 or so slaves needed for them to embark on the Atlantic crossing.

Each captain was personally responsible for the buying of slaves – and might be part owner of his ship with the right to trade ten 'privilege' slaves himself. Each country

claimed their ships to be of a higher quality and better run than those of their rivals – 'it is pitiful to see,' wrote Jean Barbot's nephew, James, 'how they [the Portuguese] crowd those poor wretches . . . in a ship,' and William Bosman, writing in 1701, said 'You would really wonder to see how these slaves live on board . . . yet by careful management of our masters of ships they are so regulated that it seems incredible: And in this particular our nation [in his case, the Dutch] exceeds all other Europeans; for as the French, Portuguese and English slave-ships are always foul and stinking; on the contrary ours are for the most part clean and neat.'

Before, however, any slaves could be taken aboard a guineaman the ship's carpenter had to make slave decks in the space which had been, on the journey out, previously allocated to manufactured goods. These slave decks were slotted in between the lower and upper decks, the distance between which being, on an average Newport slaver, not more than four and on the average European ship about five, feet high. Dutch ships, many of which had been built especially for the slave trade, had the advantage of being, as Barbot put it, 'very wide, lofty and airy betwixt decks, with gratings and scuttles.'

While the carpenter was at work the slaves waited on land, in barracoons belonging to the various companies or merchants, existing on bread and water, the men chained, the women and children running loose. Some captains preferred to build a makeshift house on the upper deck – a dangerous and often

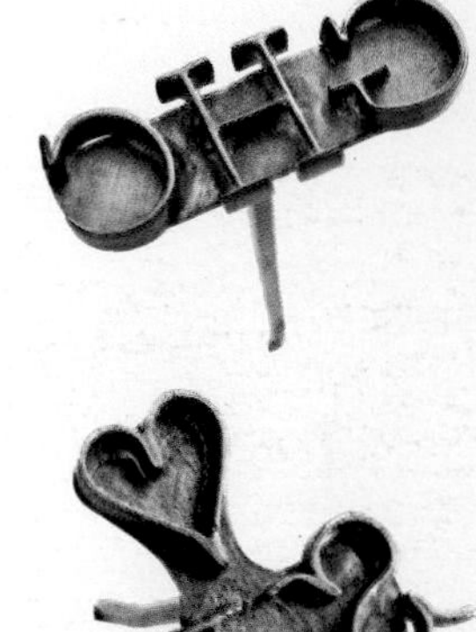

The branding: before embarkation slaves were branded with irons, like those above, so that dealers could identify their own slaves when property belonging to several dealers were shipped together.

STOWING HUMAN CARGOES

Of all the details of the slave trade that appalled anti-slavers, the most immediate – because the easiest to visualize – were those of how the human cargoes were stowed. The arrangements were made widely known in drawings like those reproduced here and by the evidence of slavers themselves.

This account of loading newly captured slaves is taken from a recently discovered manuscript by Theophilus Conneau. One version of his memoirs was published in 1854; it was heavily rewritten and was generally considered of doubtful authenticity. Now the original manuscript has been discovered and published by Howard S Mott Inc as *A Slaver's Log Book*.

Cross section of an embarkation canoe.

Conneau was born in Italy, went to sea, and ended up in Boston. His memoirs describe his adventures as a slaver between 1829 and 1847, when the trade was illegal.

'Two of the officers have the charge of stowing them. At sundown the Second Mate and Botswain descend, cat in hand, and stow the Negroes for the night. Those on the starboard side face forward and in one another's lap, vulgarly called spoon fashion. On the port side they are stowed with face aft; this position is considered preferable for the free pulsation of the heart. The tallest are selected for the greatest breadth of the vessel, while the short size and youngsters are stowed in the fore part of the ship. Great precaution is also taken to place those such as may have sores or boils on the side most convenient for their distemper. Tubs are also distributed on the sleeping deck and so placed that both sides have access. (The sick are never placed below.)

This lower deck once full, the rest are stowed on the deck, which is prepared with loose boards to keep the water from under them; they are then covered in fair weather with spare sails and with tarpaulins in rainy nights. In this manner they are made to remain all night, if possible. This discipline of stowing them is of the greatest importance on board slavers; otherwise every Negro would accommodate himself with all the comfortability of a cabin passenger....

Billets of wood are sometimes distributed to them, but as slaves shipped are often of different nations this luxury is not granted till well assured of the good disposition of the Negroes, as on many occasions slaves have been tempted to mutiny only by the opportunity at hand of arming themselves with those native pillows – indeed a very destructive missile in case of revolt.

As it may appear barbarous that slaves should be made to lie down naked on a hard board, let me inform the reader that native Africans know not the use of mattresses.... Therefore slaves cannot find great inconvenience in laying down on hard boards.'

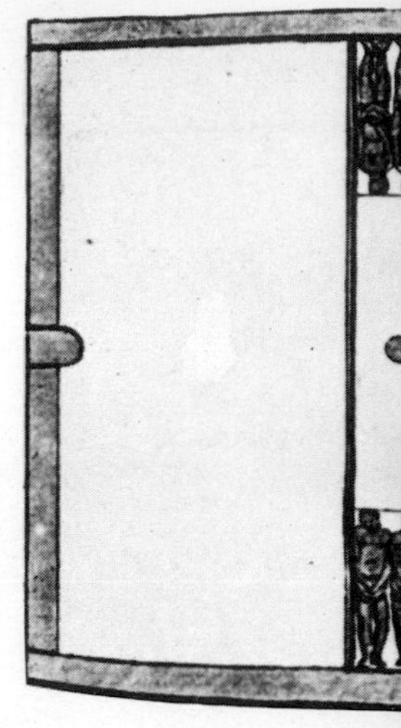

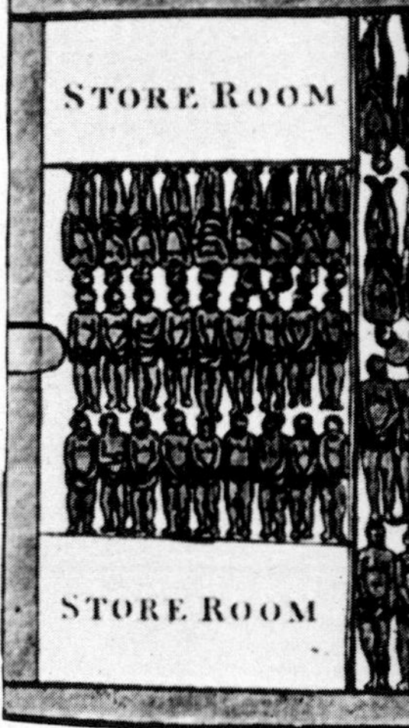

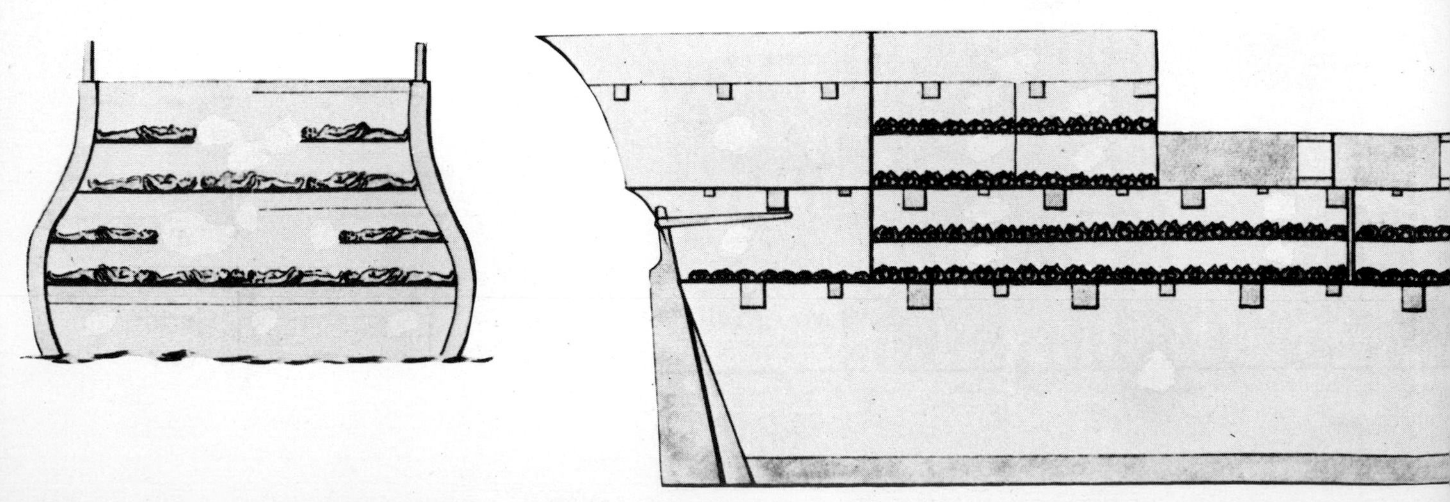

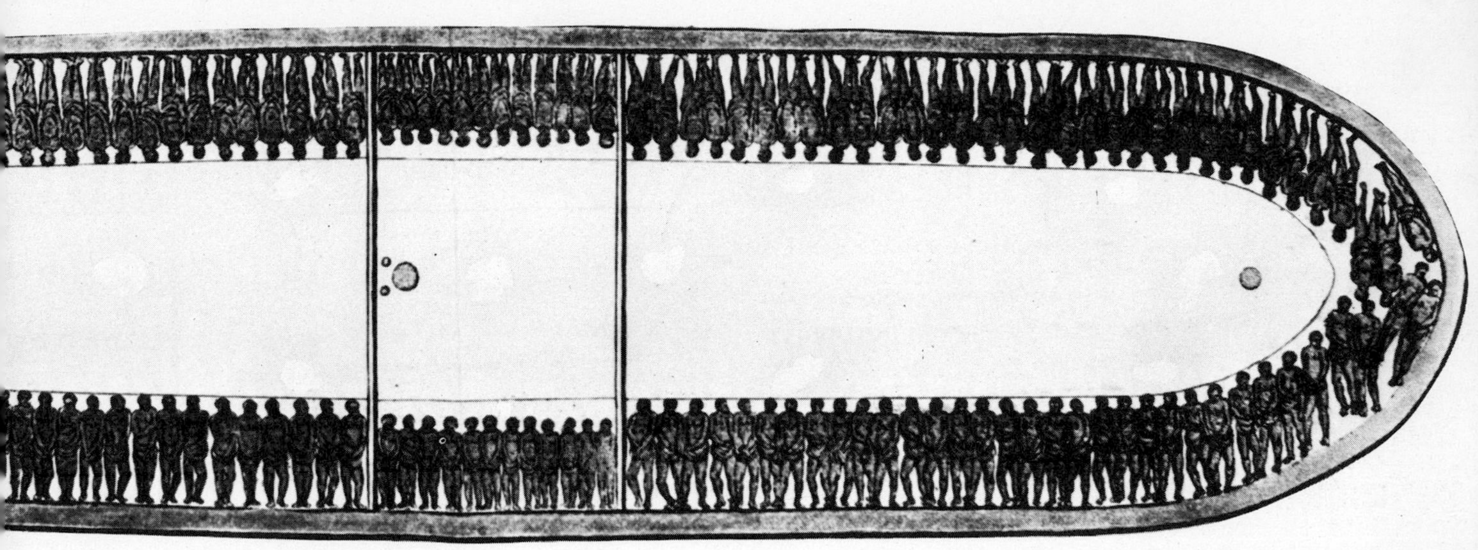

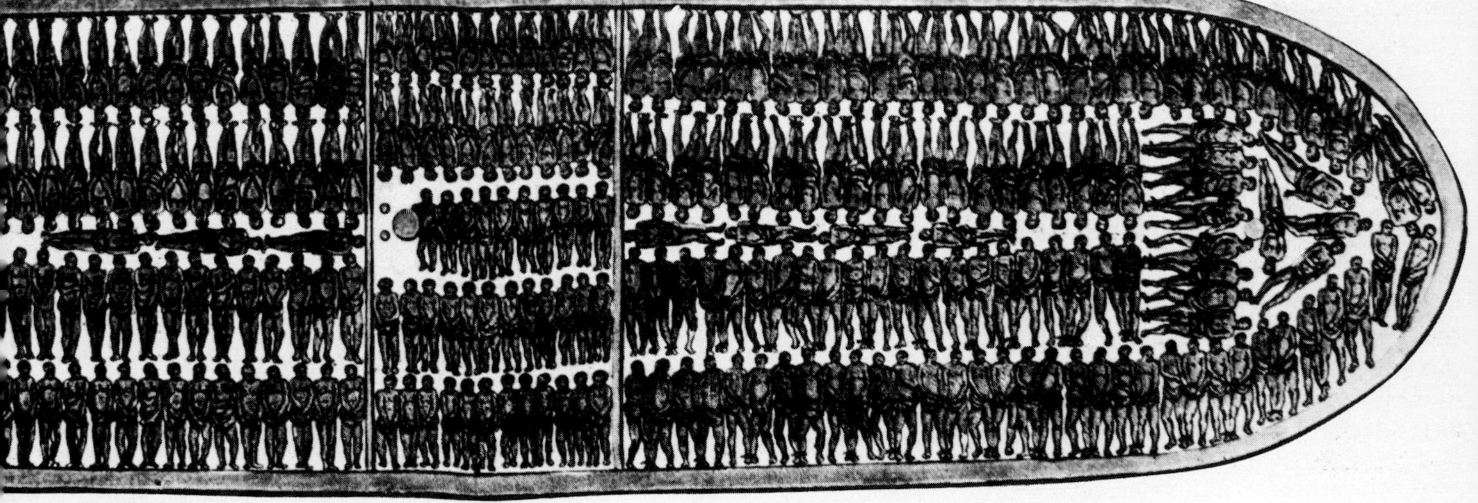

A deck (*below*) and a half deck (*above*) illustrate how slaves were made to lie 'spoon fashion' in appalling and unhygienic proximity.

These cross sections through the stern, beam and bows of a slaver show the head room – a mere two feet six inches – available to most slaves when stowed.

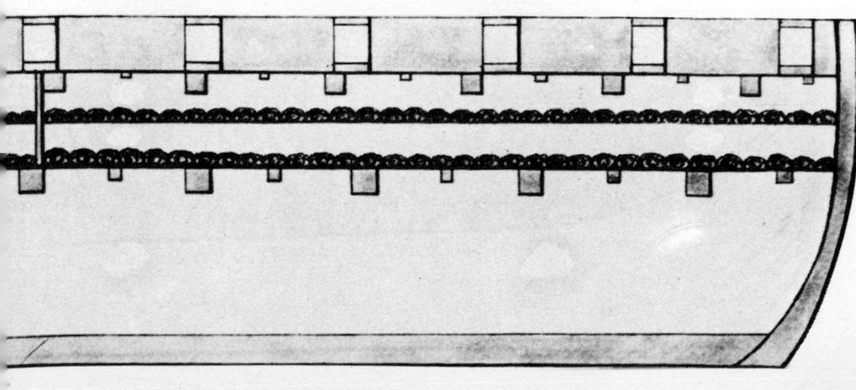

Slave quarters: this rare authentic view of the inside of a slaver, *The Albany*, was painted after its capture by a British anti-slavery vessel, *Albatross*. The slaves are relaxed in the knowledge that they will soon be free.

fatal job delegated to seamen, who had, according to one writer, to cut building materials standing 'in muddy slime up to their waists, covered with clouds of mosquitos and in danger of being bitten by poisonous snakes.' In these houses constructed between the masts, their roofs thatched with mangrove branches and reeds, their walls made from woven bamboo shoots, were penned terrified blacks, many of whom had never seen the sea and most of whom were convinced they were going to be eaten alive.

After having been stripped naked, subjected to a full and humiliating medical examination by the ship's surgeon, and branded on the breast, the men were shackled together in twos, the right wrist and ankle of one to the left wrist and ankle of the other. The women and children, also having been examined and branded, were allowed the run of the ship by day, by night sleeping between decks, strictly segregated from their own countrymen, but fair game for the seamen.

The Africans did not always submit passively to their fate. Many mutinies occurred while the ships were lying at anchor. Captain Phillips wrote: 'When our slaves are aboard we shackle the men two and two while we lie in port, and in sight of their own country, for 'tis then they attempt to make their escape, and mutiny.' Despite the ships being for the most part heavily armed, a few succeeded, but many more failed with consequent loss of crew and slaves.

James Barbot was involved in a mutiny off Cabinda, at the mouth of the river Congo. The male slaves, who had unwisely been issued with knives so that they could cut their meat, had put them to better use – cutting the cook's throat, murdering the boatswain and three seamen and nearly overpowering the ship. But knives are no defense against firearms, and although the crew was racked and weakened by fever, the mutiny was put down, the ringleaders suffering a good whipping 'by all that were capable of doing that office.'

While the slavers lay offshore there was some glimmer of hope for the blacks interned on them, but as soon as the anchor was weighed and the ship made sail there was no way out of their predicament but death. For the captain and his crew, released from the seemingly endless days of haggling, tension and sickness, it was the welcome second leg of their three-cornered voyage. But for their cargo it was the beginning of that fearful journey into the unknown, that prelude to subjection and endless toil – otherwise known as 'The Middle Passage.'

Eric Williams has written that 'The "horrors" of the Middle Passage have been exaggerated,' and he has also pointed out that white indentured servants were transported across the Atlantic under equally uncomfortable conditions – conditions which he has asserted should be seen 'not as something unusual or inhuman but as part of the age.'

It is, however, as difficult to become reconciled to this point of view as it is to believe that the African was less susceptible to pain than his white counterpart, or more accustomed to savage practices in his everyday life – both common prejudices, still not entirely eradicated. Even judged by the standard of sentences meted out to poor white criminals, who could hang for as little as 'picking a pocket for more than a shilling' and be transported for 'the stealing of cloth,' 'burning stacks of corn,' or 'hindering customs officers in the execution of their duty,' the punishments endured by innocent black slaves on board many slaveships seem harsh.

No petty criminals would have expected to suffer the penalty for madness paid by male slaves – who were either beaten to death 'to make sure they were not malingering,' or clubbed to death and thrown overboard. Slaves often tried to commit suicide for by starving themselves, as Captain Phillips explained, ''tis their belief that when they die they return home to their own country and friends again.' No whites had to endure one 'remedy' for self-starvation, which was to burn and scorch the offenders' lips with red-hot coals, beat them repeatedly, and, if this had no effect, apply the 'speculum oris.' This device, a combination of dividers and a thumbscrew, was hammered between the slave's teeth to force open his mouth, food then being poured down his throat through a funnel. And none would expect to suffer reprisals such as those inflicted on the slaves

A Singular View of the 'Middle Passage'

One of the most extraordinary documents of the great era of slavery is that by a tribal chieftain named Zamba. Zamba was a son of a local 'king' who ruled a small community 200 miles up the Congo. The king, Zembola, acquired considerable wealth as a slave dealer, selling to an American captain named Winton. At about the age of 20, in 1800, Zamba himself became king and, having acquired a rudimentary education, determined to extend his horizons by traveling to America with Winton. Winton readily agreed to the suggestion, accommodated Zamba in style on his slave ship – and then, as the ship neared Charleston, imprisoned him and sold him into slavery. Zamba was lucky; he managed to preserve some of his wealth which was invested by his humanitarian owner. He later wrote an account of his life and – since slaves were not allowed to read or write – smuggled his manuscript out with the help of a white friend. It was published in England in 1847. In this extract, he describes conditions on board the slaver from a unique point of view: that of one who suffered as a slave, but who was, at the beginning of the voyage, being given the rights and privileges of a prince.

'After many tears and lamentations on both sides, and an assurance on my part that after visiting America and England, I should return with Captain Winton, bringing home as much property as would make me the richest king on the banks of the Congo, I bade adieu to Africa. Little did I then think that I should no more see dear Africa for ever! ... but when I reflect upon the way in which a merciful Providence has acted towards me, I feel my heart swell with gratitude and love. Out of seeming evil, how much good hath fallen to my lot is not to be reckoned. The Almighty ... hath since repaid me with that inestimable treasure, which is from heaven ... which will never perish, nor rust, nor fade away.

Captain Winton accommodated me with a handsome state-room and we left the Congo on the first day of October 1800. I found that, including my own thirty-two, there were in all four hundred and twenty-two slaves on board: but as the vessel was of 500 tons burthen, they were not so crowded for space as I have since learned has often been the case with emigrants from Europe to America; their accommodation, however, was very miserable. The ship's lower deck was divided fore and aft into compartments of about six feet square, by planks raised about six inches; and into each of these divisions four slaves were put; to lie down, or sit, or take it as they chose. The planks were intended to keep them from rolling when the sea was rough. Of course, they had nothing but the hard deck to lie upon. In regard to clothing they were very scantily supplied: in general, both male and female had a yard and a half, or two yards of Osnaburghs wrapped round their loins; and some of them had a piece of cloth, or a handkerchief, bound round their heads. The males were all linked two and two by a small chain round the ankle. As for provision, they of the American ship *Kentucky* in 1844, after an insurrection, when 46 men and one woman were hanged, mutilated while still alive and then shot 'in the breast and the bodies thrown overboard . . . sometimes they shot at the body while it still hung living, and all kinds of sport was made of the business.'

To a large extent, fear governed the behavior of the captain and his crew – fear of disease and death, and fear of mutiny. And with only five or six officers and about 30 men on a ship carrying up to 500 slaves they had some grounds for anxiety. 'The white men knew,' wrote one man, 'that once the "blackbirds" burst the hatches they would soon master the ship.' Most slaveships left the Guinea coast by night – as a surgeon, Dr Trotter, said – 'when all the slaves were secured below, to prevent them from murmuring or showing any signs of discontent at leaving the coast.' For often in the night the slaves 'were heard making a howling melancholy kind of noise, something expressive of extreme anguish.' Dr Trotter guessed they would dream of their own country and 'when they woke up to find themselves in reality on a slaveship they began to bay and shriek.' Dr Trotter continued: 'This exquisite degree of sensibility was particularly observable among the women, many of whom I found in

were much better off than in the generality of slave-ships; and this, strange as it may appear, they owed to the avarice rather than the humanity of the captain. The motives of the latter, however, were of little moment to the poor slaves, provided the end was for their advantage. The slaves were supplied for breakfast with a fair ration of ground Indian corn boiled, with a spoonful of molasses to each; they generally had boiled rice for dinner; and supper was the same as breakfast. Sometimes for dinner they received each about half a pound of ship biscuit, with a little morsel of beef or pork; too much of this latter would, no doubt, have created thirst. Although this captain (as will be shown in the sequel of my narrative) acted in a most dishonorable and treacherous manner towards me, and was totally devoid of all Christian principle, yet, to serve his own ends in the matter of the slaves, he acted the part of a humane and considerate man. He told me, in the course of our voyage, that, in the early part of his experience in the slave-trade, he had seen as many slaves as he had with him at present shipped on board a vessel of 200 tons, where they were literally packed on the top of each other; and, consequently, from ill air, confinement, and scanty or unwholesome provision, disease was generated to such an extent that in several cases he had known only one-half survive to the end of the voyage; and these, as he termed it, in a very unmarketable condition. He found, therefore, that, by allowing them what he called sufficient room and good provisions, with kind treatment, his speculations turned out much better in regard to the amount of dollars received; and that was all he cared for.

For the first few days, the most of us – I mean the blacks – were laid down with seasickness: but, the weather being fine, that was soon got over. The captain caused the hatches to be kept open night and day (except only upon two occasions) during the whole voyage; and after daylight set in he allowed about one-fourth of his cargo to come on deck for two hours by rotation. He had always four of his men, with loaded muskets and fixed bayonets, day and night on deck; but during this trip there never was the slightest attempt at rioting and mutiny. The only misfortune that befell us was this: After being about 15 days out to sea, one evening, about sunset – the ship with all sail set, going down the trades at the rate of five knots an hour – in the clap of a hand, or at least more suddenly than a stranger to these latitudes could imagine, a heavy squall struck the ship, carrying away great part of the loftier spars and sails, and laying her very nearly on her beam ends. In a few minutes a tremendous sea rose, and although the squall blew over in about a quarter of an hour, and the ship regained her position, the poor slaves below, altogether unprepared for such an occurrence, were mostly thrown on the lee-side, where they lay heaped on the top of each other; their fetters rendered many of them helpless, and before they could be arranged in their proper places, and relieved from their pressure on each other, it was found that 15 of them were smothered or crushed to death, besides a great number who were cruelly bruised. The captain seemed considerably vexed; but the only (or at least the chief) grievance to him was the sudden loss of some five or six thousand dollars. ’

SLAVES IN MUTINY

William Snelgrave, a slaver, comments on slave mutinies. The book was written for general interest in 1734, long before the slave trade came under critical scrutiny.

❛ These Mutinies are generally occasioned by the Sailors ill usage of these poor People, when on board the Ship wherein they are transported to our Plantations. . . .

The first Mutiny I saw among the Negroes, happened during my first Voyage, in the Year 1704. It was on board the *Eagle* Galley of London, commanded by my Father, with whom I was as Purser. We had bought our Negroes in the River of Old Callabar in the Bay of Guinea. At the time of their mutinying we were in that River, having four hundred of them on board, and not above ten white Men who were able to do Service; For several of our Ship's Company were dead, and many more sick; besides, two of our Boats were just then gone with twelve People on Shore to fetch Wood, which lay in sight of the Ship. All these Circumstances put the Negroes on consulting how to mutiny, which they did at four a clock in the Afternoon, just as they went to Supper. But as we had always carefully examined the Mens Irons, both Morning and Evening, none had got them off, which in a great measure contributed to our Preservation. Three white Men stood on the Watch with Cutlaces in their Hands. One of them was on the Forecastle, a stout fellow, seeing some of the Men Negroes take hold of the chief Mate, in order to throw him over board, he laid on them so heartily with the flat side of his Cutlace, that they soon quitted the Mate, who escaped from them, and run on the Quarter Deck to get Arms. I was then sick with an Ague, and lying on a Couch in the great Cabbin, the Fit being just come on. However, I no sooner heard the Outcry, That the Slaves were mutinying, but I took two Pistols, and run on the Deck with them; where meeting with my Father and the chief Mate, I delivered a Pistol to each of them. Whereupon they went forward on the Booms, calling to the Negroe Men that were on the Forecastle; but they did not regard their Threats, being busy with the Centry, (who had disengaged the chief Mate), and they would have certainly killed him with his own Cutlace, could they have got it from him; but they could not break the Line Wherewith the Handle was fastened to his Wrist. And so, tho' they had seized him, yet they could not make use of his Cutlace. Being thus disappointed, they endeavored to throw him overboard, but he held so fast by one of them that they could not do it. My Father seeing this stout Man in so much Danger, ventured amongst the negroes to save him; and fired his Pistol over their Heads, thinking to frighten them. But a lusty Slave struck him with a Billet so hard, that he was almost stunned. The Slave was going to repeat his Blow, when a young Lad about seventeen years old, whom we had been kind to, interposed his Arm, and received the Blow, by which his Arm-bone was fractured. At the same instant the Mate fired his Pistol, and shot the Negroe that had struck my Father. At the sight of this the Mutiny ceased, and all the Men-negroes on the Forecastle threw themselves flat on their Faces, crying out for Mercy. . . .

[On another occasion, talking with Captain Messervy of the *Ferrers*] and understanding from him, that he had never been on the Coast of Guinea before, I took the liberty to observe to him, "That as he had on board so many Negroes of one Town and Language, it required the utmost Care and Management

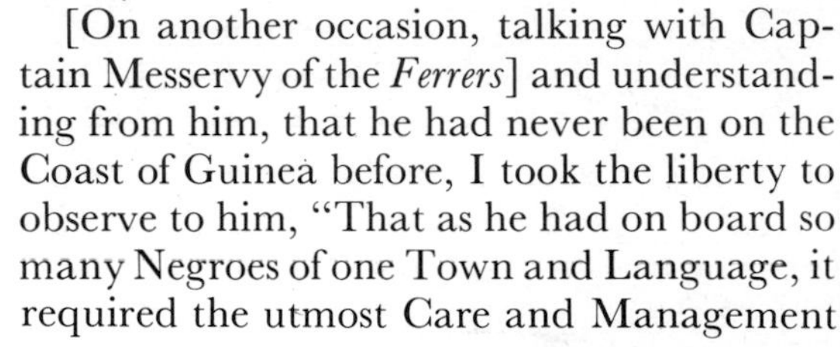

The supression of mutiny: crew members fire on hapless slave mutineers from behind a baricade set up by the security conscious captain.

to keep them from mutinying. . . ."

This he took kindly, and having asked my Advice about other Matters, took his leave, inviting me to come next day to see him. I went accordingly on board his Ship, about three a clock in the afternoon. At four a clock the Negroes went to Supper, and Captain Messervy desired me to excuse him for a quarter of an hour, whilst he went forward to see the Men-Negroes served with Victuals. I observed from the Quarter-Deck, that he himself put Pepper and Palm Oyl amongst the Rice they were going to eat. When he came back to me, I could not forbear observing to him, "How imprudent it was in him to do so: For tho' it was proper for a Commander sometimes to go forward, and observe how things were managed; yet he ought to take a proper time, and have a good many of his white People in Arms when he went; or else the having him so much in their Power, might incourage the Slaves to mutiny: For he might depend upon it, they always aim at the chief Person in the Ship, whom they soon distinguish by the respect shown him by the rest of the People.". . .

He sailed three days after for Jamaica. Some Months after I went for that place, where at my arrival I found his Ship, and had the following melancholy account of his Death, which happened about ten days after he left the Coast of Guinea.

Being on the Forecastle of the Ship, amongst the Men-Negroes, when they were eating their Victuals, they laid hold on him, and beat out his Brains with the little Tubs, out of which they eat their boiled Rice. This Mutiny having been plotted amongst all the grown Negroes on board, they run to the forepart of the Ship in a body, and endeavored to force the Barricado on the Quarter-Deck, not regarding the Musquets or Half Pikes, that were presented to their Breasts by the white Men, through the Loopholes. So that at last the chief Mate was obliged to order one of the Quarter-deck Guns laden with Partridge-Shot, to be fired amongst them; which occasioned a terrible Destruction: For there were near eighty Negroes kill'd and drowned, many jumping overboard when the Gun was fired. This indeed put an end to the Mutiny, but most of the Slaves that remained alive grew so sullen, that several of them were starved to death, obstinately refusing to take any sustenance. , violent hysteric fits.'

It was hardly surprising that there should have been some protest, and, given the conditions aboard many slaveships, it would have been more remarkable if the blacks had remained silent. Women slaves, apart from the constrictions of the slave decks, had to endure rape and 'other brutal excesses as disgrace human nature' from the sailors. 'The license allowed,' as John Newton wrote, 'in this particular, was almost unlimited.' And both men and women were obliged to endure the crossing, which lasted on average five weeks but, if becalmed, could take up to three months, chained to one another in twos or sometimes more, lying either on their backs or on their sides according to the captain's preference, with little more than 16 inches between them.

John Newton, that most complex of slave captains, who left the sea to become a clergyman, and who later became a firm advocate of abolition, wrote: 'The cargo of a vessel of a hundred tons or a little more is calculated to purchase from 220 to 250 slaves. Their lodging rooms below the deck, which are three (for the men, the boys and the women) besides a place for the sick, are sometimes more than five feet high and sometimes less; and this height is divided toward the middle for the slaves lie in two rows, one above the other, on each side of the ship, close to each other like books upon a shelf . . . The poor creatures, thus cramped, are likewise in irons for the most part which makes it difficult for them to turn or move or attempt to rise or to lie down without hurting themselves . . . Each morning perhaps more

The Amistad Affair

In the spring of 1839 Singbe, the son of a Mende chief in Sierra Leone, was seized, sold to Portuguese slavers and shipped off to Cuba. At Havana, Singbe and some 50 of his companions were bought by two Spaniards, who chartered the *Amistad* to carry the slaves to Principe. One night, after their departure, the slaves seized weapons from the sleeping sailors and killed the Captain, Ramon Ferrer, and the cook. With Singbe now in command, they set the sailors adrift and ordered the owners to head for Africa.

Instead the Spaniards steered north and west, and 63 days later the *Amistad* arrived off Long Island. The Africans were imprisoned to await trial for possible piracy. In addition the owners sued for their return.

A Yale professor located a Mende sailor who could serve as an interpreter. Soon, American newspapers were filled with articles about the Africans. Abolitionists flocked to their defense, charging that they had been kidnapped and that they had the right of free people anywhere to use force to preserve their freedom. The court proceedings lasted all winter and public opinion became increasingly divided. Singbe even gave a speech in Mende so impassioned it helped swing the verdict in his favor. The decision was appealed to the US Supreme Court.

The case was taken by the former President John Quincy Adams. Weak and almost blind at the age of 73, he made an eight-and-a-half-hour speech that won the day. The Supreme Court ordered Singbe and his fellow Africans freed. They returned to Sierra Leone in 1842.

A contemporary view of the death of the *Amistad*'s captain, Ramon Ferrer.

instances than one are found of the living and the dead fastened together.'

Overcrowding affected vessels of all sizes. In 1788 a law was passed permitting a vessel of 320 tons to carry 454 slaves, but a ship of that tonnage, the *Brookes,* was reported to have carried 609 slaves on one voyage.

Twice a day, weather permitting, the slaves, the men in chains the women and children free, were allowed up on deck to eat their meals and to take some exercise. Under the watchful eye of the crew and, in many cases, with a cannon pointing at them, a seaman alongside holding a lighted match, they consumed their diet of boiled rice, millet or cornmeal, stewed yams (for those from the Bight of Biafra) and manioc or plantains (for the Congolese and Angolans), or beans, washed down with half a pint of water. Occasionally a benevolent captain would allow them a little salt beef, tobacco or rum, or some beads to play with. On most ships, they were given sticks with which to clean their teeth and palm oil with which to wash.

Exercise consisted of a macabre 'dance,' designed to keep at bay the strange state of 'fixed melancholy' into which many blacks lapsed – 'a condition from which,' one doctor said, 'none . . . was ever cured' – and to combat scurvy. All slaves, the men still in irons, were obliged to jump up and down as best they could to the music of a drum, set of bagpipes or fiddle, supervised by sailors carrying cat-o'-nine-tails, with which they lashed those reluctant or unable to perform. The slaves were also ordered to sing, but, as another doctor said, they 'sing, but not for their amusement. The captain ordered them to sing and they sang songs of sorrow.'

In the late afternoon, when the slaves were once more lying side by side in the slave decks, the wailing and protesting would begin – over their nearness or otherwise to the air-gratings, over the lavatory buckets, or over the women. The difficulties of getting to the latrines was a constant problem. Dr Falconbridge, a surgeon on several ships, wrote: 'It often happens that those who are placed at a distance from the buckets, in endeavoring to get to them, tumble over their companions, in consequence of their being shackled. These accidents, although unavoidable, are productive of continual quarrels . . . In this situation, unable to proceed and prevented from going to the tubs . . . and as the necessities of nature are not to be resisted, they ease themselves as they lie.' It was said that the smell of a slaveship was 'often unmistakable at a distance of five miles downwind.'

A *danse macabre*: under the threat of the lash, slaves – temporarily released from their niches below deck – are forced to jig about to exercise their cramped limbs.

If routine day-to-day conditions on board the guineamen were harsh, in times of epidemic, or in squally weather, they became unbearable. Slaves were not allowed up on deck at all, tarpaulins were thrown over the air-gratings and, as Dr Falconbridge wrote, 'fluxes and fevers among the negroes ensued . . . . The deck, that is, the floor of the rooms, was so covered with the blood and mucus which had proceeded from them in consequence of the flux that it resembled a slaughterhouse . . . . Numbers of the slaves having fainted they were carried upon deck where several of them died and the rest with great difficulty were restored.'

Dr Falconbridge himself suffered the reactions of so many ordinary seamen. His brief visit below decks 'nearly proved fatal to me also . . . . I was so overcome with the heat, stench and foul air that I nearly fainted; and it was only with assistance that I could go on deck. The consequence was that I soon after fell sick of the same disorder from which I did not recover for several months.'

There were a few – very few – exceptions. Some late 18th century slaveships managed to get across the Atlantic without any loss of life. James Barbot took great pride in the hygienic conditions aboard his ship: 'We were very nice in keeping the places where the slaves lay clean and neat . . . Thrice a week we perfumed betwixt decks with a quantity of good vinegar in pails.' And Captain Crow, last of the English slavers, said. 'I always took great pains to promote the health and comfort of all on board, by

A SLAVE DESCRIBES HIS CAPTURE

Olaudah Equiano, renamed Gustavus Vassa – slave, author and abolitionist.

Virtually all those who wrote accounts of the African slave trade were traders; the African view-point was totally absent. In 1789 Olaudah Equiano's autobiography redressed the balance somewhat: it included the best description of enslavement ever written by one of its victims.

An Ibo of a prosperous father, himself a slave-holder, Equiano was born in Biafra about 1745. First seized by slavers at the age of ten, he came eventually into the hands of Benin traders and was shipped successively to Barbados, Virginia and England. Baptised and renamed Gustavus Vassa, he was for many years a mariner, fighting in the Seven Years' War and sailing frequently to the Mediterranean, the Caribbean and North America. He purchased his freedom in 1766 for £40, on the profits of private trade and became, until his death in 1797, a prominent opponent of the slave trade, working actively towards its abolition.

‘One day, when all our people were gone out to their works as usual and only I and my dear sister were left to mind the house, two men and a woman got over our walls, and in a moment seized us both, and without giving us time to cry out or make resistance they stopped our mouths and ran off with us into the nearest wood. Here they tied our hands and continued to carry us as far as they could till night came on, when we reached a small house where the robbers halted for refreshment and spent the night . . . I was now carried to the left of the sun's rising through many different countries and a number of large woods. The people I was sold to used to carry me very often when I was tired either on their shoulders or on their backs. I saw many convenient well-built sheds along the roads at proper distances, to accommodate the merchants and travellers who lay in those buildings along with their wives, who often accompany them; and they always go well armed. . . . All the nations and people I had hitherto passed through resembled our own in their manner, customs, and language: but I came at length to a country the inhabitants of which differed from us. . . . Thus I continued to travel, sometimes by land, sometimes by water, through different countries and various nations, till at the end of six or seven months after I had been kidnapped I arrived at the sea coast.

The first object which saluted my eyes when I arrived on the coast was the sea, and a slave ship which was then riding at anchor and waiting for its cargo. These filled me with astonishment, which was soon converted into terror when I was carried on board. I was immediately handled and tossed up to see if I were sound by some of the crew, and I was now persuaded that I had gotten into a world of bad spirits and that they were going to kill me. Their complexions too differing so much from ours, their long hair and the language they spoke (which was very different from any I had ever heard) united to confirm me in this belief. Indeed such were the horrors of my views and fears at the moment that, if ten thousand worlds had been my own, I would have freely parted with them all to have exchanged my condition with that of the meanest slave in my own country. When I looked round the ship too and saw a large furnace or copper boiling and a multitude of black people of every description chained together, every one of their countenances expressing dejection and sorrow, I no longer doubted of my fate; and quite overpowered with horror and anguish, I fell motionless on the deck and fainted. When I recovered a little I found some black people about me, who I believed were some of those who had brought me on board and had been receiving their pay; they talked to me in order to cheer me, but all in vain. I asked them if we were not to be eaten by those white men with horrible looks, red faces, and loose hair. They told me I was not, and one of the crew brought me a small portion of spirituous liquor in a wine glass, but being afraid of him I would not take it out of his hand. One of the blacks therefore took it from him and gave it to me, and I took a little down my palate, which instead of reviving me, as they thought it would, threw me into the greatest consternation at the strange feeling it produced, having never tasted any such liquor before. Soon after this the blacks who brought me on board went off, and left me abandoned to despair.

I now saw myself deprived of all chance of returning to my native country or even the least glimpse of hope of gaining the shore, which I now considered as friendly; and I even wished for my former slavery in preference to my present situation, which was filled with horrors of every kind, still heightened by my ignorance of what I was to undergo. I was not long suffered to indulge my grief; I was soon put down under the decks, and there I received such a salutation in my nostrils as I had never experienced in my life: so that with the loathsomeness of the stench and crying together, I became so sick and low that I was not able to eat, nor had I the least desire to taste anything. I now wished for the last friend, death, to relieve me; but soon, to my grief, two of the white men offered me eatables, and on my refusing to eat, one of them held me fast by the hands and laid me across I think the windlass, and tied my feet while the other flogged me severely. I had never experienced anything of this kind before, and although, not being used to the water, I naturally feared that element the first time I saw it, yet nevertheless could I have got over the nettings I would have jumped over the side, but I could not; and besides, the crew used to watch us very closely who were not chained down to the decks, lest we should leap into the water: and I have seen some of these poor African prisoners most severely cut for attempting to do so, and hourly whipped for not eating. This indeed was often the case with myself. In a little time after, amongst the poor chained men I found some of my own nation, which in a small degree gave ease to my mind. I inquired of these what was to be done with us; they gave me to understand we were to be carried to these white people's country to work for them. I then was a little revived, and thought if it were no worse than working, my situation was not so desperate: but still I feared I should be put to death, the white people looked and acted, as I thought, in so savage a manner; for I had never seen among my people such instances of brutal cruelty, and this not only shewn towards us blacks but also to some of the whites themselves. One white man in particular I saw, when we were permitted to be on deck, flogged so unmercifully with a large rope near the foremast that he died in consequence of it; and they tossed him over the side as they would have done a brute. This made me fear these people the more, and I expected nothing less than to be treated in the same manner. I could not help expressing my fears and apprehensions to some of my countrymen: I asked them if these people had no country but lived in this hollow place (the ship): they told me they did not, but came from a distant one. . . . At last, when the ship we were in had got in all her cargo, they made ready with many fearful noises, and we were all put under deck so that we could not see how they managed the vessel. But this disappointment was the least of my sorrow. The stench of the hold while we were on the coast was so intolerable loathsome that it was dangerous to remain there for any time, and some of us had been permitted to stay on the deck for the fresh air; but now that the whole ship's cargo were confined together it became absolutely pestilential. The closeness of the place and the heat of the climate, added to the number in the ship, which was so crowded that each had scarcely room to turn himself, almost suffocated us. This produced copious perspirations, so that the air soon became unfit for respiration from a variety of loathsome smells, and brought on a sickness among the slaves, of which many died, thus falling victims to the improvident avarice, as I may call it, of their purchasers. This wretched situation was again aggravated by the galling of the chains, now become insupportable, and the filth of the necessary tubs, into which the children often fell and were almost suffocated. The shrieks of the women and the groans of the dying rendered the whole scene of horror almost inconceivable. Happily perhaps for myself I was soon reduced so low here that it was thought necessary to keep me almost always on deck, and from my extreme youth I was not put in fetters. In this situation I expected every hour to share the fate of my companions, some of whom were almost daily brought upon deck at the point of death, which I began to hope would soon put an end to my miseries. . . .

One day, when we had a smooth sea and moderate wind, two of my wearied countrymen who were chained together (I was near them at the time), preferring death to such a life of misery, somehow made through the nettings and jumped into the sea: immediately another quite dejected fellow, who on account of his illness was suffered to be out of irons, also followed their example; and I believe many more would very soon have done the same if they had not been prevented by the ship's crew, who were instantly alarmed. Those of us that were the most active were in a moment put down under the deck, and there was such a noise and confusion amongst the people of the ship as I never heard before, to stop her and get the boat out to go after the slaves. However two of the wretches were drowned, but they got the other and afterwards flogged him unmercifully for thus attempting to prefer death to slavery. In this manner we continued to undergo more hardships than I can now relate . . . [until] at last we came in sight of the island of Barbados. , proper diet, regularity, exercise and cleanliness' – unlike some captains, some of whom only cleaned out the hold once a week and others who simply left things as they were until they arrived at their destination.

An overall average figure for deaths during the Middle Passage over the 360 year period of the slave trade has been estimated at 12.5 percent which amounted to 40,000 a year at the height of the trade. Specific numbers of slaves from Nantes between 1716 and 1775 have been put at 35,000 dead out of the 240,000 slaves carried on 762 ships, that is 14.5 percent. But bald statistics conceal the human realities – the diseases that killed seamen and slaves alike – the flux, the plague and smallpox, that most feared of all illnesses, which could kill more than half the slaves. Captain Wilson, of the *Hero* lost 360 slaves, mostly from smallpox: 'When moved from one place to another they left marks of their skin and blood upon the deck, and the . . . surgeon told me it was the most horrid sight he had ever seen.' They conceal the eccentric acts of inhuman captains; when the slaves on the French ship *Rodeur,* sailing to Guadeloupe in 1819, contracted ophthalmia, an irritating but not usually serious eye infection, the captain had 36 blacks thrown alive into the sea 'to save the unaffected and to ground a claim on the underwriters.' They conceal the desperate attempts by slaves to cut their own throats, to starve, or hang themselves. And they conceal the dangers of the prolonged calm – the *Hero* was delayed for so long that the captain wrote, 'we were so straitened for provisions that if we had been ten more days at sea, we must either have eaten the slaves that died, or have made the living slaves walk the plank.'

One of the worst atrocities occurred in 1781, when the captain of the *Zong* found himself plagued with poor winds and a slow passage, and with dysentery spreading through his 440 slaves and 17 crew. Sixty blacks and seven seamen died. His water supply began to run low. He decided to save the owners of the ship any unnecessary loss by throwing his whole cargo of 'sick wretches into the sea,' intending to turn useless slaves into legal jettison that was covered by insurance. One hundred and thirty-two slaves were disposed of in this way, but when, on the ship's return to England, the owners claimed their insurance money, the underwriters refused to pay. In court, the jury supported the owners, saying 'they had no doubt . . . that the case of slaves was the same as if horses had been thrown overboard.' A later court, however, appealed to by the underwriters reversed this decision – thus legally recognizing for the first time that slaves were human beings and not just merchandise.

When the slaveships finally arrived within sight of the Caribbean, the blacks, taken out of their chains, were fattened up, rubbed with oil 'until their black skins shone in the clear cool dawn.' On easy-going ships there were even parties, 'the women slaves dancing in the sailors' cast off clothing.' Such pleasures were only too brief. Even while the slaves were still being given the outward appearance of good health, the captain would be ashore negotiating for the disposal of his cargo. Almost immediately after came the rude awakening of the slave sales.

The weak and the sick were sold first – the 'refuse' slaves, who were bought by 'Jews as a speculation, or by surgeons.' The most usual form of selling the remainder was the fixed-price sale, or 'scramble.' Dr Falconbridge described a typical 'scramble': 'On a day appointed, the negroes were landed, and placed altogether in a large yard belonging to the merchants to whom the ship is consigned. As soon as the hour agreed on arrived, the doors of the yard were suddenly thrown open and in rushed a considerable number of purchasers, with all the ferocity of brutes. Some instantly seized such of the negroes as they could conveniently lay hold of with their hands. Others, being prepared with several handkerchiefs tied together, encircled with these as many as they were able. While others, by means of a rope, effected the same purpose. It is scarcely possible to describe the confusion of which this mode of selling is productive.' This traumatic experience proved too much for many blacks, who escaped, and ran wild about the town.'

It was, as one writer put it, a 'shattering prelude to life on the old plantation,' and bore out Ottobah Cugoano's forebodings, when he wrote: 'But I may safely say that all the poverty and misery that any of the inhabitants of Africa meet with among themselves is far inferior to those inhospitable regions of misery which they meet with in the West Indies, where their hard-hearted overseers have neither regard to the laws of God, nor the life of their fellow-men.'

THE ZONG ATROCITY

Of all the recorded horrors of the Atlantic slave trade, perhaps the most appalling is that of the *Zong*, whose master, Luke Collingwood, threw 132 slaves overboard to collect the insurance. Its significance was two-fold. Firstly it exemplified the extreme barbarities of the trade, and secondly, when the facts became known, it was adopted as a test case by the great English abolitionist, Granville Sharpe, to show the inhumanities of English law.

The incident occurred in September 1781. Granville Sharpe heard about it only two years later when the claim by the owners against the insurers came to court. He was told of the incident by the former slave and ardent abolitionist, Olaudah Equiano (Gustavus Vassa). His account runs as follows:

'19 March 1783. Gustavus Vassa called on me with an account of 132 negroes being thrown alive into the sea, from on board an English slave-ship.

The circumstances of this case could not fail to excite a deep interest. The master of a slave-ship trading from Africa to Jamaica, and having 440 slaves on board, had thought fit, on a pretext that he might be distressed on his voyage for want of water, to lessen the consumption of it in the vessel, by throwing overboard 132 of the most sickly among the slaves. On his return to England, the owners of the ship claimed from the insurers the full value of those drowned slaves, on the ground that there was an absolute necessity for throwing them into the sea, in order to save the remaining crew, and the ship itself. The underwriters contested the existence of the alleged necessity; or, if it had existed, attributed it to the ignorance and improper conduct of the master of the vessel. This contest of pecuniary interest brought to light a scene of horrid brutality which had been acted during the execution of a detestable plot. From the trial it appeared that the ship *Zong*, Luke Collingwood master, sailed from the island of St Thomas, on the coast of Africa, 6 September 1781, with 440 slaves and fourteen whites on board, for Jamaica, and that in the November following she fell in with that island; but instead of proceeding to some port, the master, mistaking, as he alleges, Jamaica for Hispaniola, ran her to leeward. Sickness and mortality had by this time taken place on board the crowded vessel: so that, between the time of leaving the coast of Africa and the 29th of November, sixty slaves and seven white people had died; and a great number of the surviving slaves were then sick and not likely to live. On that day the master of the ship called together a few of the officers, and stated to them, that, if the sick slaves died a natural death, the loss would fall on the owners of the ship; but, if they were thrown alive into the sea, on any sufficient pretext of necessity for the safety of the ship, it would be the loss of the underwriters, alleging, at the same time, that it would be less cruel to throw sick wretches into the sea, than to suffer them to linger out a few days under the disorder with which they were afflicted.

To this inhuman proposal the mate, James Kelsal, at first objected; but Collingwood at length prevailed on the crew to listen to it. He then chose out from the cargo 232 slaves, and brought them on deck, all or most of whom were sickly, and not likely to recover, and he ordered the crew by turns to throw them into the sea. 'A parcel' of them were accordingly thrown overboard, and, on counting over the remainder the next morning, it appeared that the number so drowned had been fifty-four. He then ordered another parcel to be thrown over, which, on a second counting on the succeeding day, was proved to have amounted to forty-two.

On the third day the remaining thirty-six were brought on deck, and, as these now resisted the cruel purpose of their masters, the arms of twenty-six were fettered with irons, and the savage crew proceeded with the diabolical work, casting them down to join their comrades of the former days. Outraged

An illustration of the cramped conditions below decks: such treatment almost guaranteed the rapid spread of the dreaded 'flux' or dysentery which afflicted the victims in the *Zong* incident.

misery could endure no longer; the ten last victims sprang disdainfully from the grasp of their tyrants, defied their power, and leaping into the sea, felt a momentary triumph in the embrace of death.'

The court case that followed underlined the cynicism of English law at the time, which was summarized by an insurance lawyer in 1781 as follows:

'The insurer takes upon him the risk of the loss, capture, and death of slaves, or any other unavoidable accident to them: but natural death is always understood to be expected: – by natural death is meant, not only when it happens by disease or sickness, but also when the captive destroys himself through despair, which often happens: but when slaves are killed ... to quell an insurrection ... then the insurers must answer.'

The owners of the *Zong* claimed from the insurers the full value of the murdered slaves – £30 a piece – on the grounds that there was an absolute necessity to throw them into the sea in order to save the remaining crew. The necessity given was scarcity of water. As it turned out, there was no lack of water. When the first 'parcel' of slaves was thrown overboard, no one in the ship, white or black, had been on short allowance. The ship arrived in Jamaica on 22 December with 420 gallons to spare. The 'absolute necessity' was in fact Collingwood's avarice. If the disease-ridden slaves died, there would be no insurance forthcoming and Collingwood's commission would be forfeit.

What horrified Sharpe was that the law concerned itself only with the narrow question of whether Collingwood had acted out of necessity or not. As the Solicitor-General, John Lee, for the owners, brutally put it:

'What is all this vast declamation of human people being thrown overboard? The question after all is, Was it voluntary, or an act of necessity? *This is a case of chattels or goods.* It is really so: it is the case of throwing over goods; for to this purpose, and the purpose of the insurance, *they are goods and property: whether right or wrong, we have nothing to do with it.* This property ... [has] been thrown overboard: whether or not for the preservation of the rest, that is the real question.'

At one point in the course of his tirade Lee, turning to Granville Sharpe, who attended all the hearings, was even more vulgar. He exclaimed somewhat violently to the Judges, that: "A person was in Court (at the same time turning round and looking at me) who intended to bring on a criminal prosecution for murder against the parties concerned: *but*", said he, "*it would be madness: the Blacks were property*... If any man of them was allowed to be tried at the Old Bailey for a

murder, I cannot help thinking, if that charge of murder was attempted to be sustained, *it would be folly and rashness to a degree of madness*: and, so far from the charge of murder lying against these people, *there is not the least imputation – of cruelty I will not say, but – of impropriety: not in the least!!!*"'

As a result of the *Zong* case, no one who examined the evidence could deny the injustices either of the trade itself or of English law. Although the owners won the case, the judgment was overturned on appeal.

Slave dealers throw overboard mutinous and diseased slaves.

CHAPTER III

KING SUGAR'S SLAVES

SLAVERY IN THE WEST INDIES

In a Jamaican 'House of Correction': this composite view of slave punishments shows a treadmill, lashing and a woman having her hair shorn.

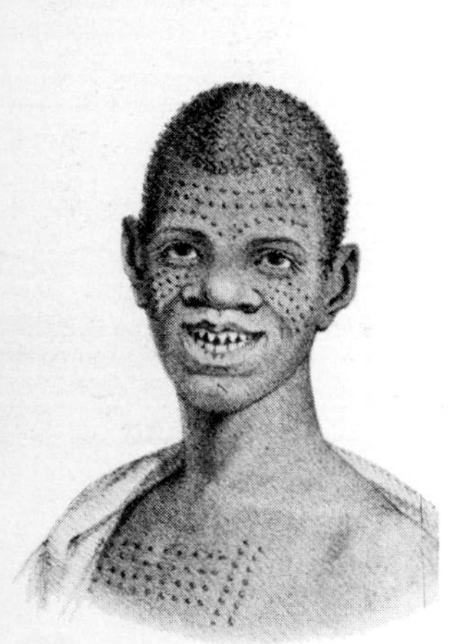

The merchant and planter, Bryan Edwards, whose *History of the British Colonies in the West Indies* was published in 1793, thought that the West Indian planters were 'entirely innocent and ignorant of the manner in which the slave trade is conducted (having no other concern therein than becoming purchasers of what British acts of Parliament have made objects of sale),' a strangely blinkered view, but by no means an isolated one.

Plantation profits founded some spectacular fortunes, both private and municipal, and it was therefore in the interests of factors, slave captains, merchants and planters alike to rationalize their actions in the interests of public and private gain, and to reassure one another that what they were doing was for the good not only of themselves but also of the African blacks.

James Boswell echoed the opinions of many planters when he said that slavery saved the blacks from 'massacre or intolerable bondage in their own country and introduces them to a much happier state of life.' And an American trader, Richard Drake, spoke for many slave captains when he recorded in his journal: 'Leclerc and I had a chat about this African business. He says he's repugnant to it, and I confess its not a thing I like. But... slaves must be bought and sold; somebody must do the trading; and why not make hay while the sun shines?' When the trade had the support of monarchs, governments and churches, who was to deny him his right to a share of the profits?

Anyway, Drake could also have argued, it was not an easy business. As Captain Phillips of the *Hannibal* complained: 'No gold-finders can endure so much noisome slavery as they do who carry Negroes; for those have some respite and satisfaction, but we endure twice the misery; and yet by their mortality our voyages are ruin'd, and we pine and fret our selves to death to think we should undergo so much misery, and take so much pains to so little purpose.' In 1694, the *Hannibal* lost 320 slaves out of 700 during the Middle Passage, representing a total loss of £6560, borne equally by the Royal African Company and the owner of the ship.

In the late 17th century, slaves could be bought on the Guinea coast for about £3 a head and fetched £16–£17 in the West Indies – the price of a ton of sugar. One hundred years later the price had risen to between £20–£25 in Africa and £40–£50 in the main American market, Jamaica. Although the monopoly companies rarely made profits – the cost of maintaining their forts in Africa was a constant drain on their resources – a private merchant with between three and five ships could make a profit of 100 percent, and the average, according to one modern writer, 'even considering losses from wreck, piracy, mutiny and disease, must have been well over 30 percent on each voyage.'

Not all investors received such a handsome return on their outlay. The successful sale of slaves in the West Indies did not automatically guarantee either cash payment or profit for the owners of a ship. Some planters, themselves heavily in debt, offered post-dated bills of exchange which in many cases were dishonored. And sugar was often unobtainable, either because it was too early in the season, or because commission merchants trading directly with the islands had cleaned up the market. Ships had then to complete the third stage of their 'triangular' voyage in ballast, which could mean a considerable loss for the owners. James Pope-Hennessy quotes the example of the *Africa*, owned by a syndicate of eight merchants, which sailed from Bristol to New Calabar in 1774. The *Africa* had been stocked with trade goods and fitted out at a total cost of £5692, the slaves fetched £5128 12s 6d at St Vincent, but due to the fact that the ship returned home empty, the proceeds of the voyage were only £5650 8s 0d, which 'by deducting miscellaneous operating charges left a net balance of £5442 8s 0d.' In this case, the gamble for the owners of the *Africa* had not paid off. Thomas Leyland, a Liverpool merchant, was luckier. One of his six ships, the *Enterprise*, stocked and fitted in 1803 at a cost of £17,045, was also obliged to return home empty, but the 392 slaves who survived the Atlantic crossing were sold at about £62 a head (roughly £25,000) and despite various operating charges Leyland's profit amounted to a comfortable £6428.

'Slaves and sugar,' commented one writer, 'seldom made poor men prosperous,' adding, 'what they did in a number of cases was to make comfortable men extremely rich.'

The slave business remained an eminently respectable one until the end of the 18th century, when the murmurs occasionally to be heard against either its usefulness or its morality grew louder and put many of those involved on the defensive. But ignorance of the conduct of the slave trade and the conditions under which slaves worked on the remote plantations, together with the unshakeable conviction that 'hot countries cannot be cultivated without negroes,' put such views firmly in the minority. Few opponents of the trade were as forthright as Dr Johnson who, at an Oxford dinner, proposed a toast to 'the next insurrection of the negroes in the West Indies!' (Dr Johnson, however, was notorious for his violent hatred of both West Indian and American slave owners, opinions which his chronicler, Boswell, attributed to 'zeal without knowledge.') And with the Society for the Propagation of the Gospel, the Baptists, the Quakers, the Jesuits, the Dominicans, the Franciscans, Bishops, Members of Parliament, Mayors, Aldermen and Peers all jostling for a corner of the lucrative market, and all assuring themselves, like Lord St Vincent, that 'life on the plantations was for the Negro a veritable paradise as compared with his existence in Africa,' it was small wonder that so few consciences were troubled.

Slavery was accepted unthinkingly by 18th century Englishmen. Small black boys were much sought after as pets by ladies of fashion; slaves were sold openly at auctions; and freed or discarded blacks swelled the ranks of the poor and destitute in London, Bristol and Liverpool. The gruesome accessories of the slave trade were on display in shop windows: 'chains and manacles, devices for forcing open Negroes' mouths when they refused to eat, neck-rings enhanced by long projecting prongs . . . thumbscrews and all the other implements of oppression.' Even the Customs House in Liverpool 'sported carvings of Negroes' heads.' A Victorian essayist wrote, 'It was the capital made in the African slave trade that built some of our docks. It was the price of human flesh and blood that gave us a start.'

Three ports dominated the British slave trade – London, Bristol and Liverpool. During the first half of the 18th century, Bristol superseded London as the principal slaving port (in 1739 52 ships sailed for the Guinea Coast). But by the end of the century, Liverpool, formerly an insignificant little port, was handling, according to one authority, five-eighths of the English trade in slaves and three-sevenths of the whole slave trade of all the European nations. Liverpool's population rose from 5000 in 1700 to 34,000 in 1773, and by 1798, 150 ships were carrying 52,557 slaves – a total gross turnover of approximately £2.5 million. Eric Williams estimated that in 1783 the city's annual profit from the slave trade alone was £300,000.

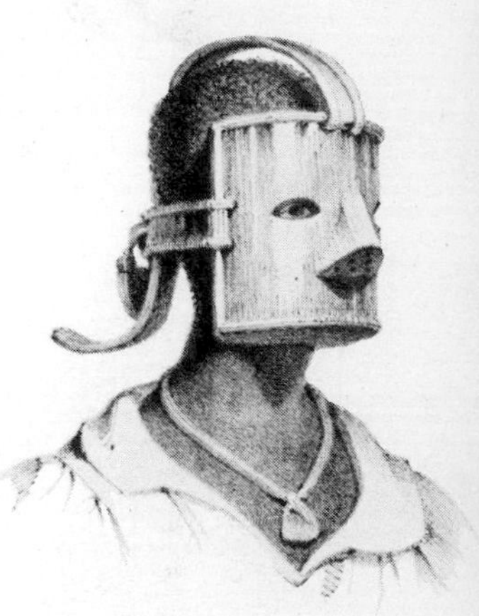

'This great annual return of wealth,' wrote a citizen of Liverpool in 1797, 'may be said to pervade the whole town . . . contributing to the support of the majority of the inhabitants; almost every man in Liverpool is a merchant . . . it will therefore create little astonishment that the attractive African meteor has from time to time so dazzled their ideas that almost every order of people is interested in a Guinea cargo.'

As the private slave merchants prospered, they bought, among other things, public recognition through philanthropy; Brian Blundell, twice mayor of Liverpool, founded

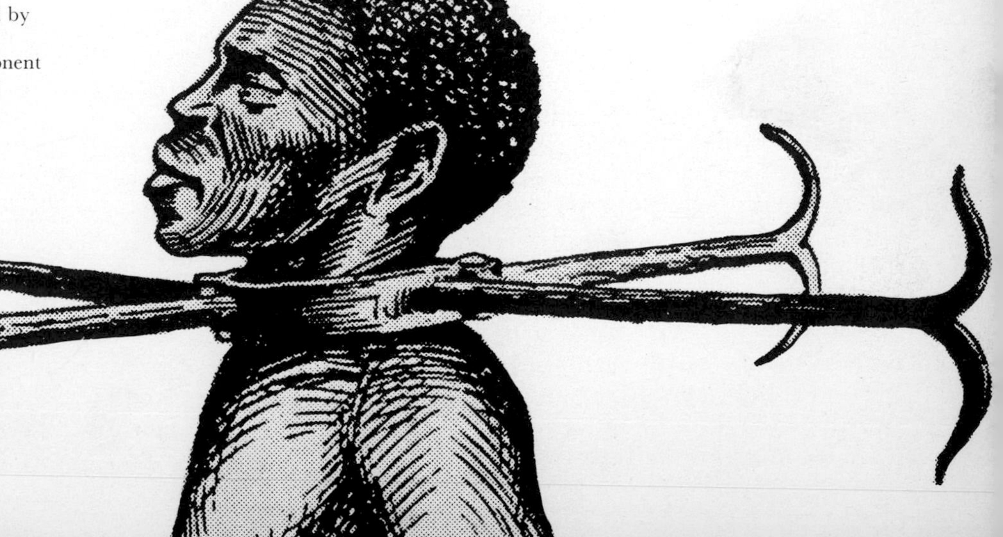

Slaves innocent and punished: these drawings record tribal markings on West Indian slaves (*far left*) and three modes of punishment for recalcitrant slaves (*right and below*) – a mask, neck-lock and neck-ring. The last was drawn from a specimen owned by William Wilberforce, England's leading opponent of slavery and the slave trade.

the Bluecoat School and, together with Foster Cunliffe (a pioneer of the Liverpool slave trade), the Liverpool Infirmary and the Warrington Academy. Sixty-four of the 81 mayors of the city, according to one historian, were actively engaged in the slave trade, as was one of Liverpool's two Members of Parliament.

Indeed, buying a seat in Parliament and a country estate was the surest way for a returned West Indian planter or a successful merchant to gain admittance to that hitherto unattainable charmed circle, the influential landowning class. He could afford to pay handsomely for the privilege – Eric Williams cites the instances of two West Indian planters, one who 'successfully spent £18,000 getting himself elected in Bristol' and the other squandering £50,000 on a Liverpool seat which he failed to win. George III's sour remark to his Prime Minister when overtaken on the seafront at Weymouth by a planter driving a coach-and-six altogether more magnificent than his own: 'All that sugar! How are the duties, eh, Pitt, how are the duties?' echoed the sentiments of most of the English aristocracy, who were obliged to swallow their resentment at the sight of nouveaux riches planters worming their way into polite society.

Like it or not, the aristocracy had to bow to the West Indian interest in Parliament, for by 1764 there were between 50 and 60 West Indian voters 'who could turn the balance any way they pleased.' It was a powerful lobby, with voices like those of the flamboyant and immensely rich absentee landlord, William Beckford, Member for Shaftesbury and twice Lord Mayor of London, and John Gladstone, father of William (who made his maiden speech in 1833 in defense of the family plantations in Guiana). With support from such allies as the Earl of Chatham, George Canning and Wellington, the planters were well able to protect their interests with prolonged opposition to any rise in sugar duties, any weakening of their monopoly and the slightest hint of abolition or emancipation.

Thus the slave-trading interest wove its way into the fabric of the British economy. Slave merchants diversified to become sugar refiners, bankers and insurers.

It was until recently generally believed that there was a strong financial link between slave trading and the Industrial Revolution.

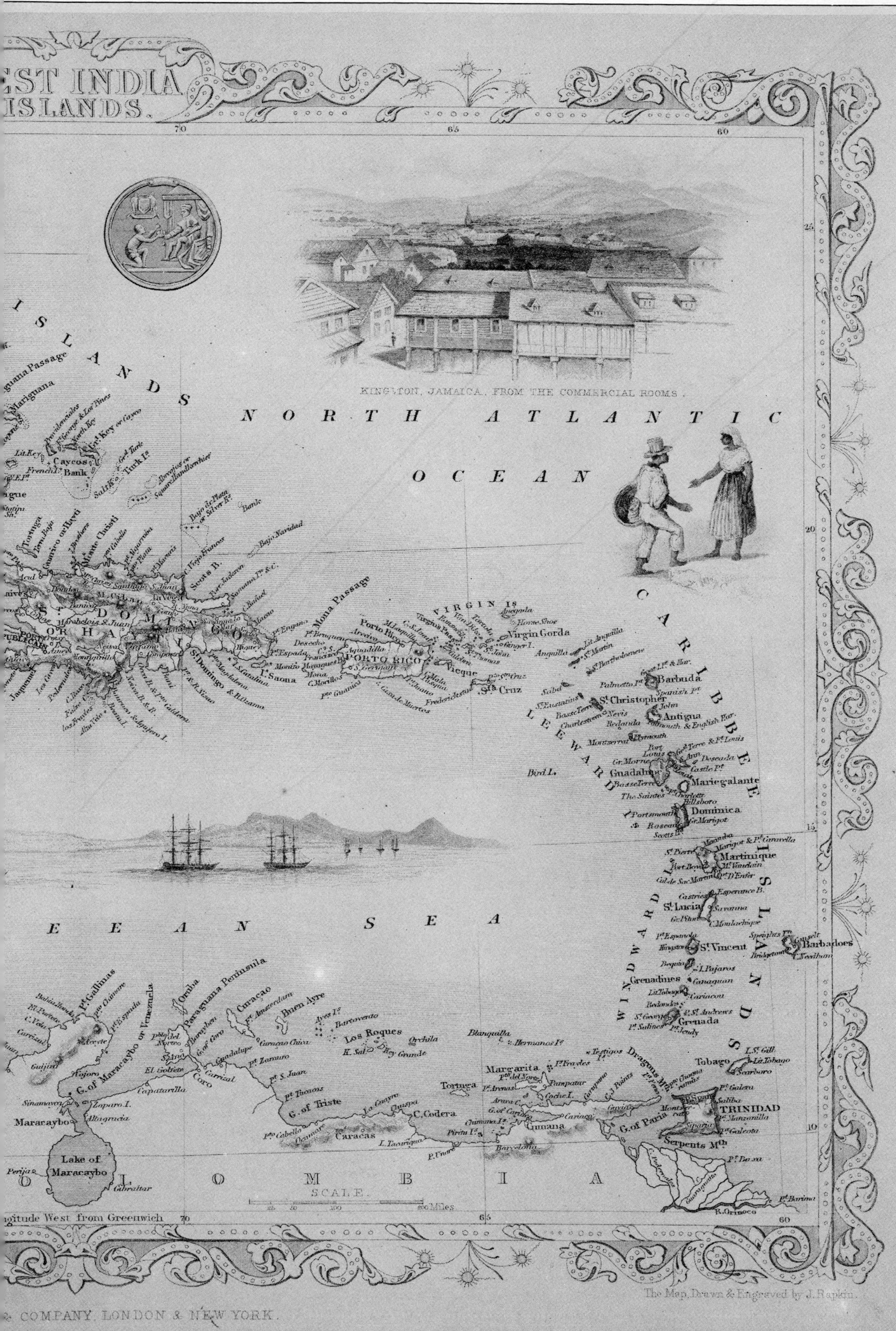

European power in the West Indies, as indicated in a map of 1841:

British
Bahama Islands
Jamaica
Leeward Islands (including Anguilla, St Kitts, Barbuda, Nevis, Antigua, Montserrat, Dominica)
Windward Islands (including St Lucia, St Vincent, Barbados)
Trinidad
Tobago
Virgin Islands (Tortola)

French
Guadeloupe
Martinique

Spanish:
Cuba
Puerto Rico
Santo Domingo (called San Domingo by English speakers)

Dutch
St Martin
St Eustatius
Curaçao

Danish
Virgin Islands (St Thomas, St John and St Croix)

On the plantation: this engraving shows West Indian slaves picking cotton and packing it in bags ready for export.

This view is now under attack. Duncan Rice, author of *The Rise and Fall of Black Slavery*, recognizes that the Atlantic trade 'clearly gave a boost to the European economy as a whole,' but calculated Liverpool's profits on the slave trade in the second half of the 18th century to have been only 7.5 percent and estimated that if all English slave trading profits had been re-invested they would only have amounted to 1.5 percent of the total national investment.

In France, the second largest slaving nation, huge fortunes were made from the slave trade, particularly after the seizure of San Domingo from the Spanish (after which it has been estimated that between 1748 and 1792, 246,800 slaves were taken to the Caribbean from Nantes alone). But across the Channel the link between slave capital and industrialization was even weaker than in England. The great slaving dynasties of Nantes (the Liverpool of France), the families of Nairac, de Luyne, Montaudoin, de Guest and Bouteiller, were predominantly Huguenot in origin and as such excluded from membership of city guilds, so weakening their political power. Connected both by marriage and business interests, they formed a separate, incestuous elite, plowing back their vast profits into insurance or West Indian mortgages and investing in direct trading rather than in industry. For instance, owing to the comparatively underdeveloped state of French manufacturing industries in the 18th century, French slave traders had to import their trading goods – like mirrors, knives, arms and clay-pipes – from Flanders, Holland and Germany.

Planters and merchants of both nations shared a common aim – to leave the West Indies and their sugar plantations, as soon as they could afford it, and return home. 'The climate of our sugar colonies is so inconvenient for an English constitution,' wrote William Beckford, 'that no man will choose to live there, much less will any man choose to settle there.'

However, William Beckford apart, the average absentee planter seldom prospered. Christopher Jeaffreson, whose plantation in St Kitts (as St Christophers was called) was let to a Mr Worley (who was not only a bad planter but behind with his rent), said: 'It is so difficult a matter to find an honest and sufficient tenant that I cannot resolve upon it. For a poor tenant may soon be disabled, and

TO BE SOLD & LET
BY PUBLIC AUCTION,
On MONDAY the 18th of MAY, 1829,
UNDER THE TREES.
FOR SALE,
THE THREE FOLLOWING
SLAVES,
VIZ.
HANNIBAL, about 30 Years old, an excellent House Servant, of Good Character.
WILLIAM, about 35 Years old, a Labourer.
NANCY, an excellent House Servant and Nurse.
The MEN belonging to "LEECH'S" Estate, and the WOMAN to Mrs. D. SMIT
TO BE LET,
On the usual conditions of the Hirer finding them in Food, Clot in , and Medical ance,
THE FOLLOWING
MALE and FEMALE
SLAVES,
OF GOOD CHARACTERS.
ROBERT BAGLEY, about 20 Years old, a good House Servant.
WILLIAM BAGLEY, about 18 Years old, a Labourer.
JOHN ARMS, about 18 Years old.
JACK ANTONIA, about 40 Years old, a Labourer.
PHILIP, an Excellent Fisherman.
HARRY, about 27 Years old, a good House Servant.
LUCY, a Young Woman of good Character, used to House Work and the Nursery.
ELIZA, an Excellent Washerwoman.
CLARA, an Excellent Washerwoman.
FANNY, about 14 Years old, House Servant.
SARAH, about 14 Years old, House Servant.
Also for Sale, at Eleven o'Clock,
Fine Rice, Gram, Paddy, Books, Muslins,
Needles, Pins, Ribbons &c. &c.
AT ONE O'CLOCK, THAT CELEBRATED ENGLISH HORSE
BLUCHER,
ADDISON PRINTER GOVERNMENT

Above: A sale poster advertising slaves, domestic items and a horse reveal the way in which slaves were dehumanized to be treated as objects. *Below*, a planter in Surinam (Dutch Guiana) with his newly acquired young slave girl.

a dishonest one will never be willing to comply with his lease. And I am sensible the law is more favorable to a tenant than an attorney. So that in my case would be so much the worse. I should profit nothing by good years, and bear the whole loss of the bad.'

The returned planters on their Dorset or Wiltshire estates might torment themselves with profits lost or embezzled by their colonial overseers, but for the slaves who worked on the plantations it mattered little who was in charge of them. Cultivation of sugar cane, which flourished so abundantly in the rich soil, tropical heat and humidity of many West Indian islands, was a backbreaking and infinitely laborious undertaking carried out, from sunrise to sunset, apart from a two-hour break from midday until two o'clock. A Swiss traveler, describing the digging of ditches in a cane field, wrote, 'There were about a hundred men and women of different ages . . . the majority of them naked or covered with rags. The sun shone down with full force on their heads. Sweat rolled from all parts of their bodies . . . Exhaustion was stamped on every face . . . The pitiless eye of the Manager patrolled the gang and several foremen armed with long whips moved periodically between them, giving stinging blows to all who, worn out by fatigue, were compelled to take a rest, men or women, young or old.'

The French practice of slavery differed significantly in form from the British. Under the *Côde Noir* (Black Code) of 1685, a slave law drawn up by the French mainly to uphold Catholicism in their West Indian colonies, black slaves, although still recognized as chattels and given no protection against personal physical abuse from their owners, were at least entitled to be prosecuted criminally 'without their masters becoming parties' and to be condemned to death, prison or mutilation within the normal framework of justice. French planters were under an obligation to have their slaves baptized, legally married if they so wished, to feed and clothe them properly, and to give them a rest on Sundays.

In contrast, slaves in British possessions were not considered part of their charge by the Anglican clergy, were rarely, if ever, baptized, never instructed, never legally married and discouraged if found attending church. 'I saw a slave receive twenty lashes of a whip,' wrote Ottobah Cugoano, 'for being seen in church on Sunday instead of going to work.'

It was also forbidden under the *Côde Noir* to sell separately a mother and child if the child was under the age of puberty. Owners, however, although urged to treat their slaves humanely, retained the right to chain and flog their slaves with rods or cords if and when they considered it necessary, and to administer the punishments for running away: for absenteeism once in a month both ears were cut off and one shoulder branded, the second time the buttocks were cut off and the other shoulder branded; if the slave ran away a third time, the punishment was death.

Though the *Côde Noir* represented a genuine attempt to bring slavery under the sanctions of law, with planters living in constant fear of insubordination and uprising among the slaves who so heavily outnumbered them, the system of plantation slavery

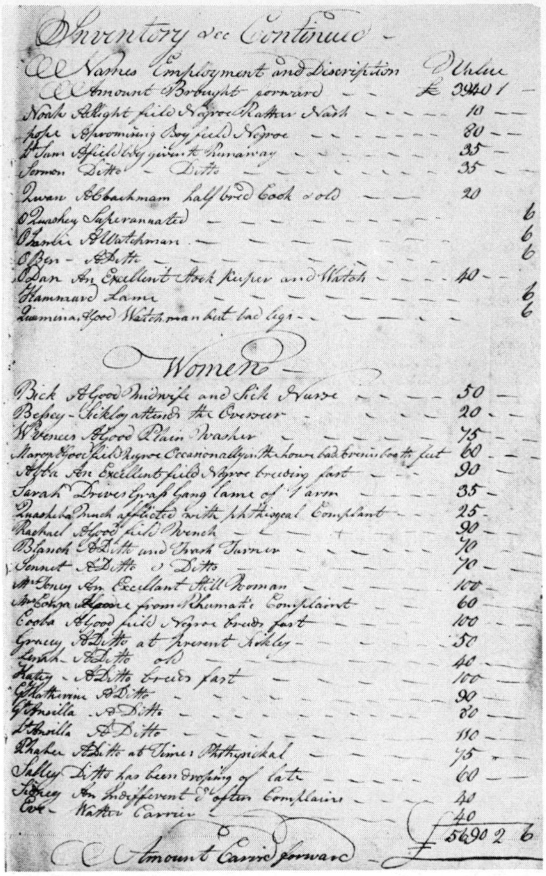

Inventory &c Continued

Names Employment and Discription	Value
Amount Brought forward	£ 3940 1
Noah A slight field Negroe Ratter Nash	10
Pope A promising Boy field Negroe	80
Sam A field boy given to Runaway	35
Simon Ditto Ditto	35
Quan A Coachman half bred Cook & old	20
Quashey Superannuated	6
Charlie A Watchman	6
Ben A Ditto	6
Dan An Excellent Stock Keeper and Watch	40
Hammard Lame	6
Quamina A good Watchman but bad legs	6

Women

Bick A good Midwife and Sick Nurse	50
Bessey Sickly attends the Overseer	20
Venus A good Plain Washer	75
Mary A good field Negroe Occasionally in the house bad breeds both fast	60
Abba An Excellent field Negroe breeding fast	90
Sarah Drives Grass Gang lame of 1 arm	35
Quasheba Much afflicted with phthisical Complaint	25
Rachael A good field Wench	90
Blanch A Ditto and Trash Turner	70
Sennet A Ditto & Ditto	70
Mrs Toney An Excellant Still Woman	100
Mrs Cohyn Alone from Rheumatic Complaint	60
Cooba A good field Negroe breeds fast	100
Gracey A Ditto at present Sickley	50
Lenah A Ditto old	40
Katey A Ditto breeds fast	100
G Katherine A Ditto	90
G Amoilla A Ditto	80
L Amoilla A Ditto	110
Phaber A Ditto at Times Phthysickal	75
Salley Ditto has been droping of late	60
Sidney An Indifferent & often Complains	40
Eve Watter Carrier	40
Amount Carried forward	£ 5690 2 6

The inventory of blacks on a West Indian plantation reveals in details (*below*) those qualities admired by plantation owners. 'A good field Negroe,' reads one line, 'breeds fast.'

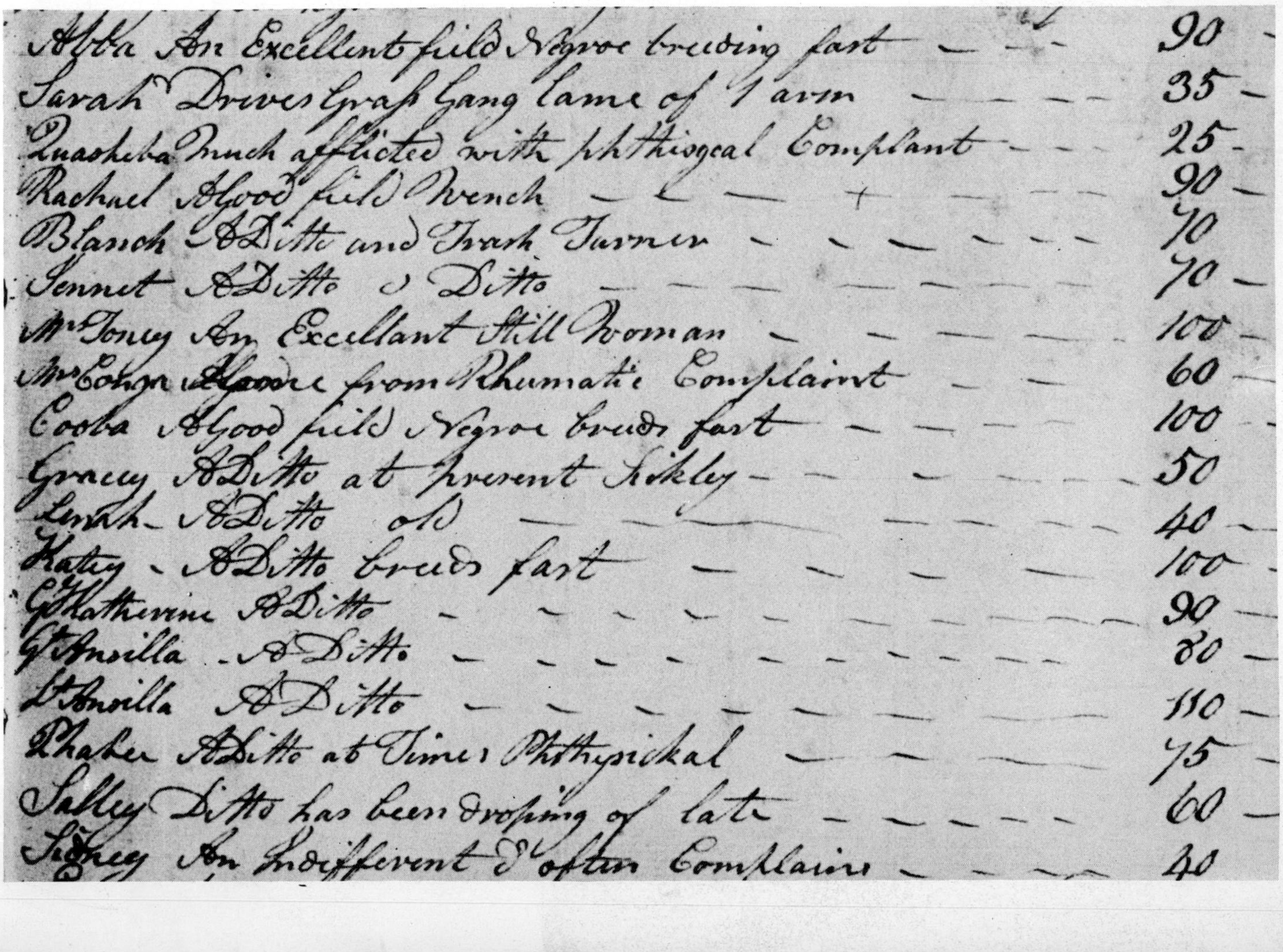

Abba An Excellent field Negroe breeding fast 90
Sarah Drives Grass Gang lame of 1 arm 35
Quasheba Much afflicted with phthisical Complaint 25
Rachael A good field Wench 90
Blanch A Ditto and Trash Turner 70
Sennet A Ditto & Ditto 70
Mrs Toney An Excellant Still Woman 100
Mrs Cohyn Alone from Rheumatic Complaint 60
Cooba A good field Negroe breeds fast 100
Gracey A Ditto at present Sickley 50
Lenah A Ditto old 40
Katey A Ditto breeds fast 100
G Katherine A Ditto 90
G Amoilla A Ditto 80
L Amoilla A Ditto 110
Phaber A Ditto at Times Phthysickal 75
Salley Ditto has been droping of late 60
Sidney An Indifferent & often Complains 40

inevitably became one of terror and oppression. 'The safety of the whites,' wrote a Governor of Martinique, 'demands that we keep the Negroes in the most profound ignorance. I have reached the stage of believing firmly that one must treat the Negroes as one treats beasts.'

To justify their often excessively vicious and cruel behavior towards their slaves, both French and English owners reassured themselves that blacks were not the same as whites. Many, indeed, believed, with one planter, Edward Long, that 'when we reflect on the nature of these men, and their dissimilarity to to the rest of mankind, must we not conclude that they are of a different species of the same genus?' Mr Long (who was the author of a *History of Jamaica*) also concluded that the blacks were 'unjust, cruel, barbarous, half-human, treacherous, deceitful thieves, drunkards, proud, lazy, unclean, shameless, jealous to fury, and cowards.'

Vilify and abuse their slaves though they might, Mr Long and his fellow plantation owners were forced to rely on them for the cultivation of the sugar cane upon which their livelihood depended. Three hundred acres was generally considered to be the minimum size for a sugar plantation, and one slave was needed for every two acres (as opposed to one slave for every five to ten acres on a cotton plantation, and one slave for every 30 or 40 acres of corn).

The cane was planted in holes or trenches about five or six inches deep, made by a black with a hoe – an able field hand was expected to make at least 120 of these holes in the course of a 12-hour day. It was then left to grow for between 14 and 18 months until it was 'as high as a man, or higher' – unless, of course, the crop had been ruined by hur-

A record of cruelty: this late 18th century engraving by a Christian abolitionist records an incident in which a woman slave was lashed. The scene was described in doggerel: 'For mercy she aloud did cry/But nevertheless by cruel whipping/Next day in agony she did die.'

ricanes, disease, drought, earthquakes, rebellion, epidemic, or any other of the natural or human disasters to which it was vulnerable. After having been cut down with a knife or a billhook, the cane was taken to the sugar-mill (worked either by water, cattle, man-power, or the wind) where it was crushed between heavy rollers to extract the juice, which then flowed along a pipe to the nearby boiling-house. After clarification, it went to the curing house and 'was then barreled up into hogsheads, tierces or smaller barrels, carted down to a port or bay, and put on shipboard.' The monotonous cycle would then begin again. It was not, however, always necessary to replant the canes afresh after each cutting – new shoots would spring from the old and although not quite as productive as new canes, most planters let these ratoons stand for two seasons before grubbing them up.

On some plantations provisions were grown for the slaves, such as yams or corn, but blacks were also expected to cultivate their own plots in order to supplement the standard low calorie rations of grain or dried horse beans. In 1791, William Wilberforce, speaking to the House of Commons after visiting the West Indies, said: 'They [the blacks] were in general underfed. They were supported partly by the produce of their own provision ground, and partly by an allowance of flour and grain from their masters. In one of the islands, where provision grounds did not answer one year in three, the allowance to a working negro was but from five to nine pints of grain per week: in Dominica, where it never failed, from six to seven quarts: in Nevis and St Christophers, where there was no provision ground, it was but eleven pints. Add to this that it might be less, as the circumstances of their masters might become

A mode of West Indian punishment: a black suspected of theft or of wishing to run away is stripped, staked out and whipped by another slave, while the master looks on.

PROFIT AND LOSS

In all colonies, the plantation system brought about a moral deterioration in white attitudes. Only blacks could be fully enslaved and thus there grew up almost absolute equations between plantations and slavery, slavery and race. These were justified by legal fictions or a spurious claim to ethnic superiority, both rooted in economic necessity or simple greed. Slaves were evaluated by their cost of purchase and upkeep, their productivity and expectation of life. Their often contemptuous names were listed in record alongside, and with little differentiation from, those of steers and mules.

Though an absentee Jamaican planter, Bryan Edwards (1743–1800), author of the best-selling *History, Civil and Commercial of the British Colonies in the West Indies*, was a notably honest commentator. He provided the best description of a representative Jamaican sugar plantation and its capitalization. He shows that the business was not easy, thus providing the reasons behind the planters' economic justifications of slavery.

'A sugar plantation consists of three great parts; the Lands, the Buildings, and the Stock: but before I proceed to discriminate their relative proportions and value, it may be proper to observe, that the business of sugar planting is a sort of adventure in which the man that engages, must engage deeply. There is no medium, and very seldom the possibility of retreat. A British country gentleman, who is content to jog on without risk on the moderate profits of his own moderate farm, will startle to hear that it requires a capital of no less than 30,000 pounds sterling to embark in this employment with a fair prospect of advantage....

As therefore a plantation yielding, *on an average*, 200 hogsheads of sugar annually, requires, as I conceive, not less than 300 acres to be planted in canes, the whole extent of such a property must be reckoned at 900 acres. I am persuaded that the sugar plantations in Jamaica making those returns, commonly exceed, rather than fall short of, this estimate; not as hath been ignorantly asserted, from a fond and avaricious propensity in the proprietors to engross more land than is necessary; but because, from the nature of the soil, and rugged surface of the country, the lands vary greatly in quality, and it is seldom that even 300 acres of soil in contiguity, fit for the production of sugar, can be procured....

The stock on a plantation of the magnitude described, cannot prudently consist of less than 250 negroes, 80 steers and 60 mules.... The cost of the stock, therefore, may be stated as follows:

	Jamaica Currency
250 negroes, at £70 each	17,500
80 steers, at £15	1,300
60 mules, at £28	1,680
Total in currency equal to £14,557 sterling	£20,380

Let us now bring the whole into one point of view

LANDS	14,100
BUILDINGS	7,000
STOCK	20,380
Total in currency	41,480

Which is only £520 short of £42,000 Jamaica

Inside a sugar mill: the raw material of the planter's business.

currency, or £30,000 sterling, the sum first mentioned....

The produce of such a plantation...

	Sterling
300 Hogshead of sugar, at £15 sterling per hogshead	3,000
130 puncheons of rum, at £10 sterling per puncheon	1,300
Gross returns	£4,300

But the reader is not to imagine that all this, or even the sugar alone, is so much clear profit. The annual disbursements are first to be deducted, and very heavy they are; nor is any opinion more erroneous than that which supposes they are provided for by the rum.

ANNUAL SUPPLIES from Great Britain & Ireland.

1st Negro clothing; viz

1,500 yards of Osnaburgh cloth, or German linen.

650 yards of blue bays, or pennistones, for a warm frock for each negro.

350 yards of striped linseys for the women

250 yards of coarse check for shirts for the boilers, tradesmen, domesticks and the children.

3 dozen of coarse blankets for lying-in women, and sick negroes.

18 dozen of coarse hats.

2d Tools

For the carpenters and coopers, to the amount of £25 sterling, including 2 or 3 dozen of falling axes.

3d Miscellaneous articles

To the sum of £850 sterling. To the sum are to be added the following very heavy *Charges within the Island*; viz

	Jamaican currency
Overseer's or manager's salary	200
Distiller's ditto	70
Two other white servants, £60 each	120
A white carpenter's wages	100
Maintenance of five white servants exclusive of their allowance of salted provisions, £40 each	200
Medical care of the negroes (at 6s *per annum* for each negro) and *extra* cases, which are paid for separately	100
Millwright's coppersmith's, plumber's, and smith's bills, annually	250
Colonial taxes, publick and parochial	200
Annual supply of mules and steers	300
Wharfage and storeage of goods land and shipped	100
American staves and heading, for hogsheads and puncheons	150
A variety of small occasional supplies of different kinds, supposed	50
Equal to £1,300 sterling; being in currency	£1,840

The total amount, therefore, of the annual contingent charges of all kinds, is £2,150 sterling, which is precisely one-half the gross returns; leaving the other moiety, or £2,150 sterling, and no more, clear profit to the planter, being seven *per cent* on his capital.... With these and other drawbacks (to say nothing of the devastations which are sometimes occasioned by fires and hurricanes, destroying in a few hours the labor of years) it is not wonderful that the profits should frequently dwindle to nothing; or rather that a sugar estate, with all its boasted advantages, should sometimes prove a mill-stone about the neck of its unfortunate proprietor.'

Stocks which double as a bed: a West Indian punishment for drunken slaves.

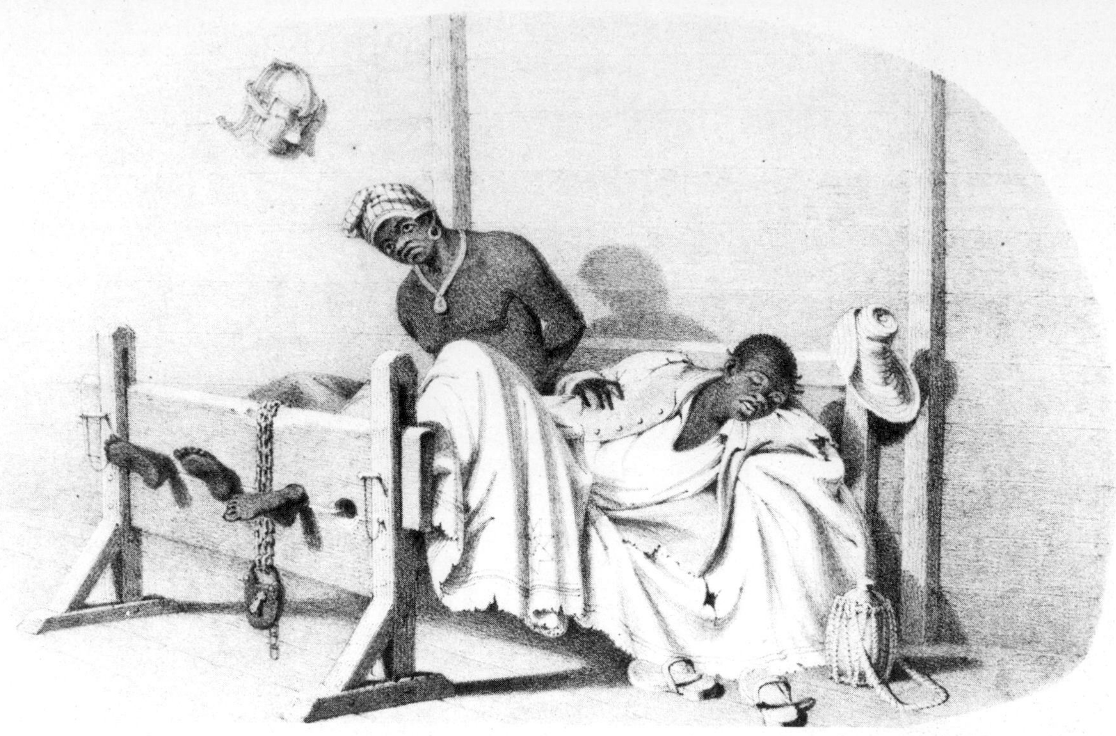

embarrassed; and in this case both an abridgement of their food and an increase of their labor, would follow.'

In British possessions the slaves took their homegrown vegetables and fruit, together with the pigs, goats and chickens raised by the harder-working blacks, to the local market on Sunday mornings, where they were traded for tobacco or rum.

The death rate among slaves on the plantations was high – Eric Williams, in his *History of the Caribbean*, estimated that one-third of all blacks reaching the West Indies died within three years. He also calculated that although there were 70,706 slaves in Barbados in 1764 and 41,840 were imported between 1764 and 1783, in that year the black population was 62,258. Some 50,000 out of a grand total of about 112,000, had died in the 20-year period.

Such figures, however, supply only a bare outline for the framework of misery and hopelessness which surrounded the slaves' lives – the unbearably taxing regime on minimal rations, the intolerably cramped living conditions, the vicious and random punishments and the dissimulation and deception practised by blacks to conceal the bitterness and hatred they felt for their masters.

For day after day, month after month, the relentless toil continued – the rise at dawn to the sound of the blowing of the conch shell, the drudgery of work in the fields or in the intense heat of the boiling house, 'the most unhealthy to which a negro can be applied,' the unappetizing midday meal, the return after sundown to the tiny windowless huts for the meager evening meal of coarse flour, salt herrings or peas.

These huts, about 20–25 feet in length and 12 feet wide, were made of wattle and plaster, with earth floors and palm-thatched roofs. Inside, some were not high enough for a man to stand upright, most were divided into two or more compartments, the occupants sleeping either on the floor on beds of straw or, as James Pope-Hennessy wrote: 'on good estates the bedstead was of boards, with a mat and a blanket; a rough table, two or three stools, some earthen jars, a pail, an iron pot and a pile of calabashes for use as plates and cups completed the equipment of these hovels.'

By contrast, the lot of the domestic slave was one of comparative ease. Both they and the craftsmen on the estate were allowed larger houses than the field hands and 'if of a thrifty turn, could buy linen sheets and mosquito nets, and acquire a plate or two of Staffordshire ware which they proudly displayed on a crude shelf.' If the black women of the household such as maids, hairdressers and cooks, were prepared to put up with the importuning of their masters, who not only made use of them themselves, but made them available to inexperienced sons and to male guests, they could enjoy comforts undreamed of by the women existing in airless cabins on the plantation. Dressed in the cast-off clothing of their mistresses they even 'gave balls in which, like trained monkeys, they danced minuets and quadrilles, and bowed and

A BITTER SWEET HARVEST

From the time the first plantations sprang up in Barbados in 1627, the economy of the British West Indies was dominated by sugar. The population rose from 100,000 to 700,000 in 1820, when sugar production was running at about 80,000 tons a year. In the late 18th century, on some 1500 British West Indian plantations, the whites – outnumbered anything up to 12 to 1 by their slaves – did their best to wring profits from what was at best a precarious industry. As Michael Craton wrote in *Sinews of Empire*, cultivating sugar with slaves was 'a losing game.' But the planters could see no other way of operating and continuing to run their estates as outlined by these pictures, painted in Antigua in 1823. By then, abolitionist sentiment and the ending of the slave trade had led to an improvement in conditions, but harvesting methods were largely unchanged.

On the approach of the autumn rains, gangs of slaves were marched to the fields to plant the cane. Each gang, accompanied by a black driver with a long whip, was set to work hoeing the well-manured squares. If the roots of the previous planting had failed to send up fresh, new shoots, the old plants were dug up and replaced with cuttings from mature cane stalks. The dormant buds soon sprouted and – barring hurricanes, drought and disease – the crop was ready for harvesting a little over a year later.

Harvest time: slaves fell ripe sugar with machetes. After cutting, the oozing canes were transported to the mill.

The vertical rollers of the crusher squeeze the juice out of the bundles of cane.

Fresh from the mill, the cane juice was piped into the boiling house where the slaves, laboring in steamy heat, began the complex operations that produced sugar and rum.

In huge simmering vats, the raw juice was boiled and cleared of its impurities. Then slaves ladled the now transparent liquid along adjoining lines of smaller vats, each hotter than the last. The juice, now thick and clear, was led off to cooling trays, where the sugar crystalized on the surface of the brownish residue, the molasses. The sugar encrusted mass was tipped into perforated barrels and the molasses drained out, leaving the sugar. The molasses was then turned into rum and the two products were ready for export.

Below: Outside the boiling house, crushed canes are spread out ready to be used as fuel for the furnaces.

Bottom: Slaves ladle steaming juice from vat to vat to clear it of the scum which is carried away in a brick channel. The juice flows into cooling trays beneath the windows.

Inside the distillery, slaves tap the barrels of spirit for the planter to test its strength. Rum under 25 percent proof was redistilled.

In London's West India Docks, sugar and rum from the British West Indies are unloaded ready for distribution.

Sunday morning market: a slave wife, on the way to trade her wares to supplement her family's diet, chats with a friend.

curtseyed in the fashion of Versailles.'

For the men, too – the butlers, valets, footmen and coachmen – there were occasional opportunities for self-advancement – the father of Toussaint L'Ouverture, who led the great revolt in San Domingo in the 1790s, was apparently allowed the use of five slaves to cultivate his own plot of land. But house slaves were as much at the mercy of their master's or mistress's caprice as the field hands – if the cause of the slightest annoyance or discontent, a hitherto cosseted maid or valet was liable, at least, to be 'sold away,' or at worst relegated to one of the field gangs where they would receive harsh treatment from those who had seen and envied their previous prosperity.

Though the behavior of most planters and overseers towards their blacks was brutal, there were a few 'good' masters, who emphasized the need for humane treatment when dealing with slaves. One such was John Pinney, owner of the largest single plantation in Nevis, in the Leeward Islands, who stated that 'he would not have a severe manager on his plantations.' By his own testimony, he was the most thoughtful and kindly of masters: 'I flatter myself,' he wrote in instructions to his managers, 'to say a word respecting the care of my slaves and stock – your own good sense must tell you they are the sinews of a plantation and must claim your particular care and attention. Humanity tempered with justice towards the former must ever be exercised, and when sick I am satisfied they will experience every kindness from you, they surely deserve it, being the very means of our support.'

His blacks apparently enjoyed a high standard of medical care – he had a hospital (an old boiling house) with a lying-in room for serious cases, and for a time he even retained the services of a qualified doctor. Later, however, for reasons of economy, he reverted to the more common practice of dosing the slaves himself, with the assistance of his black driver 'who was especially skilled in compounding roots into remedies for venereal disease.' As he later wrote: 'From experience, I know it is better to depend on the administration of the simples of the country . . . than to rest your dependence on medical gent in the island . . . . When I took upon myself the care of my negroes . . . I found my deaths not much more than one-third what they were before.'

Like many planters, he gave his slaves a holiday and a present of pork or beef at Christmas, but like most of his class was glad when it was over – coming as it did between the heavy seasons of planting and cropping, it often developed into a 'kind of Saturnalia' with owners, like their Roman counterparts, watching anxiously for signs of unrest or insurrection among their slaves.

Although John Pinney was in favor of flogging his slaves for laziness, disobedience or insolence, he declared that he would not 'suffer any human being committed, by Providence, to my care to be treated with cruelty.'

His definition of 'care' and 'cruelty' seems bizarre today; indeed – as the following incident shows – he was clearly aware that his standards were not as humanitarian as he would wish them to appear. When Tom Wedgwood, son of Josiah the famous potter, paid a visit to the island in 1800, Pinney was careful not to allow Wedgwood to see anything of which he might disapprove. He instructed his manager not to 'suffer a negro to be corrected in his presence, or so near for him to hear the whip – and if you could allowance the gang at the lower work, during his residence at the house, it would be advisable – point out the comforts the negroes enjoy beyond our poor in this country, show him the property they possess in goats, hogs, and poultry . . . By this means he will leave the island possessed with favorable sentiments.'

Other visitors saw plantation life more directly. Sir Hans Sloane went to the West Indies in 1686 as personal physician to the Governor of Jamaica. In his *Voyage to the Islands of Madeira, Barbados, Nevis, St Christophers and Jamaica*, published in two volumes in 1707 and 1725, he recorded some of the slave punishments he had witnessed. For certain 'flagrant' crimes slaves were 'nailed to the ground, with crooked sticks strapped to each limb. They were then slowly burned alive, first the hands and the feet, and then . . . gradually up to the head.' 'Lesser' crimes were dealt with by castration, or chopping off part of the foot with an axe. In French territories, whipping, authorized un-

A grim punishment: stocks that prevent movement and rest typify the tortures inflicted on some slaves by their owners.

der the *Côde Noir*, was loosely restricted to between 39 and 50 lashes. English colonists had no such restrictions. Slaves were occasionally flogged to death, and often whipped until their bodies were raw, the more sadistic planters ordering salt, pepper or hot ashes to be rubbed into the wounds of their victims. Sometimes melted wax was applied or burning wood passed over the afflicted parts.

The list of tortures meticulously documented by Sir Hans Sloane and, later, accumulated by supporters of abolition such as William Wilberforce and Thomas Clarkson, remained depressingly consistent for over a hundred years. Slaves were castrated, encased in irons, forced to wear a tinplate mask (to stop them eating the sugar cane), blown up with gunpowder, or tied up near wasp or ants' nests. No allowances were made either for age or sex – James Pope-Hennessy quotes the case reported in the *Jamaica Gazette* of a 14-year-old girl late for work, who was 'so unmercifully whipped . . . that she fell motionless to the ground, and was dragged by her heels to the hospital, where she expired.' Pregnant women were made to lie face down on the ground with a hole 'dug in the earth to accommodate the unborn child' and then beaten. A six-month-old baby had its mouth slit from ear to ear by one planter. And the punishment for attempted abortion was the wearing of an iron collar until the child was born.

In their turn, the slaves resisted. They revenged themselves against the atrocities inflicted on them by their masters in any way they were able. To release themselves from the crushing burden of their lives, and in the firm belief that they would return to Africa, they committed suicide. They lied to placate their owners. They stole to supplement their diet. The more intrepid ran away into the hills, where they lived as outlaws. To avenge the torture and death of their families and friends, they poisoned their torturers and their dependents. In the hope of obtaining their freedom, they rose in open rebellion against their oppressors.

The two most powerful secret weapons were those of poison and of murder by fetish (or *Obeah* as it was called in the West Indies). A black cook, expert in vegetable poisons, would contaminate her owners' food, a slave would poison his master for alienating the affections of his wife or lover, a discarded black mistress would poison her seducer, black nurses would either poison the white children entrusted to their care or murder them by other, untraceable means – often stabbing them through the head with a slim scarf pin. And to save their own children from growing up to suffer the fate of their elders, slaves sometimes killed them, either by the same means or by inducing a state of starvation known as 'jaw sickness' in a newly-born child. This disease, thought to have been caused by black midwives who operated on the mouths of babies at birth, was responsible for one third of the deaths of babies born on the plantations.

Obeah, to which an 18th century expert on the subject ascribed 'a very considerable portion of the annual mortality among the negroes of Jamaica,' was a practice at first ridiculed but later – after the Jamaican uprising of 1760 – said to have been inspired by an 'old Coromantee oracle, who had administered the fetish oath to the conspirators' – feared and hated by all Europeans. Although a law was passed forbidding its practice, it retained its pervasive influence – even threats of hanging failed to deter its exponents.

Ultimately, however, although poison and fetish supplied outlets for the oppressed, they did not set them free. That could only come from revolt, which gave the slaves the chance, however slim, of seizing power from their master and overthrowing the system.

During the 17th century, there were various uprisings – in 1639 in the French part of St Kitts, in 1649 in Barbados, in 1656 in Guadeloupe, in 1679 in San Domingo and in 1690 in Jamaica, when 300 slaves attacked a planter's house and killed an overseer on the adjoining plantation. All of these insurrections were comparatively easily dealt with – although it needed 500 men to subdue the 60 blacks who fled to the mountains of St Kitts. Few islands escaped – in the 18th century St John, Antigua, Guadeloupe, Jamaica (six times), Martinique, Nevis, and Cuba – all sustained revolts. In Jamaica the British, unable to defeat the runaways, or Maroons as they were called, against whom the militia

SLAVES IN REBELLION

Slave revolts seem to have broken out wherever there were opportunities and chances of success – where the forces of control were weak, where slaves had possibilities of organization, and where opportunities existed to escape into the wilds. The Gold Coast blacks proved particularly dangerous.

Tacky's ferocious Jamaican uprising in 1760, described by Bryan Edwards in this extract, was the closest the British islands came to such a general slave revolt as that which destroyed French San Domingo in the 1790s.

‘The circumstances which distinguish the Koromantyn, or Gold Coast, Negroes, from all others, are firmness both of body and mind; a ferociousness of disposition; but withal, activity, courage, and a stubbornness, or what an ancient Roman would have deemed an elevation, of soul, which prompts them to enterprizes of difficulty and danger; and enables them to meet death, in its most horrible shape, with fortitude or indifference ... the Negro rebellion which happened in Jamaica in 1760 arose at the instigation of a Koromantyn Negro of the name of Tacky, who had been a chief in Guiney; and it broke out on the Frontier plantation in St Mary's parish. . . .

An 18th century freedom fighter: this runaway, Leonard Parkinson, was one of many Maroon guerrillas that were a permanent menace to Jamaica's white society.

Having collected themselves into a body about one o'clock in the morning, they proceeded to the fort at Port Maria, killed the sentinel, and provided themselves with as great a quantity of arms and ammunition as they could conveniently dispose of. Being by this time joined by a number of their countrymen from the neighboring plantations, they marched up the high road that led to the interior parts of the country, carrying death and desolation as they went. At Ballard's Valley they surrounded the overseer's house about four in the morning, in which finding all the White servants in bed, they butchered every one of them in the most savage manner, and literally drank their blood mixed with rum. At Esher, and other estates, they exhibited the same tragedy; and then set fire to the buildings and canes. In one morning they murdered between thirty and forty Whites and Mulattoes, not sparing even infants at the breast, before their progress was stopped. Tacky, the Chief, was killed in the woods by one of the parties that went in pursuit of them; but some others of the ring-leaders being taken, and a general inclination to revolt appearing among all the Koromantyn Negroes in the island, it was thought necessary to make a few terrible examples of some of the most guilty. Of three who were clearly proved to have been concerned in the murders committed at Ballard's Valley, one was condemned to be burnt, and the other two to be hung up alive in irons, and left to perish in that dreadful situation. The wretch that was burnt was made to sit on the ground, and his body, being chained to an iron stake, the fire was applied to his feet. He uttered not a groan, and saw his legs reduced to ashes with the utmost firmness and composure; after which, one of his arms by some means getting loose, he snatched a brand from the fire that was consuming him, and flung it in the face of the executioner. The two that were hung up alive were indulged, at their own request, with a hearty meal immediately before they were suspended on the gibbet, which was erected in the parade of the town of Kingston. From that time, until they expired, they never uttered the least complaint, except only of cold in the night, but diverted themselves all day long in discourse with their countrymen, who were permitted, very improperly, to surround the gibbet. On the seventh day a notion prevailed among the spectators, that one of them wished to communicate an important secret to his master, my near relation; who being in St Mary's parish, the commanding officer sent for me. I endeavored, by means of an interpreter, to let him know that I was present; but I could not understand what he said in return. I remember that both he and his fellow-sufferer laughed immoderately at something that occurred, I know not what. The next morning one of them silently expired, as did the other on the . . . ninth day. ’

A Maroon leader, Cudjoe, is persuaded to make peace.

had fought a running battle for over 50 years, were obliged to sign a treaty with them. In 1739 the Maroons were declared free and were given 1500 acres in which they could plant any crop except sugar. It was the first successful slave revolt and a prelude to the greatest revolt of all – that of San Domingo – whose aim, as Eric Williams said, 'was the total abolition of slavery and the independent existence of an entire Negro state.'

For its size, San Domingo was the wealthiest of all the West Indian colonies. The extraordinary fertility of the soil allowed the same number of slaves to cultivate five times the amount of cane as that grown in Jamaica, and San Domingo's sugar price undercut Jamaica's by 20 percent. After the American Revolution in 1783, with the connection severed between the British West Indies and North America, the French were conveniently able to fill the gap in the market. From 1779 to 1789, the black population and the total production of San Domingo almost doubled. British planters were forced to admit that they could not compete. To cut their losses, many sold off surplus slaves to the French. The French economy was heavily dependent on San Domingo. As one French politician put it: 'Follow the cask of sugar which goes to pay for copper in Sweden, silk in the Levant, and see how many workers employed to make copper and silk owe their subsistence to that exchange.'

A gruesome execution witnessed after an uprising against the Dutch in Surinam in 1730.

For slaves, San Domingo in 1789 has been described as the 'worst hell on earth'; 40,000 slaves a year came into the island to labor under conditions which made a mockery of the *Côde Noir*. The mortality rate was unequaled anywhere in the West Indies. It was, one French aristocrat said, 'a second Sodom which will be consumed by the wrath of God': 482,000 slaves lay at the bottom of a complex social hierarchy, with planters and white officials at the top, craftsmen and professional men coming a poor second and below them the various degrees of miscegnation to be found among the mulattoes, who were coupled with the free blacks in having no political rights.

The French Revolution with its stirring slogan of Liberty, Equality and Fraternity, sparked changes. In May 1791, the mulattoes born of free parents (only about 400 in all) were granted political and social rights by the National Assembly. This progressive step was rejected outright by the planters. The mulattoes decided to take matters into their own hands. They incited the vast downtrodden army of slaves to rise, exterminate their white masters and take over the colony for themselves.

The revolt took place against the background of international unrest and upcoming war between Britain, France and Spain. To preserve the status quo, the planters were prepared to secede from France and pledge their allegiance to England and this they told William Pitt the younger, then British Prime Minister. Pitt, disturbed at the losses incurred by British planters and by the resultant re-export of slaves to the French, which only served to prop up France's booming economy still further, was well aware of the significance of the offer – it would more than compensate England for the loss of the thirteen American colonies. But tempting though the prospect of a British monopoly of the sugar, indigo, cotton and coffee which grew so abundantly in San Domingo was, its acquisition was too delicate an operation to be performed in time of peace. Within a year, however, Britain and France were at war. Allegiances polarized: the British promised all planters and poor whites in the French West Indies continued political and social superiority; the revolutionary French decreed the total abolition of slavery in the French dominions, and enlisted the willing aid of the mulattoes and slaves, who fought alongside them in the firm belief that victory guaranteed their freedom.

Of all the leaders to emerge from the bitter struggle that followed, the most remarkable was the former slave, Pierre Dominique Toussaint L'Ouverture. Born in 1743, the eldest son of a captured African chieftain, he had acquired some education from his missionary-educated godfather, Pierre

The Demerara Uprising

Grisly reprisals: three of the scores of slaves hung in Demerara (British Guiana) after an uprising in 1823.

Slave liberator: Toussaint L'Ouverture who led a slave rebellion in Haiti against both the Spanish and the French and whose military genius led to the proclamation of Haitian independence in 1804.

Baptiste, who had taught him not only to read and write but the rudiments of Latin, French, geometry and drawing. This knowledge, combined with the information passed on to him by his father about medicinal plants, was enough to attract his master's attention – he was first chosen to be his coachman and later put in charge of all the other blacks on the plantation. He was, as C L R James put it, 'very small, ugly and ill-shaped, but although his general expression was one of benevolence, he had eyes like steel and no one ever laughed in his presence. His comparative learning, his success in life, his character and personality gave him an immense prestige among all the Negroes who knew him . . . Knowing his superiority he never had the slightest doubt that his destiny was to be their leader, nor would those with whom he came in contact take long to recognize it.'

With innate political sense and steadfastness of purpose, Toussaint wove his way through the maze of jealousies, proposals and counter-proposals which surrounded him. Concentrating on his mission to free his comrades, he rallied them in August 1793: 'Brothers and friends, I am Toussaint L' Ouverture . . . I have undertaken vengeance. I want Liberty and Equality to reign in San Domingo. I work to bring them into existence. Unite yourselves to us, brothers and fight with us for the same cause.' To achieve his aim, Toussaint co-operated with the Spanish until 1794, when the French ratified the act declaring freedom for the slaves, after which he turned on his former allies, expelling them from the Northern Province, and at the head of 5000 troops, pledged his loyalty to the French.

For the British the campaign was an unmitigated disaster. Although they captured the islands of Martinique, Tobago and St Lucia, they lost Grenada and St Vincent and the troops that were poured into San Domingo quickly became weakened and decimated by yellow fever, proved no match for the acclimatized and fervent followers of Toussaint L'Ouverture. In 1798, the British agreed to evacuate San Domingo and in return Toussaint (who in 1796 had become Commander-in-Chief of the Army) promised he would not attack Jamaica.

By 1798, he was in effect ruler of the island, but despite the victories he had obtained on behalf of the French and despite his undoubted status, he remained wary of French intentions – he wrote to the French on 5 November 1797: 'France will not revoke her principles, she will not withdraw from us the greatest of her benefits . . . . But if, to re-establish slavery in San Domingo this was done, then I declare to you it would be to attempt the impossible; we have known how to face dangers to obtain our liberty, we shall know how to brave death to maintain it. This, Citizen, is the morale of the people of San Domingo, those are the principles that they transmit to you by me.'

In the end Toussaint was betrayed by another military genius – Napoleon Bonaparte, who in 1801 seized power in France by a *coup d'etat.* Disliking the sight of an independent colony, under a black leader, who, by his own admission had pronounced himself the 'Bonaparte of San Domingo,' Napoleon determined to bring San Domingo back to its former dependence on France by abolishing the constitution, disarming the blacks, deposing Toussaint and restoring slavery. With this in mind, he sent a force to the island commanded by his brother-in-law, Leclerc. Toussaint was captured. As he was bundled unceremoniously aboard a French warship he remarked, 'In overthrowing me you have cut down in San Domingo only the trunk of the tree of liberty. It will spring up again by the roots for they are numerous and deep.' He was taken to France, where he was imprisoned 'without trial . . . high up in the French Alps, where the rigors of the climate and a semi-starvation diet soon had the inevitable effect.' He died on 17 April 1803 and his corpse was thrown into a common grave.

His words on his capture proved to be only partially prophetic. His successors fought with unsurpassed fervor against what Leclerc referred to as a 'war of extermination.' Fifty thousand Frenchmen died in the attempt to restore San Domingo to its former status – from the yellow fever that had been the downfall of the British, and from the strength of the opposition, led by Jean Jacques Dessalines and Henri Christophe, and on 19 November 1803, the French Army surrendered. But the victory was a Pyrrhic one. Though the new Republic of Haiti (the ancient Indian name of San Domingo) erased from its flag the white of the French *tricolor* and created an Emperor, Dessalines, its independence was only nominal.

BRAZIL'S 'BARBAROUS TRAFFIC'

After the United States, Brazil was the greatest slave holding nation in the New World. In the early 19th century, there were at any one time some two million slaves, mainly working the country's sugar plantations and exploiting the country's mineral wealth. The institution died very slowly. The slave traffic ceased only in the 1850s and the slaves were finally emancipated only in 1888.

Among a row of slaves washing for diamonds in Brazil's mineral rich *Minas Gerais* ('general mines') district, one worker signals a find.

From the time the Portuguese formally acquired Brazil from the Dutch in 1661, they used slaves. At first the local Indian population was employed, but the aboriginals, whom the settlers referred to disparagingly as *burgres* (buggers), were unable to withstand enslavement; they died rapidly from smallpox, measles, respiratory infections and venereal diseases. The only other source of labor was Africa.

The facts of Brazilian slavery have been notoriously difficult to come by, for in 1891 all the records of slavery – the log books of slave ships, custom house records, documents of sale, ownership papers – were ordered to be destroyed to prevent any stigma attaching to the families of former slaves. But in 1825 the great German explorer, Alexander von Humboldt, set Brazil's slave population at nearly two million – out of a total of four million. In 1830 the English abolitionist, Thomas Fowell Buxton, estimated imports at 100,000 a year, but recent estimates place the average import of slaves in the 1830s at about 34,000 a year.

Slaves rest on their way to a Brazilian plantation.

Slave quarters inland.

Slaves in transit arrive at a staging post.

Preparing a meal of cassava.

Until the end of Brazilian slavery in 1888 (and beyond) sugar was vital to the country's economy. The industry was based on family owned plantations known as *engenho*. Indeed much of the chief sugar growing area, northeastern Brazil, was made up of a series of rural *engenhos*. Each was almost a world in itself. It had a *casa grande*, or mansion house, where the family and the domestic slaves lived. It often had a chapel with a resident priest, who was sometimes a member of the family and who might serve also as a teacher of religion, arithmetic, music, Portuguese and French to the children of the plantation owner. Each *engenho* had its *senzala*, or row of slave houses. Each had its *engenho* proper – the installation for the refining of sugar – after which the whole establishment was named.

In Brazil, as in other Roman Catholic nations, slaves were on the whole better treated than in Protestant countries. There were a number of reasons for this. For one thing, Spain, Portugal and France all had detailed laws concerning the treatment of slaves. For another, the Church took a close interest in the lot of the slaves, encouraging church marriages and opposing the separation of families. Thirdly, the Portuguese – like the Spanish – had little race or color prejudice. In the British West Indies and in the southern United States, the child of a slave woman by her owner was born and remained a slave. It was customary, however, in Roman Catholic lands for the master to manumit both his child and, occasionally, the mother as well. In Brazil, a number of free blacks reached positions of relatively meaningful authority.

Emancipation came to Brazil in a number of stages. Direct Portuguese rule ended in 1822. In 1826, Brazil gave Britain the right to search ships suspected of carrying slaves, and in 1830 Brazil declared the trade to be piracy. Little changed, however, until 1851, when in a well coordinated political and naval campaign, Britain made a conclusive move that cut imports to a mere 3000. In 1871, Brazil passed a partial abolition act; complete emancipation followed in 1888, when the remaining 700,000 slaves were freed.

Sugar cane is carried to a mill powered by water.

Slaves feed the furnaces with the crushed sugar cane.

An overseer brings slaves to their master for punishment.

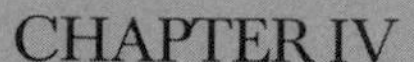

CHAPTER IV

IN SERVITUDE TO COTTON

SLAVERY IN THE SOUTHERN STATES 1700-MID 19th CENTURY

In the fields: slaves plant out sweet potatoes on James Hopkinson's plantation in South Carolina, 1862.

The establishment of slavery in America in the 17th century brought with it all the arbitrary and repressive laws fundamental to an institution within which a master could enjoy absolute rights over his property. In 1669, the Assembly of Virginia put forward the proposal that if a slave, when being punished by his master, 'by the extremity of his correction should chance to die,' it should not be seen as a case of felony. South Carolina adopted equally sweeping laws, its Constitution ruling that an owner should have 'absolute power and authority over his negro slaves.'

Soon, blacks as a whole – whether free or not – were subjected to legal restrictions previously intended for slaves. The social phenomenon of slavery spawned the legal trappings that were to buttress racial prejudice and oppression for the next two centuries.

The 1705 slave code of Virginia limited the assembly of black slaves, and forbade traveling without a pass, escape and striking white persons. It also restricted the activities of free blacks by denying them the right 'to bear witness in court proceedings against any but other blacks' and stressed that 'no Negro, molatto [sic] or Indian shall presume to take upon him, act in or exercise any office, ecclesiastic, civil or military.'

Nevertheless, the courts had to face the legal paradox that the slave was both a chattel and a human being. As one judge said: 'Negroes are under the protection of the laws, and have personal rights, and cannot be considered on a footing only with domestic animals.' South Carolina adapted its constitution sufficiently to concede that a white master could be found guilty of the murder of a slave. The penalties meted out for such a crime were seldom severe, being to a large extent dependent on the vagaries of public opinion, but at least there were penalties. Eugene Genovese quotes the case of a master in South Carolina believed responsible for the deaths of several slaves. 'A committee of local citizens waited on [him] to suggest . . . with grave courtesy and respect, that he leave the area immediately. He did.' And in 1791, when a white was convicted of murdering a slave and fined £700 which he could not pay, he was sentenced instead to seven years in prison. Despite the undoubted incidence of

The cotton gin: a 19th century engraving celebrates the invention by Eli Whitney of a machine to separate the soft cotton lint from the seed inside. The gin guaranteed the expansion of cotton cultivation and of the slave system.

Maryland Legalizes Slavery

In this Maryland statute of 1664 on the status of slaves, the phrase *durante vita* appeared, stipulating service for life. At the same time, the statute sought to separate the races by imposing severe penalties on any white woman marrying a slave: any white woman who became a slave wife would herself become a slave and her children would be born slaves. In addition, there is, even at this stage, an implication that all blacks were necessarily to be considered as slaves.

'Bee itt Enacted by the Right Honble the Lord Proprietary by the aduice and Consent of the upper and lower house of this present Generall Assembly That all Negroes or other slaues already within the Prouince And all Negroes and other slaues to bee hereafter imported into the Prouince shall serue Durante Vita. And all Children born of any Negroe or other slaue shall be Slaues as their ffathers were for the terme of their liues. And forasmuch as divers freeborne English women forgettfull of their free Condicion and to the disgrace of our Nation doe intermarry with Negro Slaues by which alsoe diuers suites may arise touching the Issue of such woemen and a great damage doth befall the Masters of such Negroes for preuention whereof for deterring such freeborne women from such shamefull Matches Bee itt further Enacted by the Authority advice and Consent aforesaid That whatsoever free borne woman shall inter marry with any slaue from and after the Last day of this present Assembly shall Serue the master of such slaue dureing the life of her husband And that all the Issue of such freeborne woemen soe marryed shall be Slaues as their fathers were. And Bee itt further Enacted that all the Issues of English or other freeborne woemen that haue already marryed Negroes shall serve the Masters of their Parents till they be Thirty yeares of age and noe longer.'

large numbers of undetected crimes of violence against slaves and the many obstacles placed in the way of the enforcement of the law, 'white killers,' as Professor Genovese has said, 'probably faced justice more often in the Old South than elsewhere.'

Within a few years of the adoption of the Declaration of Independence in 1776, trafficking in slaves – there were then about half a million in North America – had been prohibited in every state except Georgia (where it was abolished in 1798). The discrepancy between the ideals of the new American States and the practising of the slave trade had produced an outcry – from the Quakers in Pennsylvania, from Thomas Jefferson in Virginia and from Luther Martin in Maryland, who protested that 'the traffic was inconsistent to the Revolution and dishonorable to the American character.' New York banned the importation of slaves in 1788; 'nor,' it was announced, 'should any be purchased in the State for export' and a penalty of £100 a slave was imposed on those found evading this law. Massachusetts forbade the African slave trade, but the act omitted to mention any other areas where they might be obtained. Pennsylvania was more specific – it prohibited trading 'to, from, or between Europe, Asia, Africa, or America, or any places or countries whatever.' South Carolina temporarily prohibited the trade until 1793. North Carolina slapped an exorbitant tax on all imported slaves.

Neither the outcry nor the banning of the slave trade proved much of a deterrent to those willing and able to bend the law. By the end of the 18th century, after the invention by Eli Whitney of the cotton gin and the reopening of the South Carolina slave trade, other states did covertly what South Carolina did openly: they smuggled in their slaves.

During the first half of the 19th century, cotton was king in the Southern States. Between 1815 and 1861, the cotton crop increased from 160 million pounds to over 2300 million pounds (two-thirds of all United States' exports). Pioneer farmers devoured the countryside westward 'eating the fat of the land and leaving devastation behind.' The established cotton planters, together with the sugar planters of Lousiana, the tobacco planters of Virginia and Kentucky or the rice planters of South Carolina were at one with the raw entrepreneurs who invaded the South in such large numbers – all agreed that, once the initial investment had been made, slaves were the most economical form of labor, and all those who could afford to buy them did so.

It is important to remember, however, that slaveholders represented only a quarter of the white population of the Southern States. Of this minority, according to one authority, about a quarter owned from one to ten slaves, half owned more than ten but less than 50 leaving only a quarter to make up the so-called 'planting aristocracy.' As Clement Eaton said, 'This small privileged class of planters [one-sixteenth of the white population] tended to think of themselves as "the South"; they confused their narrow class interests as identical with the welfare of the whole South.'

Sectionally self-interested and reactionary though some Southern planters were, and doggedly opposed to the move towards emancipation which had already freed many slaves in the North, their views on slave-holding were often ambivalent. While recognizing their own need for and dependence on the labor of their slaves, they frequently complained of being in the grip of circumstance. Mrs Mary Chestnut, whose husband's father owned a large plantation at Camden, South Carolina, severely criticized Harriet Beecher Stowe's view of the South, as portrayed in *Uncle Tom's Cabin.* Mrs Stowe and her like, she declared, 'live in nice New England homes, clean, sweet-smelling, shut up in libraries, writing books which ease their hearts of their bitterness against us. What self denial they practise is to tell John Brown to come down here and cut our throats in Christ's name. Now consider what I have seen in my mother's life, my grandmother's, my mother-in-law's. These people were educated at Northern schools, they read the same books as their Northern contemporaries . . . they have the same ideas of right and wrong, while they of the South are doomed to live in Negro villages the inhabitants of which walk through their houses whenever they see fit, dirty, slatternly, idle, ill-smelling by nature. These women I love have less chance to live their own lives in peace than if they were African missionaries. They have a swarm of blacks about them like children under their care ... and they hate slavery as much as Mrs Stowe does.'

A small farmer in Virginia, quoted by Frederick Law Olmsted in *The Cotton Kingdom* held much the same opinions. 'I only wish,' he said, 'your philanthropists would contrive some satisfactory plan to relieve us of it [slavery]; the trouble and the responsibility of properly taking care of our negroes . . . is anything but enviable. But what can we do that is better? Our free negroes – and I believe it is the same at the North as it is here

THE REAL FACE OF SLAVERY

The daguerreotypes reproduced on these pages are extraordinary historical documents. Made in Columbia, South Carolina in 1850, they are among the earliest known photographs of Southern slaves. They are almost certainly the earliest for which the subjects are identified. In addition, the three slaves shown here were all born in Africa.

The pictures were found in 1976 in the attic of Harvard's Peabody Museum of Archaeology and Ethnology. They were made at the behest of Louis Agassiz, a prominent scientist, who as a part of the debate on the evolution of species then gathering momentum, wished to prove that the various races of mankind were separate species and had all been created independently. To establish this, he argued, would help substantiate the Biblical account of the creation of life and undermine the suggestion that species evolved one from another.

To back his theory, he conducted field research on Southern plantations. He concluded that he had identified and recorded in pictures differences between black Africans and white Americans sufficient to justify labeling them as separate species.

The theory never had much popularity. Even then, it was generally accepted that mankind formed a single species. His theory was seized upon only by defenders of slavery who saw in it 'a scientific basis for racial inequality.' It now seems somewhat ironic that pictures taken for such a dubious purpose should preserve such a telling portrait of the reality of slavery.

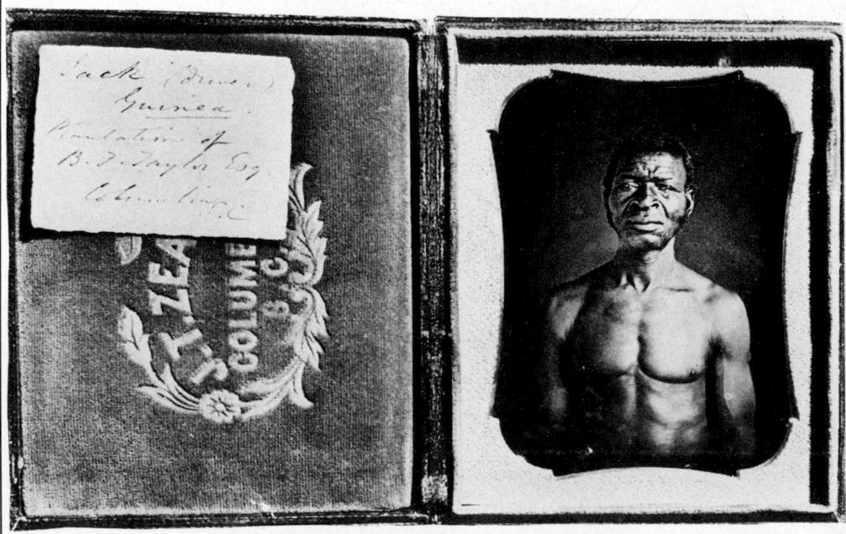

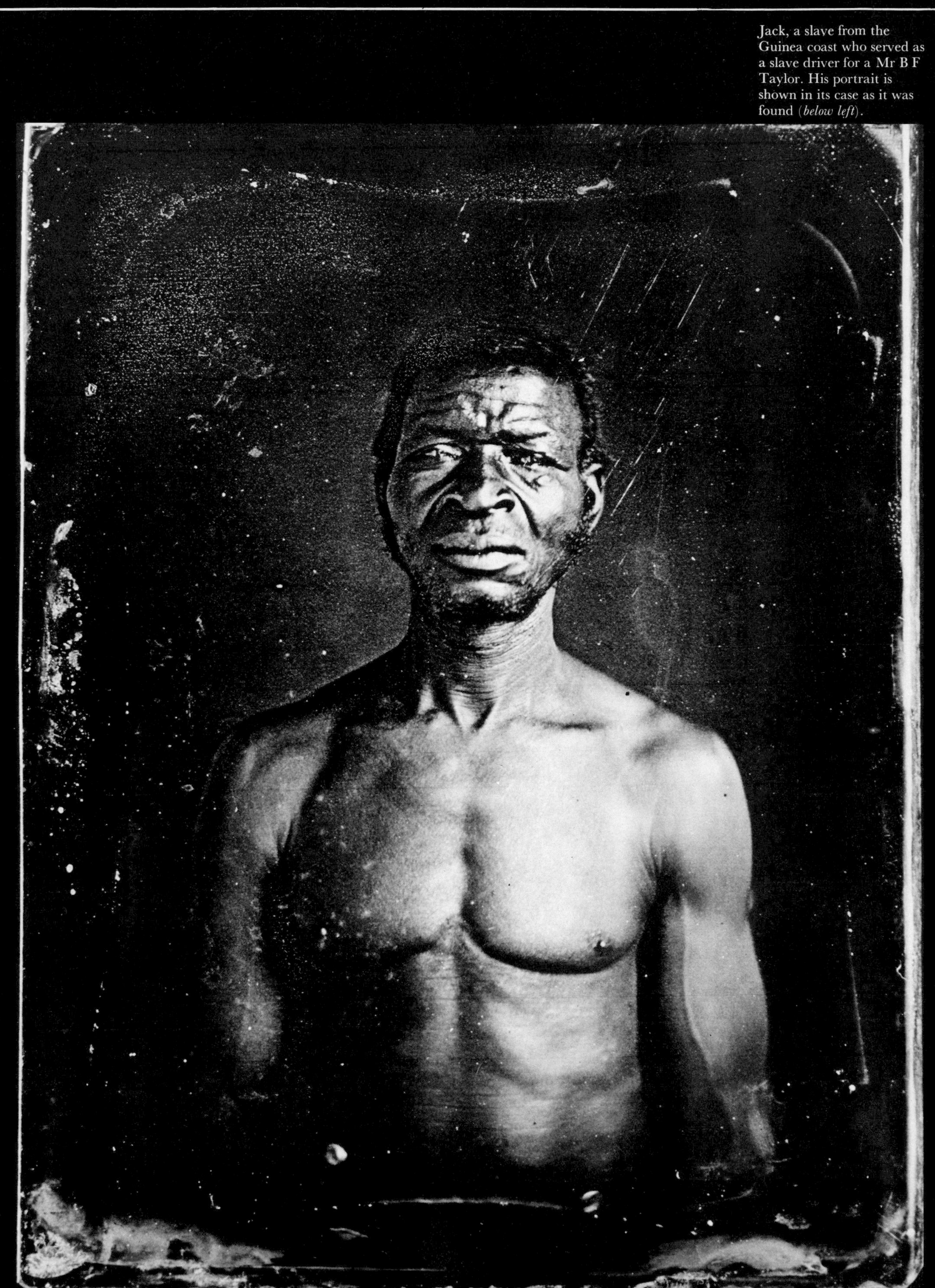

Jack, a slave from the Guinea coast who served as a slave driver for a Mr B F Taylor. His portrait is shown in its case as it was found (*below left*).

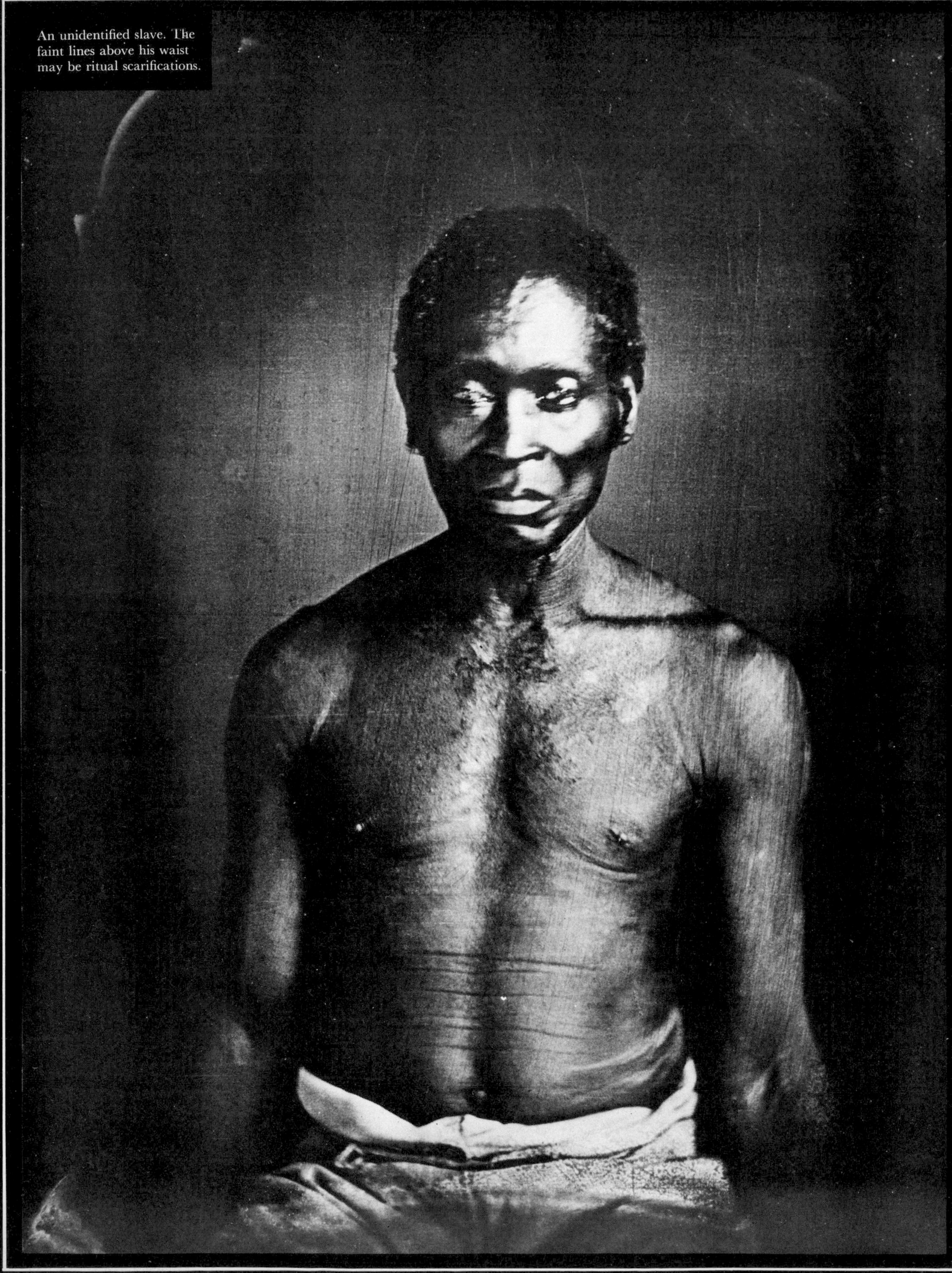

An unidentified slave. The faint lines above his waist may be ritual scarifications.

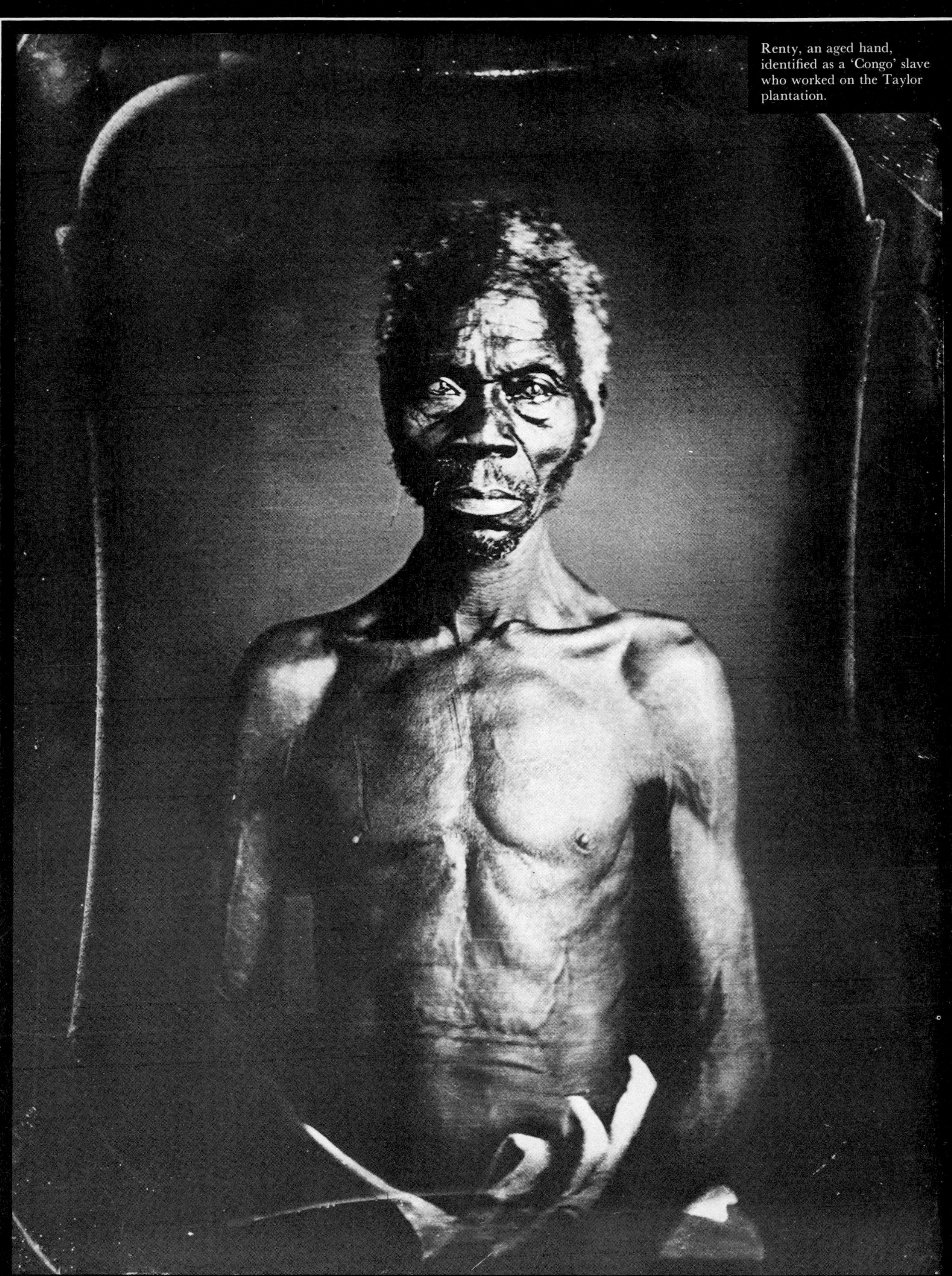

Renty, an aged hand, identified as a 'Congo' slave who worked on the Taylor plantation.

– are a miserable set of vagabonds, drunken, vicious, worse off, it is my honest opinion than those who are retained in slavery.'

Possibly the most unctuous (and certainly the most wordy) sentiments were those expressed by another plantation owner, Patrick Henry, in a letter to a friend: 'Would anyone believe that I am Master of Slaves of my own purchase! I will not, I cannot justify it. However culpable my Conduct, I will so far pay my devoir to Virtue, as to own the excellence and rectitude of her Precepts and to lament my want of conformity to them. I believe a time will come when an opportunity will be offered to abolish this lamentable Evil . . . if not let us transmit to our descendents together with our Slaves a pity for their unhappy lot, and an abhorrence for Slavery.'

There were also attempts to justify slavery philosophically. To most Southerners, slavery was justified by the very existence of the black 'who was naturally too deficient in forecasting capacity to be able to learn how to take civilized care of himself,' and by the opportunities provided for a slave's advancement through daily contact with his more fortunately-endowed white masters.

Some of the more intelligent Southern planters, faced with the difficulties posed by reconciling autocracy with paternalism and absolute rights with a sense of duty, turned to classical arguments. To the Greeks, slavery was justified by its capacity to free a leisure class from the petty considerations of everyday life; and the flowering of classical Greek literature and ideas provided visible evidence of what such a class could achieve when so liberated.

This argument carries little weight. The Southern plantation society was one based on chivalry, personal bravery, hospitality and an elaborately formal code of manners, adhered to by both black and white, which, as Professor Genovese said, 'contributed to the South's deserved reputation for that formal courtesy and graciousness which helped define its aristocratic ethos.' But it did not include, except in outstanding cases, many of the 'necessities' of civilized life – Frederick Olmsted found, on his travels through the Slave States in the 1850s, hardly any newspapers or books, or, indeed, anyone prepared to discuss 'literature, or art, science or foreign affairs.' Social gatherings were the only form

Slaves in Transit

One of the most vivid descriptions of slave coffles on the move was written by George W Featherstonhaugh, an English author and geographer who was employed by the US War Department to make geological surveys of the lands west of the Great Lakes. His unequivocal – if self-righteous – disgust with the internal slave traffic is plain from the following observations, recorded during his travels from Virginia through Alabama to the south-west in September, 1834.

'Just as we reached New River, in the early gray of the morning, we came up with a singular spectacle, the most striking one of the kind I have ever witnessed. It was a camp of negro slave-drivers, just packing up to start; they had about three hundred slaves with them, who had bivouacked the preceding night *in chains* in the woods; these they were conducting to Natchez, upon the Mississippi River, to work upon the sugar plantations in Lousiana. It resembled one of those coffles of slaves spoken of by Mungo Park, except that they had a caravan of nine waggons and single-horse carriages, for the purpose of conducting the white people, and any of the blacks that should fall lame, to which they were now putting the horses to pursue their march. The female slaves were, some of them, sitting on logs of wood, whilst others were standing, and a great many little black children were warming themselves at the first of the bivouac. In front of them all, and prepared for the march, stood, in double files, about 200 male slaves, *manacled and chained to each other*. I had never seen so revolting a sight before!... To make this spectacle still more disgusting and hideous, some of the principal white slave-drivers, who were tolerably well dressed ... were standing near, laughing and smoking. ...

Wishing them in my heart all manner of evil to endure ... we drove on, and having forded the river in a flat-bottomed boat, drew up on the road, where I persuaded the driver to wait until we had witnessed the crossing of the river by the "gang," as it was called.

Far right: A slave coffle in front of the Capitol, Washington.

of recreation, but there were no 'debating societies, military companies nor libraries, theaters nor concert halls, singing societies nor amateur theatricals.' Edmund Wilson, in an essay on Olmsted, came to the conclusion that 'the classical argument that the bondage of an inferior class of laborers is justified by the use of his leisure that the liberated may take has not been proved in the South.'

The cotton plantations on which so many slaves worked varied considerably in size and character. One historian estimated that 'half the cotton crop was made by small farmers with one to half a dozen slaves.' Many consisted, like the small farm described by Mark Twain in *Huckleberry Finn*, of: 'a rail fence round a two acre yard; a stile made out of logs sawed off and up-ended in steps, like barrels of a different length, to climb over the fence with, and for the women to stand on when they are going to jump onto a horse; some sickly grass-patches in the big yard . . . big double log house for the white folks – log smoke back of the kitchen; three little log nigger-cabins in a row t'other side the smoke-house; one little hut all by itself away down against the back fence, and some outbuildings down a piece the other side; . . . about three shade-trees away off in a corner; some currant bushes and gooseberry bushes in one place by the fence; outside the fence a garden and a watermelon patch; then the cotton fields begin; and after the fields, the woods.'

Frederick Olmsted found another such small plantation on the Red River tributary of the Mississippi, whose valley produced so much of the cotton crop of the United States. Searching for something to eat, he was directed by an old black ferryman to his master's house, which turned out to be 'a small square log cabin, with a broad open shed or piazza in front, and a chimney, made of sticks and mud, leaning against one end. A smaller detached cabin, 20 feet in the rear was used for a kitchen . . . About the house was a large yard, in which were two or three China trees, and two fine Cherokee roses; half a dozen hounds; several black babies, turkeys and chickens, and a pet sow, teaching a fine litter of pigs how to root and wallow. Three hundred yards from the house was a gin house and stable, and in the interval between were two rows of comfortable negro cabins.'

It was an interesting, but a melancholy spectacle, to see them effect the passage of the river: first, a man on horseback selected a shallow place in the ford for the male slaves; then followed a waggon and four horses, attended by another man on horseback. The other waggons contained the children and some that were lame, whilst the scows, or flat-boats, crossed the women and some of the people belonging to the caravan. There was much method and vigilance observed, for this was one of the situations where the gangs – always watchful to obtain their liberty – often show a disposition to mutiny, knowing that if one or two of them could wrench their manacles off, they could soon free the rest, and either disperse themselves or overpower and slay their sordid keepers, and fly to the Free States. The slave-drivers, aware of this disposition in the unfortunate negroes, endeavor to mitigate their discontent by feeding them well on the march, and by encouraging them to sing "Old Virginia never tire," to the banjo.'

A HUMAN MARKET

Most slaves' first traumatic experience of the New World was a slave auction. Whether they occurred in the West Indies or the seaboard of the United States made little difference. For 150 years, the scene described by Olaudah Equiano in the 1780s remained little changed: 'We were not many days in the merchant's custody before we were sold after their usual manner, which is this: on a signal given, (as the beat of a drum) the buyers rush at once into the yard where the slaves are confined, and make choice of the parcel they like best. The noise and clamor with which this is attended and the eagerness visible in the countenances of the buyers serve not a little to increase the apprehensions of the terrified Africans, who may well be supposed to consider them as the ministers of that destruction to which they think themselves devoted. In this manner, without scruple, are relations and friends separated, most of them never to see each other again.'

After 1807, with an official end to the trade, sales became less of a scramble and more of a business. On the mainland new territories were opened up to settlement in the southwest. White men began to move into the interior, developing cotton plantations on the rich lands that stretched westward from central Georgia through Mississippi. Slave emporiums were established to supply a need of the new lands, drawing their slaves mainly from the upper South. Alexandria, Virginia was one of the central points for the collection of slaves being sold. From there they were sent overland to Natchez or by sea to New Orleans for sale in the west.

Though slave auctions were less brutal affairs by the early 19th century and many dealers and owners advised against splitting families up, separations remained a painfully common feature of slave dealing.

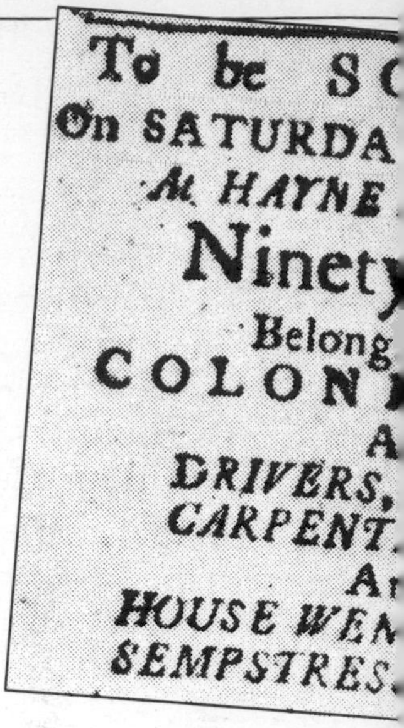

To be S
On SATURDA
At HAYNE
Ninet
Belong
COLON
A
DRIVERS,
CARPENT
A
HOUSE WEN
SEMPSTRES

An inspection before the auction, 1861.

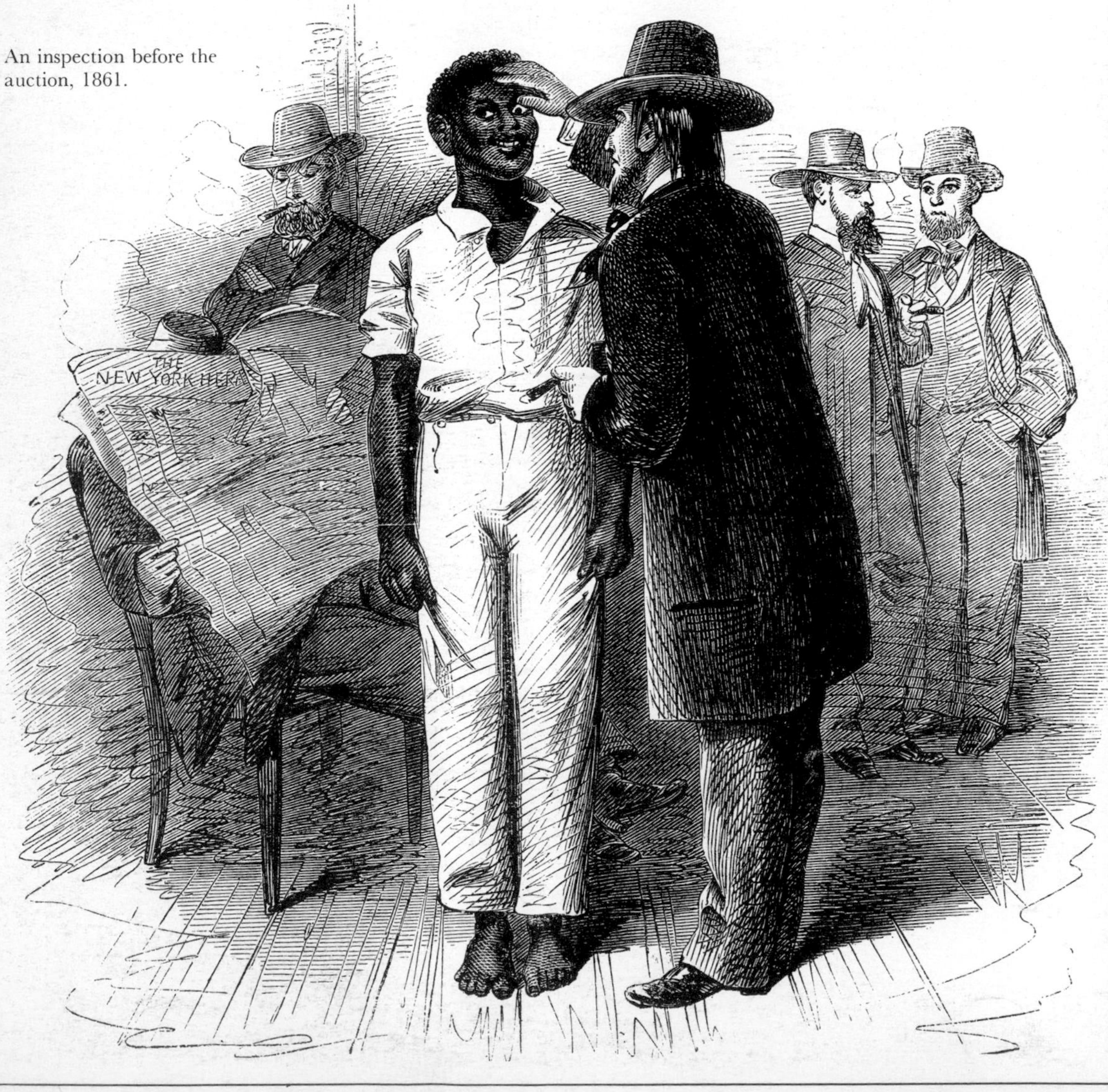

Below: At a slave sale in Virginia the auctioneer tries to whip up interest from his would be clients.

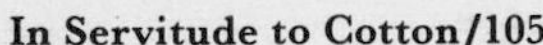

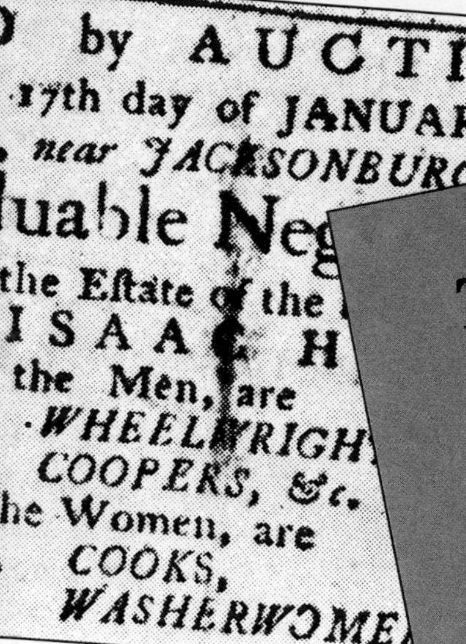
D by AUCTION,
17th day of JANUARY inst.
, near JACKSONBURGH
luable Neg
the Estate of the
ISAAC H
the Men, are
WHEELWRIGHT
COOPERS, &c.
he Women, are
COOKS,
WASHERWOME

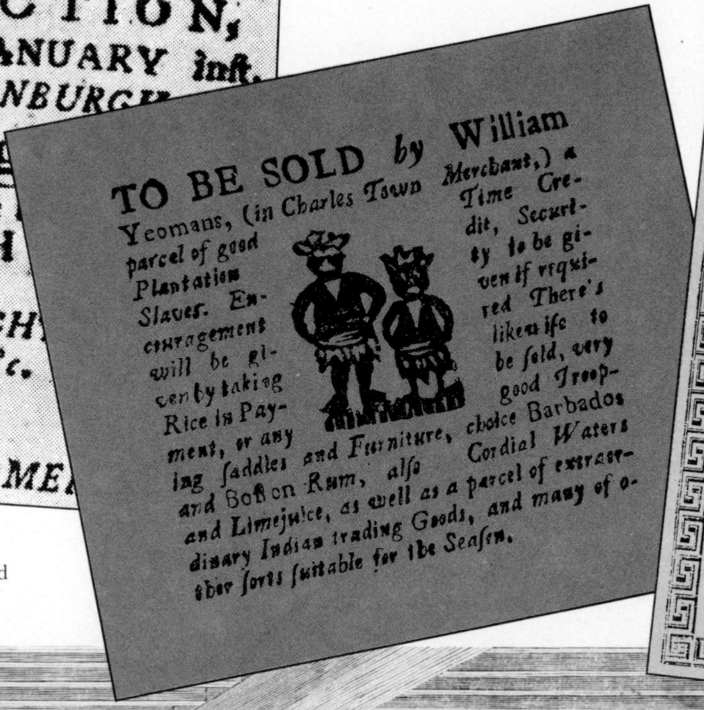

TO BE SOLD by William Yeomans, (in Charles Town Merchant,) a parcel of good Plantation Slaves. Encouragement will be given by taking Rice in Payment, or any Time Credit, Security to be given if required. There's likewise to be sold, very good Trooping Saddles and Furniture, choice Barbados and Boston Rum, also Cordial Waters and Limejuice, as well as a parcel of extraordinary Indian trading Goods, and many of other sorts suitable for the Season.

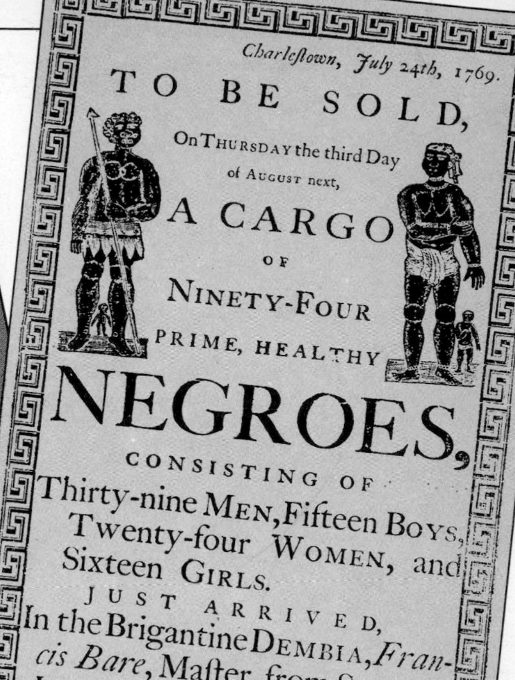
Charlestown, July 24th, 1769.

TO BE SOLD,

On THURSDAY the third Day of AUGUST next,

A CARGO OF NINETY-FOUR PRIME, HEALTHY

NEGROES,

CONSISTING OF

Thirty-nine MEN, Fifteen BOYS, Twenty-four WOMEN, and Sixteen GIRLS.

JUST ARRIVED,

In the Brigantine DEMBIA, *Francis Bare*, Master, from SIERRA-LEON, by

DAVID & JOHN DEAS.

Sale posters seen in Jacksonburg (*above*) and Charleston (*right*).

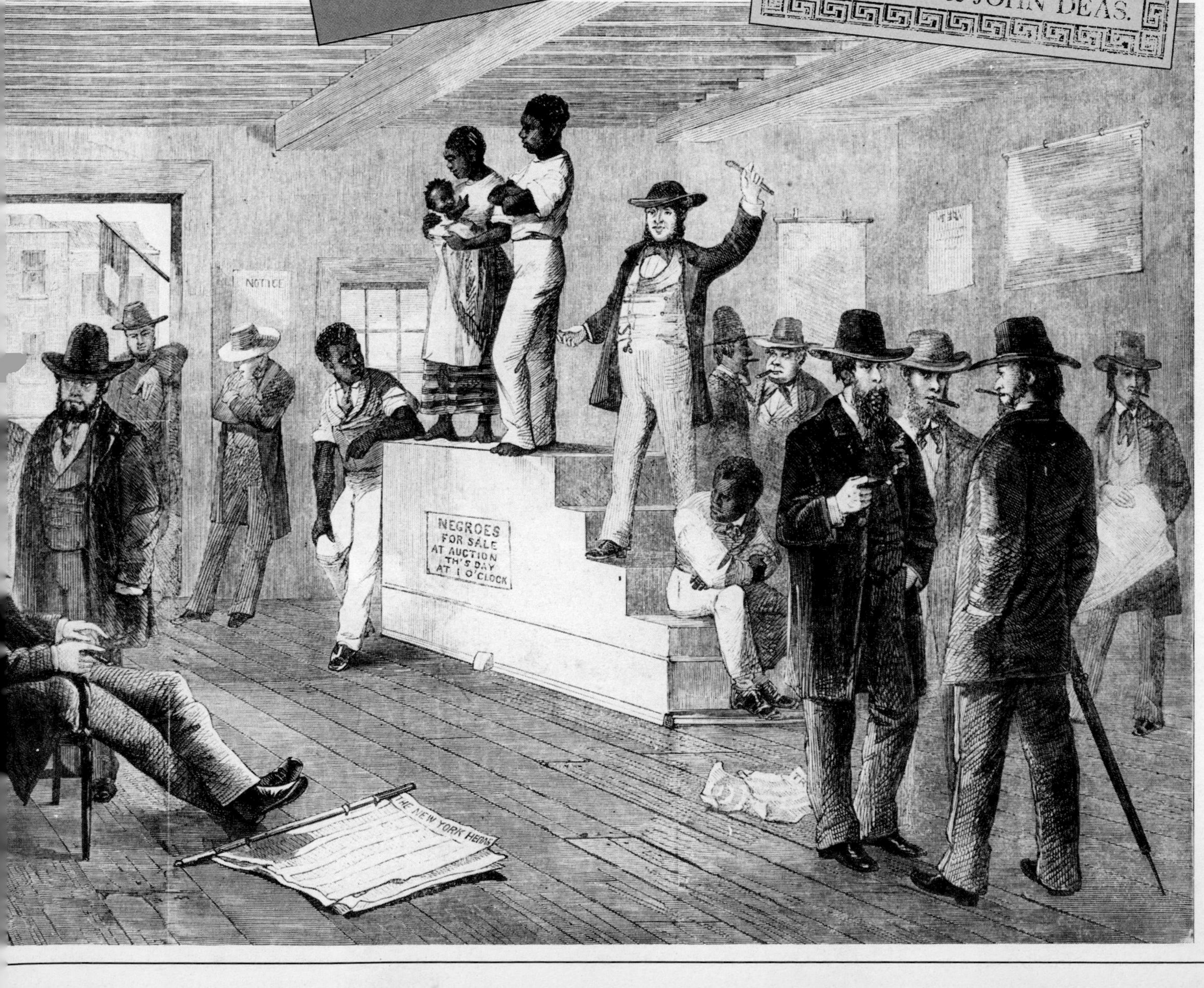

After the sale: in a painting by Eyre Gowe, dealers agree terms and slave families part in sadness before heading south from Richmond, Virginia.

Slave quarters: cabins at the Hermitage Plantation, Savannah, Georgia.

Inside, the house consisted of only one room 'about twenty feet by sixteen,' a large proportion of this space being taken up by a four-poster bed, which had a small camp bed alongside it. At the other end of the room was a fireplace, a dresser, a table, a bureau, two chairs with deer-skin seats, and a rocking chair. Olmsted, observant as ever, noticed the 'literature and knick-knacks on the mantelpiece,' finding them to consist of 'a Bible, five other books, a powder-horn, the sheath of a bowie-knife, a whiplash, and a tobacco-pipe.' Nevertheless, this farm supported 'ten or eleven field hands, such as they was,' and, besides growing all the corn and making all the pork that was needed, raised cattle and produced enough cotton to sell 60 to 70 bags.

The expectations of a larger planter were correspondingly higher. Under ideal conditions – a competent overseer, healthy slaves, good implements and strong mules – each field hand could cultivate ten acres of cotton or ten of corn and, according to one historian 'with a proper division of labor, five bales (two thousand pounds) or more of cotton per field hand could be produced.'

The economic facts of life on the average small plantation were harsh. The price of cotton in Liverpool rose to 12 cents a pound from 1850 until the Civil War, but a planter, with the high costs of transport, brokerage and interest on advance-money, could not expect to take home even half the Liverpool price. Smaller planters depended heavily on moneylenders to tide them over between crops, but even the largest had difficulty in keeping out of debt. A planter's most valuable assets were his slaves – an 18-year-old bought for $650 in 1845 could be sold five years later for $1000, and for nearly $2000 just before the Civil War. Many planters, anxious to increase their capital in this way, lived lives of spartan self-denial in order to support their slave investments. Too poor to replace outworn stock or implements, they struggled to keep going merely to keep their slaves in good enough condition to pass on to their children; as Edmund Ruffin, President of the Virginia Agricultural Society said, 'a man so situated may be said to be a slave to his own slaves.'

The larger planters managed to achieve a measure of prosperity. Frederick Olmsted visited a flourishing plantation in Mississippi owned by a planter who had not been to the estate for over two years – a situation frequent in the lower South. Managed by an overseer, the cultivated land consisted of between 1300 and 1400 acres and the whole estate supported 135 slaves. Thirty men manned the plows, there were 30 hoers (mainly women), and – among others – a black driver, three mechanics, two seamstresses, one cook, one stable servant, one cattle-tender, one hog-tender, one teamster, one house servant (the overseer's cook), one midwife and a nurse.

On all plantations, whatever the size, both white and black were inextricably bound up in each other's lives. Inside the mansion house, slaves often slept alongside, or even shared, their master and mistress's bed. Outside, black and white children shared the intimate rough and tumble of play. A black nurse supervised white charges, a personal maid attended her mistress, a single black factotum served his hard-pressed master. Like it or not, slave and slaveholder were locked in a macabre embrace from which neither could extricate himself.

Naturally, the relationship was dominated at best by suspicion, at worst by fear and hatred. Owners, often helplessly dependent economically on their slaves, could never be wholly confident of their goodwill; and slaves, although perhaps genuinely attached to their masters or mistresses, could never be sure that for economic reasons or a moment of irritation, they would not be sold, humiliated or beaten. Mrs Chestnut recorded that her mother-in-law, who 'had been frightened in her youth by tales of the Haiti rebellion,' was terrified of being poisoned, and was given to saying to her family (in the presence of the table servants): 'I warn you, don't touch that soup! It is bitter. There is something wrong about it.' And Professor Genovese quotes the words of one black woman, whose husband had been sold away from her: 'White folks got a heap to answer for the way they've done to colored folks! So much they won't never pray it away!'

The fear of being sold away from family and friends was an ever-present one. Conscientious slaveholders respected family ties, often arranging elaborate marriages for their slaves; but the words 'until death do us part' were conspicuously absent from the marriage ceremony and the marriage had no validity in the eyes of the law. Slave mar-

Zamba Describes a Sale

When Zamba, the slave-prince, arrived in Charleston, he was duly sold, in a private deal for $600. He provided the following account of the sale of his unfortunate comrades:

'Several dray-loads of clothing for the slaves were brought alongside. Next day was still cold; but the whole of the slaves were put ashore, and obliged to wash and scour themselves. They were then provided with tolerably good clothing, made of blue or white coarse woollen cloth, of English manufacture, commonly called "plains." The owners of the ship had provided these; but, had the weather been warm, the poor slaves would have been put up for sale in the scanty clothing they were in. The captain told me they were advertised for sale, which would take place in two days. Meantime we had a considerable number of white gentlemen to visit us, mostly intending purchasers. On the appointed day, the auctioneer, a Mr Naylor, accompanied by two young clerks, came down; and, after much careful inspection, arranged the whole cargo in separate lots, some of them singly, and others in lots of fifteen or twenty. The single ones were intended for domestic servants in town, and were chosen from the youngest and smartest-looking; the larger lots for the country, or what are called "field hands." At length, a great number of white gentlemen had arrived, and a few white ladies – at least, white women; for their conduct was not such as would entitle them to be called ladies in Europe: in a calm, cool, business-like way, they went around the various groups of negroes, examining and handling their limbs in the same manner as I afterwards saw butchers examining cattle.

The sale soon began, and took up a considerable time; the prices ranging from 250 to 450 dollars a head: the 32 negroes whom I had put on board brought nearly 10,000 dollars. It will be thus seen that the owners of the ship had made an excellent speculation: by this trip, as I learned from the captain, they had cleared from 90,000 to 100,000 dollars; and it must be allowed, that great part of this arose from the prudent and humane treatment which was exercised towards the live cargo. No doubt exists in my mind, that the moving principle in all concerned was avarice; and, in this case, it showed that, even from sinister motives, Providence can cause good to be produced at last. In the course of my subsequent experience, I have known ships, of the same tonnage as the *Triton*, arrive from Africa, in which 750 slaves had been embarked; but, owing to cruel usage, scanty and unwholesome provisions, impure air, and absolute filth, which prevailed on board, not more than 400 lived to reach Charleston; and of these, one-half were in a most weakly and miserable condition, and the remainder could by no means be classed as sound and healthy. In these cases, greed and avarice joined to inhumanity were punished; but at a sad expense of life, as regarded the wretched negroes. I have seen a slave-ship arrive from Africa, in such a condition as to its freight of flesh and blood, that no mortal of ordinary nerves could put his head below the hatch; and in such a miserable state were the negroes, that I have known 30 or 40 out of one cargo sent up to the hospital in carts. I heard frequently also, from what I deemed good authority, that on board these crowded and ill-conducted slavers, it was not a rare circumstance for the captain to order such poor slaves as were evidently dying, to be thrown overboard during the night, while yet the pulse of life was beating!'

The Great House: an idyllic view of the graceful Olivier Estate, South Carolina.

riages were practical attempts to ensure social stability rather than any desire to see deep and binding Christian unions. Whether the ceremony was crowned with orange blossom in the 'Big House,' in the presence of the planter and his wife and officiated over by a black preacher, or whether it was a simple 'broomstick ceremony,' when the couple merely jumped over a broomstick, the wedding – as all slaves knew only too well – was only as binding as their master's goodwill allowed it to be. 'Don't you know a slave can't be married,' cried George to Eliza in *Uncle Tom's Cabin*, 'There is no law in this country for that: I can't hold you for my wife, if he chooses to part us.'

If the separating of husbands and wives caused heartbreak, the loss of children imposed a corresponding agony. Although some historians now claim that family separation occurred less frequently than has hitherto been believed, it happened often enough. In the words of one slave: 'I have borne thirteen chillun and seen 'em mos' all sold off into slavery, and when I cried out with a mother's grief, none but Jesus heard.' If only to keep up plantation morale, slaveholders had reason to keep their slave families together, but if hard times came, slaves were an owner's most readily realizable cash asset and in the interests of personal survival he was sometimes obliged to auction some off. And even though he might stipulate that certain 'lots' should be sold together, slave dealers were not renowned for their humanitarian instincts – Harriet Beecher Stowe's trader, Haley, bought a 14-year-old boy at an auction without his elderly mother, refusing to listen to her passionate pleas for mercy. As one observer commented on witnessing

A slave 'pen' belonging to dealers in Alexandria, Virginia, a headquarters of the Southern slave business in the mid-19th century.

The Lashing House

For slaves, the lash was often an everyday experience, as this extract from *Testimonies Concerning Slavery* (1865) by a Virginian white, M D Conway, shows:

"In the towns and villages the flogging is done by a special and legally-appointed functionary. It is only under severe emergencies or in the heat of passion that gentlemen and ladies beat their own slaves. The gentlemen shun it as a temporary descent to the social grade of the overseer or the constable, as the slave-whipper is called, and the ladies have too much sensibility to inflict complete chastisement; so they merely write on a bit of note-paper, "Mr . . . , will you give Negro-girl Nancy . . . lashes, and charge to account. . . ."

I remember no building in our village so well as the slave-whipper's old, prison-like quarters, built of brick and limestone; and I recall vividly the fascination it had for myself and the other boys. It was known as "Captain Pickett's." The captain himself, with his hard, stony look, and his iron gray hair and beard, was the very animal to inhabit such a shell. . . .

About this particular building we lingered and peered with an insatiable curiosity, all the more pertinaciously for being so often driven or dragged away. And our curiosity found enough fuel to keep it inflamed; for few hours ever passed without bringing some victim to his door. . . . Around each victim we crowded, and when he or she disappeared and the door was shut, we – the boys – would rush around to all the walls, crevices, and backyards which we knew so well, gaining many a point from which we could see the half-naked cowering slave and the falling lash, and hear, with short-lived awe, the blows and the imploring tones, swelling to cries as the flogging proceeded.

Perhaps at that moment some tourist from Old or New England traveling through the South to ascertain "the facts" about Slavery, is at the hospitable board of the writhing slave's owner, learning how merciful the treatment of the slave is. He will write in his Diary, that, during several weeks passed at the residence of this or that large slaveholder, he saw no cases of severe punishment, though he observed keenly. He does not know to this day, perhaps, that in every Southern community there is a "Captain Pickett's place," – a dark and unrevealed closet, connected by blind ways with the elegant mansions. His Diary might have had a different entry had he consulted the slaves or the boys. . . .

The slave-whipper is well paid for his ugly work, and makes a "handsome living." But the silent old man of whom I have been writing came at last to prefer no living at all to such a one; for one day a sobbing girl, bearing in her hand an order for forty lashes, was unable to gain admittance; whereupon the neighbors broke down the door, and found that Captain Picket had hung himself by his own whipping-post."

A 1796 record of an incident in which a female slave was given 200 lashes.

Slaves and overseers in the field in a Southern cotton plantation.

the separation of a family: 'I never saw such profound grief as the poor creatures manifested,' and Mrs Chestnut, passing a slave auction with a friend, told her: 'If you can stand that no other Southern thing need choke you.'

The stresses and strains of family life among slaves were not confined to the possibilities of separation. The difficulties of bringing up children to accept the fate that would inevitably overtake them placed an additionally heavy burden on their parents, already coping with the deprivations inherent in their own lives. A mother, in an attempt to prepare her child for the rigors of the overseer's lash, thrashed him regularly. For the children, whipping became as much a part of their lives as eating and drinking – it even entered into their games, 'whipping each other with switches,' being as popular as 'playing at auctions.'

With their mothers working in the fields all day, slave children were cared for either by old black nurses, or, more commonly, by other older children. Frederick Olmsted described a nursery on a rice plantation in Georgia: 'On the verandah and the steps of the nursery, there were twenty-seven children, most of them infants, that had been left there by their mothers, while they were working their tasks in the fields. They probably make a visit to them once or twice during the day, to nurse them and receive them to take to their cabins . . . when they have finished their tasks – generally in the middle of the afternoon. The older children were fed with porridge, by the general nurse. A number of girls, eight or ten years old, were occupied in holding and tending the youngest infants.' Childhood for slaves ended on their twelfth birthday. From then on they either worked in the fields alongside their parents, 'one quarter of an able-bodied hand's day's work' being allotted to them, or they were taken into the house to work as servants.

Working in the house had its advantages, but was not as soft an option as many envious field hands thought. The demands made on house servants' time were even greater than those on the field hands'. And house servants were subject utterly to the whims of their owners. The two young girls working for a slatternly mistress in central Mississippi, who (according to Olmsted) slapped them continually while they were waiting at table, might well have been happier out of her clutches, among family and friends in the fields. Of all the indignities suffered by house slaves the one that most rankled was always having to stand in the presence of whites; and over all young women's heads, whether married or single, hung the threat of rape by their masters and their sons, or by overseers. This was a continuing horror of plantation life, but there were other aspects to the problem. Occasionally, as Professor Genovese pointed out in *Roll Jordan Roll*, some liaisons developed into love affairs, and some slaveholders set up their slave mistresses in town houses. A few like David Dickson of Georgia faced social ostracism by leaving home to live openly with a slave mistress and her children. So it was widely recognized by intelligent owners that taking advantage of black women caused trouble. One planter wrote in his *General Rules to Govern Time of an Overseer*: 'Above all things avoid intercourse with negro women. It breeds more . . . neglect, more idleness, more rascality, more stealing and more lieing [sic] up in the quarters and more everything that is wrong on a plantation than all else put together.'

Contrary to the belief of white Southern men, many of their wives, sisters and daughters, exposed daily to the attractions of personable young male blades, formed equally strong attachments. Professor Genovese quoted two instances, one of a wife, who took the carriage driver for a lover and bore his child, and another of a planter's daughter who ran off with a slave, bore his child, and refused to leave him. 'White women of all classes,' he comments, 'had black lovers and sometimes husbands in all parts of the South, especially in the towns and cities.' In such cases, Professor Genovese added, blacks were not subjected to lynching (as they often were for rape) and 'the whites apparently took these matters much more in (their) stride than they were able to do later.'

Slaves as family members: this engraving illustrates the best aspect of the master–slave relationship – with the slaves shown as loyal and well-loved family retainers.

Punishments for other offences moderated somewhat in the 19th century. Branding, cutting off ears, castration and other sadistic practices common throughout the West Indies during the 18th century, were forbidden by law, and the most widespread means of correction was the whip. In theory, it was widely considered bad policy to flog too often or too harshly, for this could produce an adverse effect on the slaves: it would make them apathetic and disinclined to work, or simply drive them to run away. In practice, abuse was widespread. Frederick Olmsted witnessed the flogging of an 18-year-old girl accused by her overseer of trying to cheat him of a day's work. He beat her with a raw-hide whip, first giving her 'thirty or forty blows across the shoulder' and then, after she again refused to admit her fault, he beat her again. 'It was the first time I had seen a woman flogged,' wrote Olmsted, 'I had seen a man cudgeled and beaten, in the heat of passion . . . but never flogged with a hundredth part of the severity used in this case.' The overseer was unrepentant. If he had not beaten her, he explained, 'she would have done the same thing again tomorrow, and half the people on the plantation would have followed her example . . . They'd never do any work at all if they were not afraid of being whipped.'

Given such circumstances, slaves sometimes refused to submit at all to the lash, even if it meant risking harsher treatment. One overseer told Frederick Olmsted: 'Some negroes are determined never to let a white man whip them, and will resist you, when you attempt it; of course,' he concluded with brutal casualness, 'you must kill them in that case.'

Those who ran away from their owners were taking a desperate step into the unknown. For, however harsh the conditions, at least the plantation provided a slave with shelter and a regular supply of food. To take to the woods or the swamps was to invite not only illness from hunger or exposure, but to brave the horrors of the slaveholder's pack of bloodhounds, which was kept for just such an occasion. Poor whites, particularly in the lower South, trained these 'nigger dogs' especially for this gruesome task and hired out their packs to those who had none, asking between $10 and $250 for each recaptured runaway, depending on the length of time it took to catch him. One farmer in Alabama told Frederick Olmsted that if the slave fought, 'that generally makes them [the hunters] mad, and they'll let 'm tear him a spell. The owners don't mind having them kind o' niggers tore a good deal; runaways ain't much account nohow, and it makes the rest more afraid to run away, when they see how they are sarved.'

Some slaves who took to the woods would do so for a few days, in protest against a heavy beating, or some loss of privilege, such as protracted denial of their meat ration, or cancellation of a holiday. Many of these were helped by slaves from neighboring plantations, who would feed them, and occasionally, at great personal risk, act as intermediaries between a runaway and his master, who might be induced to promise leniency if the errant slave should return.

But the other category of runaway – the slaves who fled to join separated families, or to obtain freedom in the North, Canada, or Mexico – faced obstacles so formidable that they defeated all but the most skilled and educated. Advertisements offering rewards for their recapture show that most of these runaways were men of between 16 and 35. Slaves fleeing north from the border states obviously had an advantage over those further south, but both were frequently aided

In this painting entitled 'On to Liberty,' slave women lead their children to freedom.

RUNNING AWAY

For slaves, the only real alternative to slavery was to run away to the 'quasi-freedom' of the North (where economically, socially and politically they were hardly better off) or to a precarious life in the swamps and woods. Running away was a common feature of plantation life. Slaves – usually lone individuals – would vanish after some final, unbearable affront. Usually they were caught again rapidly, as owners mounted patrols and dogs to hunt down their property. Records of whole communities of runaways are rare. But there were countless stories of individual runaways, among them astonishing sagas of slaves and their families who hid for long periods of time. One is told here by John James Audubon, the naturalist and artist, who stumbled on a runaway in a Lousiana swamp late in the 1820s.

'A stentorial voice commanded me to "stand still, or die."... Presently a tall firmly-built Negro emerged from the bushy underwood.... "Master," said he, "I am a runaway.... My camp is close by, and as I know you cannot reach home this night, if you will follow me there, depend upon *my honor* you shall be safe until the morning.'..."

There, in the heart of the cane-brake, I found a regular camp.... The wife raised not her eyes towards mine, and the little ones, three in number, retired into a corner.... The Runaway told me a tale of which the following is the substance.

About 18 months before, a planter residing not very far off, having met with some losses was obliged to expose his slaves at a public sale.... The Runaway chanced to be purchased by the overseer of the plantation; the wife was bought by an individual residing about a hundred miles off, and the children went to different places along the river....

On a stormy night ... the poor negro made his escape, and, ... made directly for the cane brake, in the center of which I found his camp. A few nights afterwards he gained the abode of his wife, and the very next after their meeting, he led her away. The children one after another he succeeded in stealing.... I promised to accompany them to the plantation of their first master. We soon reached the plantation.... Ere an hour had elapsed, the Runaway and his family were looked upon as his own. He afterwards repurchased them from their owners.'

The agony of the lone runaway and his almost inevitable fate is well captured by Alex Haley in his bestselling *Roots*. The hero, Kunta Kinte, not long a slave, has fled: 'When he heard the distant baying of the dogs, a rage flooded up in him such as he had never felt before. . . . When they were but strides away, Kunta whirled and crouched down, snarling back at them. As they came lunging forward with their fangs bared, he too lunged at them. . . . Springing away, Kunta began running again. . . . Then there was another shot, and another – and he felt a flashing pain in his leg. Knocked down in a heap, he had staggered upright again when the toubob shouted and fired again, and he heard the bullets thud into trees by his head. Let them kill me, thought Kunta; I will die as a man should. Then another shot hit the same leg, and it smashed him down like a giant fist.' [Kunta is caught stripped and tied to a tree.] 'The lash began cutting into the flesh across Kunta's shoulder and back, with the "oberseer" grunting and Kunta shuddering under the force of each blow. After a while Kunta could not stop himself from screaming with pain, but the beating went on until his sagging body pressed against the tree. His shoulders and back were covered with long, half-opened bleeding welts that in some places exposed the muscles beneath. . . . Then . . . everything went black.

He came to in his hut, and along with his senses, pain returned . . . He boiled with fury that instead of beating him like a man, the toubob had stripped him naked. When he became well, he would take revenge – and he would escape again. Or he would die.'

$150 REWARD

RANAWAY from the subscriber, on the night of the 2d instant, a negro man, who calls himself ***Henry May***, about 22 years old, 5 feet 6 or 8 inches high, ordinary color, rather chunky built, bushy head, and has it divided mostly on one side, and keeps it very nicely combed; has been raised in the house, and is a first rate dining-room servant, and was in a tavern in Louisville for 18 months. I expect he is now in Louisville trying to make his escape to a free state, (in all probability to Cincinnati, Ohio.) Perhaps he may try to get employment on a steamboat. He is a good cook, and is handy in any capacity as a house servant. Had on when he left, a dark cassinett coatee, and dark striped cassinett pantaloons, new—he had other clothing. I will give $50 reward if taken in Louisvill; 100 dollars if taken out one hundred miles from Louisville in this State, and 150 dollars if taken out of this State, and delivered to me, or secured in any jail so that I can get him again.

WILLIAM BURKE

Bardstown, Ky., September 3d, 1838.

A slave hunt.

A slave collar for persistent runaways (the effects of a similar device are shown below). Note the label's lordly judgment that runaways were 'bad.' Few nowadays would deny that such rebelliousness expressed an admirable individuality or a despair deserving of sympathy – or both.

and abetted by sympathizers in the North, (although it is now thought that white abolitionists played less of a part in this 'underground' movement than did other slaves, free Negroes, and black abolitionists). By whatever means, large numbers escaped across the border – one judge estimated that by 1855, 60,000 slaves had slipped the net and successfully defected to the North.

That more slaves did not run away, or revolt, has been attributed by some historians to the solace provided by religion and to the prolonged and unrestrained revelry indulged in by slave communities over the Christmas holiday, on the Fourth of July, on Saturday nights, or at any other time they could persuade their masters to celebrate. As the abolitionist, Frederick Douglass, put it, 'those holidays were among the most effective means in the hands of the slaveholders of keeping down the spirit of insurrection among the slaves . . . but for these, the rigors of bondage would have become too severe for endurance and the slave would have been forced to a dangerous desperation.'

Although insurrections in the South were

Insurrection

The threat of a slave revolt was enough to stir primeaval terror in the hearts of slave holders. A number of minor revolts in the 18th and 19th centuries offered a taste of what might happen if there was a general uprising. The revolts were therefore suppressed with extraordinary brutality. In New York in 1712, a crowd of slaves set fire to several houses and killed about ten whites. Twenty-one slaves were executed by burning, hanging, and being broken on wheels. In South Carolina's Stono insurrection of 1739, about 20 whites and 40 negroes died. In 1800 in Richmond, Virginia, a planned revolt involving thousands of slaves was betrayed before it began. The would-be leader, Gabriel, was hanged. In Charleston in 1822 a free black named Denmark Vesey planned an uprising that horrified whites. Vesey was a brilliant politician who spoke freely about the need for revolution. He had a lieutenant named Gullah Jack, a grotesque and frightening Angolan who claimed supernatural powers. Again Vesey was betrayed before his plans were put into action. He was put on trial, an event that was surrounded by increasing hysteria as whites learned of the extent of the conspiracy. Thirty-five blacks were hanged.

But the most horrifying revolt (to whites) was that led by Nat Turner in Virginia in 1831. Turner was a slave preacher and a mystic. On 21 August, he and his followers swept through Southampton County, and killed nearly 60 whites within 24 hours. Troops then overpowered his small band. Fifty-five blacks were later executed and another 200 lynched.

In prison, Turner dictated a long confession in which he professed his divine inspiration: 'I saw white spirits and black spirits engaged in battle and the sun was darkened – the thunder rolled in the heavens, and blood flowed in streams – and I heard a voice saying "Such is your luck, such you are called to see".' His captors took care he saw no such thing: he was hung on 11 November.

Nat Turner with a group of conspirators during his short lived uprising in 1831.

comparatively few and never attained the magnitude of those which occurred in the Caribbean, their significance lay, as Professor Genovese pointed out, 'in their very existence as the ultimate manifestation of class war under the most unfavorable conditions.' The fact that they occurred at all, against all but impossible odds, provided 'a yardstick with which to measure the smoldering resentment of an enslaved people who normally had to find radically different forms of struggle.' It was, indeed, the ultimate protest; slaves showed their resentment of their condition mainly by feigning illness, by theft, by sporadic outbursts of arson, by poisoning or by murdering their oppressors – all effective but essentially solitary measures. Organized revolt needed leaders of high caliber, capable of inspiring and motivating a group of followers toward a course of action which, if it failed, meant certain death. Such leaders were few and far between – the Toussaint L'Ouverture of the Southern Slave States never emerged. Instead, Virginia got Nat Turner and Gabriel Prosser and South Carolina got Denmark Vesey (a free black who had, in fact, visited Haiti), and none of these three insurgents achieved more than a fraction of their original aims. Nat Turner, a religious fanatic, attained notoriety through the 57 whites that were killed when he attempted to seize the Virginia town of Jerusalem in 1831, Gabriel Prosser when he tried to take Richmond in 1800, and Denmark Vesey because of his designs on Charleston, South Carolina in 1822. All were hanged for their pains.

If they did not succeed in overthrowing their hated white masters, these revolts did succeed in causing them extreme agitation. The uprisings confirmed slaveholders' worst fears about the intentions of their slaves and many must have shared the feelings of Mary Chestnut, who, after seeing a play about the Indian Mutiny, was overcome by 'a thrill of terror' as she wondered how long it would be before all slaves 'would resist the seductive and irresistible call: Rise, kill, and be free.' All slaveholders were, however, united in their determination never to allow such things to happen again. Night patrols, already in use throughout the lower South, 'to prevent slaves roaming about at night and getting into mischief,' had their powers extended, after the Denmark Vesey uprising, to allow them to curb the movement of free blacks as well as slaves, and the upper South followed suit after the Nat Turner insurrection. Further restrictions were imposed on free blacks – those leaving their own state were not allowed to return, in case they might bring back with them 'pernicious doctrines,' and for similar reasons it became an offense to teach a slave to read. Religious instruction, however, previously regarded by many slaveholders with suspicion (it being generally felt that slaves were better left in ignorance of the Sermon on the Mount), now came to be regarded as a useful means of social control.

In the 1830s owners tried to ameliorate the conditions of their slaves. But these measures were designed primarily, as Professor Genovese said, 'to make the South safe for slaveholders by confirming the blacks in perpetual slavery and by making it possible for them to accept their fate.' Neither did their humanitarianism extend to emancipation, especially after the decisive vote against it in the Virginia debates of 1831–32, and manumissions became increasingly difficult to obtain. A petition presented to the General Assembly of Virginia in January, 1831, expressed widely-held views when it stated: 'Slaves, while kept in subjection are submissive and easily controlled, but let any number of them be indulged with the hope of freedom . . . they reject constraint and become almost wholly unmanageable. It is by the expectation of liberty, and by that alone, that they can be rendered a dangerous population.'

Try as they might, the tide of opinion was turning against the slaveholders. However much they protested that their slaves were better fed, better clothed, better looked after in sickness and old age, than the vast majority of the free laboring classes of the world, there was no escaping the fact that slavery fell into a different category altogether. As W E B du Bois put it: 'there was . . . a real meaning to slavery different from that we may apply to the laborer today. It was in part psychological, the enforced personal of inferiority, the calling of another Master; the standing with hat in hand. It was the helplessness. It was the defencelessness of family life. It was the submergence below the arbitrary will of any sort of individual.' The growing defensiveness of the slave owners' attitude to the institution was itself evidence of the swelling voice of its opponents, speaking in the name of humanity.

THE FIELD-WORKERS

Most slaves were employed in cotton fields. In the following document, accompanied by pictures taken in the early 1860s, Solomon Northup describes the culture of cotton on a large plantation on the Bayou Boeuf in Avoyelles Parish, Lousiana. Born a free man in New York State, Northup earned money as a fiddler for entertainments before two white men drugged and kidnapped him, and then sold him as a slave. Northup's family never gave up the search for him, and after 12 years his freedom was restored by their efforts.

'In the latter part of August [after several hoeings] begins the cotton picking season. At this time each slave is presented with a sack. A strap is fastened to it, which goes over the neck, holding the mouth of the sack breast high, while the bottom reaches nearly to the ground. Each one is also presented with a large basket that will hold about two barrels. This is to put the cotton in when the sack is filled. . . .

An ordinary days' work is two hundred pounds. A slave who is accustomed to picking, is punished, if he or she brings in a less quantity than that. . . .

The cotton grows from five to seven feet high, each stalk having a great many branches, shooting out in all directions, and lapping each other above the water furrow.

Sometimes the slave picks down one side of a row, and back upon the other, but more usually, there is one on either side, gathering all that has blossomed, leaving the unopened bolls for a succeeding picking. When the sack is filled, it is emptied into the basket and trodden down. It is necessary to be extremely careful the first time going through the field, in order not to break the branches off the stalks. The cotton will not bloom upon a broken branch.

The hands are required to be in the cotton field as soon as it is light in the morning, and, with the exception of ten or 15 minutes, which is given them at noon to swallow their allowance of cold bacon, they are not permitted to be a moment idle until it is too dark to see, and when the moon is full, they often times labor till the middle of the night. They do not dare to stop even at dinner time, nor return to the quarters, however late it be, until the order to halt is given by the driver.'

A slave family on a South Carolina cotton plantation.

Slaves on the James Hop... prepare to leave for the field.

In the fields on an unidentified plantation.

Slave family, Savannah, Georgia.

Returning from the field, Charleston, South Carolina.

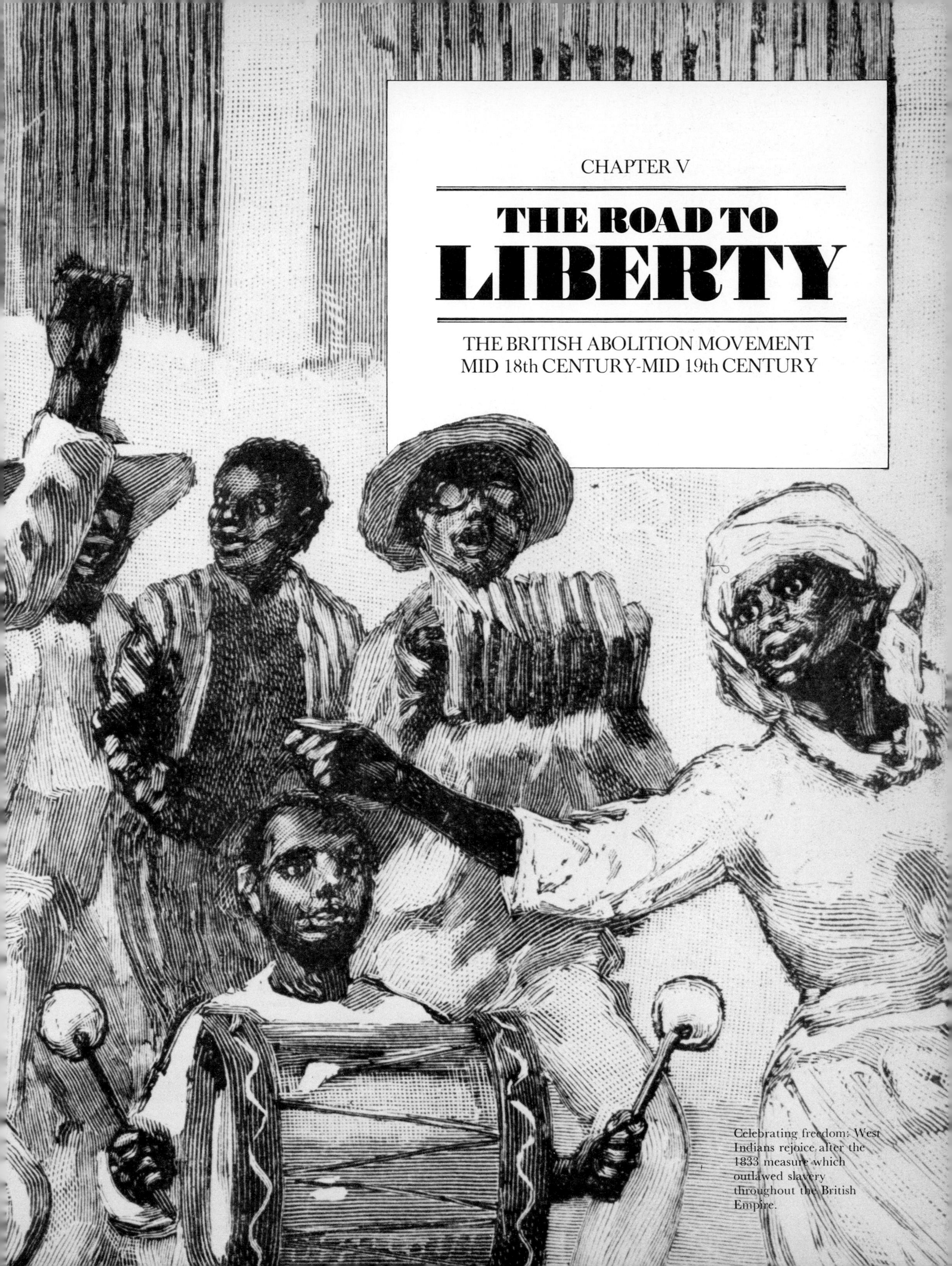

CHAPTER V

THE ROAD TO LIBERTY

THE BRITISH ABOLITION MOVEMENT MID 18th CENTURY-MID 19th CENTURY

Celebrating freedom: West Indians rejoice after the 1833 measure which outlawed slavery throughout the British Empire.

The first abolitionists were American Quakers. The *Germantown Protest*, printed in 1688 by a group of Pennsylvanian Quakers of Swiss and Dutch descent, opposed both slavery and the slave trade: 'Now, tho they are black, we cannot conceive there is more liberty to have them slaves, as it is to have other white ones . . . And those who steal or robb men, and those who buy or purchase them, are they not all alike?'

Similar sentiments were uttered in 1700 by the first non-Quaker to express anti-slavery opinions publicly, Chief Justice Sewall of Massachusetts (a colony which in 1641 had forbidden slavery 'unless it be lawful Captives taken in just Warres, and such strangers as willingly sell themselves or are sold to us'). In a pamphlet entitled *Selling of Joseph*, Sewall wrote that 'all Men, as they are the Sons of Adam are Coheirs; and have equal Right unto Liberty, and all other outward Comforts of Life. . . . So that Originally, and Naturally, there is no such thing as Slavery.' Even Quakers, however, were not prepared to take a concerted stand. True, the Society of Friends tried to prevent the importation of slaves into Massachusetts, and many, like John Woolman, began using maple sugar, instead of slave-produced cane-sugar. But the majority of early 18th century Quakers thought of slavery as being only one among many evils surrounding those who wished to lead a simple and godly life. Some of the anti-slavery tracts which were published, therefore – such as those of William Sandiford in 1733 and Benjamin Lay in 1738 – were dismissed as the rantings of fanatics and served merely to create a gulf between their authors and the Community.

But with the increase in the black population throughout the mainland colonies between 1700 and 1760, the ethical and moral problems posed for Quakers by slave-owning became more acute. In 1759 the Philadelphia Yearly Meeting of the Society of Friends decided to begin ' to disown any member involved in buying or selling slaves.' In 1761 Pennsylvania imposed a duty of £10 on every slave imported into the colony.

Anthony Benezet, a Quaker convert of Huguenot origin, whose family had emigrated first to London and then to Philadelphia, finally forced the Society of Friends to dissociate itself publicly from slave trading. He made an impassioned plea against the trade at the annual meeting of 1772, when, 'with tears running down his cheeks,' he cried 'Ethiopia shall soon stretch out her hands unto God!' So impressed was the Society that 'it condemned the trade by a unanimous vote.'

By 1772, however, Benezet had already written extensively on slavery, and been read in both France and England. In 1767, he had written *A Caution and Warning to Great Britain and her Colonies on the Calamitous State of the Enslaved Negroes in the British Dominions*. The *Caution* was circulated by English Quakers among schools (including Eton, Winchester, Harrow and St Paul's), in order that 'the rising youth might acquire a knowledge, and at the same time a detestation, of this cruel traffic.' Both this work and his next study, published the same year, on Guinea, the slave trade, and its 'Nature and Calamitous Effect,' profoundly influenced both British and French abolitionists, by then deeply involved in their humanitarian crusade.

At first British abolitionist efforts were concentrated on ending the slave trade rather than emancipating the slaves themselves. Abolitionists felt that slavery would die a natural death as soon as the trade was abolished. On the face of it, this was a natural assumption: more male slaves were shipped across the Atlantic than female (it being uneconomic to transport pregnant women and children), family life was generally discouraged, and deaths from disease or overwork kept demand high.

The slave trade came under only occasional attack before the second half of the 18th century from a few enlightened clerics, philosophers, poets and novelists. In 1688 Mrs Aphra Behn wrote *Oroonoko, or the History of a Royal Slave*, which was not only the first novel in the English language by a woman, but the first to have a slave as its hero. John Wesley called the trade 'the execrable sum of human villainy'; John Locke described it as the 'vile and miserable estate of many'; Alexander Pope condemned it; but it was nevertheless accepted by the majority as a necessary, if distasteful, fact of life. Slavery was allowed by law on British soil, and many West Indian planters, returning in affluence to their newly-acquired country estates, took advantage of the situation, by bringing with them numbers of favorite black slaves from their plantations. By the 1770s, there were some 15,000–16,000 slaves in England, conservatively valued at £700,000.

The formal movement for abolition arose as a consequence of the Evangelical revival of the mid-18th century in England, which was itself derived from the preaching of John Wesley. Wesley urged a return to an emotional commitment to the message of the Gospel, rather than a reliance on the formalism and rationality of the established Church.

One result of Wesley's teaching – which was eventually to found the Methodist Church – was an uncompromising attitude to slavery. He made a clear distinction between the legalities of slavery and the demands of justice. 'Can law, human law, change the nature of things?' he wrote, 'Can it turn darkness into light or evil into good? Notwithstanding ten thousand laws, right is right and wrong is wrong . . . there must still remain an essential difference between justice and injustice, cruelty and mercy.'

Abolition as a planned campaign dates from 1765, when Granville Sharp, a 30-year-old junior civil servant in London, came upon Jonathan Strong, a black slave, beaten and almost blinded and stumbling helplessly down the street in Mincing Lane. Sharp took him to his brother, a doctor, and the two of them nursed him back to health. Two years later his owner, a lawyer from Barbados named David Lisle, finding that his slave had recovered, kidnapped him and sold him to a West Indian planter.

While in prison awaiting transportation, Strong smuggled a plea for help out to Sharp, who filed a petition for assault. Within a few days, Lisle countered, issuing Sharp with 'a writ for robbing the original master of his slave.' The case was eventually, in the face of outraged public opinion, withdrawn by Lisle, to the disappointment of Sharp, who had been 'studying the finer points of English law as it related to property in slaves.' Sharp, although no lawyer, was so affected by the case that he determined to establish a test case.

This study was put to good use when another fugitive slave, Thomas Lewis, was seized in Chelsea and 'dragged to a boat on the Thames.' His case came up before Lord Justice Mansfield, who was notoriously reluctant to do anything which might upset the status quo or deprive the powerful West Indian sector of the community of their supposed property. In this case, the jury decided that the master had 'not established his claims,' but on the wider issue of whether slaves could exist in England, Granville Sharp was left unsatisfied. Lord Mansfield left the point open, adding, 'I hope it will never be finally discussed, for I would have all the masters think them free, and all negroes think they were not, because then they would both behave better.'

The Lord Justice was, however, forced to abandon this ambivalent view a year later, when the indefatigable Sharp produced yet another fugitive, James Somersett. Backed into a corner by the indisputable fact that Somersett's owner had a 'clear title to him under Virginia law,' Lord Mansfield tried twice to adjourn the case, strongly urged settlement out of court, and even tried to persuade Parliament to legislate on the subject of slave property. Wriggle he might, but

Granville Sharp, evangelist and humanitarian: Sharp, a leading anti-slaver, combined a passion for legal reform with zealous Christianity. The Victorian lawyer and historian, Sir James Stephen, described Sharp as having 'the most inflexible of human wills united to the gentlest of human hearts.'

The Somersett Case

The case of the slave James Somersett, brought at the instigation of Granville Sharp in 1772, was a turning point in British legal history. It finally made clear that slavery could not exist as an institution under British law (although blacks were still kept illegally as slaves – and even kidnapped for export – for many years afterward). It was only a matter of time, therefore, before the rule of law was extended to imperial possessions.

The affair began in late 1769 when Charles Stewart, a senior customs official from Boston, arrived in London with one of his slaves, James Somersett (whose name is often spelled with a double 'm' or single 't').

Two years later, in 1771, Somersett fled from his master. On 26 November 1771, the master seized his 'property' and delivered him to the commander of the *Ann and Mary*, 'to be by me safely and securely kept and carried and conveyed in the said vessel' to Jamaica. Somersett's friends moved quickly: two days later, Lord Mansfield granted a writ of *habeas corpus* against the captain of the ship, John Knowles. Granville Sharp, who had already failed to obtain from Mansfield judgment on the legality of slavery in the case of another slave, Thomas Lewis, was determined to make Somersett a test case. After the serving of the writ, Somersett could not be taken from England without the act being declared legal.

The case opened on Friday, 7 February 1772. Speaking for Somersett was the bluff and colorful William 'Bull' Davy who argued 'that no man at this day is or can be a slave in England.' He conceded that slavery was legal under colonial laws, but that this had no application to the laws of England. 'Have the laws of Virginia,' he asked, 'any more influence, power or authority in this country than the laws of Japan?' He quoted an Elizabethan verdict 'that England was too pure an air for slaves to breathe in' and concluded, 'I hope, my Lord, the air does not blow worse since.'

There was really no defense, although Mansfield writhed with embarrassment at the implications of the case. 'On the one hand,' he said, 'we are assured, that there are no less than 15,000 slaves now in England, who will procure their liberty, should the law declare in their favor, and whose loss to the proprietary, is estimated at a moderate sum of more than £700,000. On the other, should the coercion of the colony slave-laws be found binding to the extent argued, it must imply consequences altogether foreign to the object of present inquiry.'

There were a number of other hearings, but it was clear that Granville Sharp's tactics would be met with success. On 22 June 1772, Mansfield made the famous judgment that slavery 'must take its rise from positive law... the claim of slavery can never be supported... and therefore the man must be discharged.'

The abolitionists were delighted – as indeed were a crowd of free blacks who had been following the proceedings closely. The *London Chronicle* reported 'no sight could be more pleasingly affecting to the mind than the joy which shone at that instance in these poor men's sable countenances.'

Lord Mansfield.

Parliament, the owner and Sharp were not prepared to let him off the hook; on 7 February 1772, the case came to court, and on 22 June Lord Mansfield delivered his judgment: 'The power claimed never was in use here nor acknowledged by the law. . . . The state of Slavery is of such a nature that it is incapable of being introduced on any reasons, moral or political, but only by positive law, which preserves its force long after the reasons, occasion, and time itself whence it was created, are erased from the memory. It is so odious that nothing can be sufficient to support it but positive law. Whatever inconveniences, therefore, may follow from the decision, I cannot say this case is allowed or approved by the law of England, and therefore the black must be discharged.' By this verdict, slavery ceased to exist on English soil. Slavery in the colonies was unaffected, but the case marked the formal beginning of the end of slavery throughout the Empire.

In 1776, abolitionists received some additional support from an unexpected quarter – Adam Smith's classic study in economics, *The Wealth of Nations*. Smith concluded that slavery was uneconomic, firstly because it ruined the land, and secondly because slaves were more expensive to keep than free laborers. But he also made clear his belief that slavery originated in the fact that 'the pride of man makes him love to domineer . . . he will generally prefer the service of slaves to that of freemen.'

In 1783 abolitionist sentiment received a further shot in the arm when the case of the slaveship *Zong* was brought before the courts. Lord Justice Mansfield, once again confronted by the unpalatable fact of slave-trading, had this time to decide whether the 132 slaves who were thrown overboard from a slaveship, allegedly short of water and in the grip of an epidemic, were legal jettison or not. Lord Mansfield ruled that in law it was 'as if horses had been thrown overboard,' and consequently the owners were entitled to receive compensation.

This judgment served to draw the various abolitionist factions closer together. In the same year six Quakers – William Dillwyn, George Harrison, Samuel Hoare, Thomas Knowles, John Lloyd and Joseph Woods – formed a committee, its aim being 'the relief and liberation of the negro slaves in the West Indies and for the discouragement of the Slave Trade on the coast of Africa.' Links were formed with Granville Sharp, who had lobbied bishops and archbishops ceaselessly since the Somersett case, in many cases obtaining their support, and with James Ramsay, a surgeon who had (unlike his fellow abolitionists) actually had first-hand experience of the slave trade, having once treated diseased slaves on a ship. Later he became rector of two parishes on St Kitts, where for 19 years he fought to improve slave conditions. On his return to England, he published an *Essay on the Treatment and Conversion of African Slaves in the British Sugar Colonies*, the first statement of the abolitionist case to be based entirely on first-hand evidence.

In the next few years, the abolitionist cause gained its two most important recruits – Thomas Clarkson and William Wilberforce. In 1785 Clarkson won a Cambridge University prize for a Latin essay on the subject, *Is it right to make slaves of others against their will?* Ignorant of the slave trade before competing for this prize, Clarkson became converted to the abolitionist cause after reading Benezet's account of the slave trade in order to prepare himself for his essay. He also claimed to have a 'direct revelation from God ordering him to devote his life to abolishing the trade,' which inspired him not only to make contact with fellow sympathizers, but also to activate them to reorganize their hitherto well-meaning but ill-conceived plans.

Together with Granville Sharp and Josiah Wedgwood, the potter, he founded the Society for the Abolition of the Slave Trade, whose seal, designed by Wedgwood, had as its motif a supplicant African, round whom was inscribed the motto 'Am I not a man and a brother?' To further the society's aims and to substantiate his case, Clarkson embarked single-handed on the mammoth task of compiling a detailed dossier on the abuses of the slave trade, assembling a collection of shackles, thumbscrews and other instruments, and acquiring the names and histories of 20,000 seamen. He then set about interviewing the seamen, and any ship's doctors, slave-captains and merchants prepared to talk freely to him. Understandably, many were reluctant to do so – in one case, after a seaman revealed secretly to Clarkson his captain's murder of the ship's steward, Clarkson was nearly pushed off the pier at Liverpool by the vindictive captain and some

Thomas Clarkson (*right*) and William Wilberforce (*far right*) were England's two leading abolitionists. While Clarkson toured the country, Wilberforce concentrated on exposing the evils of slavery in Parliament.

other slavers, on whom he also had damning information. Fortunately, Clarkson was six feet tall and heavily built, and with an uncharacteristic show of aggression he 'put his head down and charged like a bull,' scattering his opponents. He then returned to the tavern where he had a private sitting-room and wrote up his notes for the day.

Without an effective voice in Parliament, however, the abolitionists were impotent. Only a handful of politicians had so far interested themselves in the slave trade, and their qualifications for 'parliamentary leader of the Abolitionists' were unsatisfactory. What the Society needed, as one historian said, was an 'independent man with ability, connections and reputation. He had to be important enough to have the ear and secure the sympathy of the great; he had to have the mind to master a complicated subject and to expose his opponents' lies. He needed, above all, to be prepared to devote himself, his time and his money, to the cause.'

Such a paragon was found in the 26-year-old Member for Yorkshire, William Wilberforce, who had spoken on the subject in the House, and who was known to have not only brains and religious principles, but wealth, family connections and a circle of influential friends which included the dramatist Richard Sheridan, the statesman and libertarian Charles James Fox and the Prime Minister, William Pitt. In 1787 Clarkson was sent to persuade Wilberforce to become their spokesman and he promised to undertake the leadership of the campaign 'if nobody better could be found.'

From the society's point of view by far the most important of Wilberforce's friendships was that with Pitt the Younger, a relationship which provided the political axis around which all subsequent abolitionist effort revolved. It was directly due to Wilberforce's personal influence on the Prime Minister that in 1788 a select Committee of the Privy Council was set up to investigate the slave trade.

Clarkson's findings were set before the committee, but witnesses to support his case proved suddenly reluctant to come forward. Many previously thought to be reliable hotly denied, when it came to the point, that 'slaves were captured in any but just wars,' or that, 'kidnapping took place in Africa.' Many assured their questioners that 'the Trade was a blessing to these People,' that, 'those who were transported to the West Indies were doubly fortunate in being alive at all and in being removed to a better life,' and that 'their happiness on the journey could be seen by the singing and dancing with which they expressed their delight.' Fortunately for the abolitionist cause, there was enough controversial evidence, in particular on conditions of seamen aboard the slaveships and on the despotism of some African rulers (notably the King of Dahomey) to recommend that the matter should be discussed in the House. Wilberforce unfortunately fell seriously ill and the discussion had to be postponed for over a year. Pitt, meanwhile, guaranteed his friend that he would 'take his place in promoting Abolition.'

By that time, however, the abolitionists

The Plaque of Freedom

Undoubtedly the most popular symbol of abolitionism was that devised by the potter Josiah Wedgwood. In 1787, Wedgwood decided to make his own contribution to the cause by producing a medallion (below) and distributing copies to his friends. He made some 200,000, and even sent some to Benjamin Franklin who declared himself 'much affected by contemplating the figure.' The image was reproduced in countless prints and drawings, and – in at least one case – on a child's sampler (right).

had already achieved a few tangible results. The first was the foundation of the West African colony of Sierra Leone, set up in 1787 for 'the relief of the London black poor,' a project instigated by Granville Sharp at the suggestion of the blacks themselves. A quarter of a million acres was bought from a neighboring chief, and Granville Sharp drew up a Utopian constitution, 'bristling with frank pledges and laws derived from ancient Israel.' Unfortunately, as one historian commented, 'the practical details of founding a colony were less thoroughly investigated.' The 400 blacks and 60 Europeans who sailed to the colony on 8 April 1787, arrived at the beginning of the rainy season, and were almost immediately overtaken by hunger, fever and dysentery. Half of the settlers died within a year, or fled to more hospitable regions and those that remained struggled to survive without sufficient money or livestock and with no arms with which to protect themselves.

Granville Sharp, far from feeling any twinges of conscience at his lack of foresight, wrote severely: 'The greatest blame of all is to be charged on the intemperance of the people themselves; for the most of them became so besotted during the voyage that they were totally unfit for business when they landed and could hardly be prevailed upon to assist in erecting their huts.' Sierra Leone was saved from extinction by the formation of the St George's Bay Company in 1790, which put it on a firm financial basis. Two years later, the colony was reinforced by 100 whites and some of the 4000 black loyalists resettled in Nova Scotia by the British Government after the American Revolution – 1131 of whom applied to be transferred to Sierra Leone, attracted by opportunities for landownership denied them in Nova Scotia.

Another achievement was the bill introduced by Sir William Dolben to limit the number of slaves in each ship according to its tonnage – a proposal which provoked an outcry from slave captains and other supporters of the trade (one spokesman even

A vicious campaign: these two cartoons illustrate the passions aroused by the anti-slavery campaign around the turn of the 18th century. At left is an abolitionist view of the 'barbarities in the West Indies,' dramatizing one incident reported in Parliament in 1791. At right, the famous cartoonist, James Gilray, publicizes a snide rumor that Wilberforce (on the sofa, left) kept a black mistress.

went so far as to assure the House that the holds of slaveships were 'redolent with frankincense'). The bill, which left 22 slave captains and 350 seamen unemployed in Liverpool, became law on 17 June 1788.

A third – if minor – success was the link formed between English and French abolitionists and the founding, with the assistance of the English government, of the French *Société des Amis des Noirs*. As it happened, France proved something of a disappointment to the abolitionists. The French abolitionist movement, although 'socially more substantial,' remained politically less effective then the British one. The members of the *Amis des Noirs* were liberal aristrocrats rather than Evangelical reformers and of a reflective rather than active turn of mind. French abolitionists did not commit themselves to emancipation, and only cautiously to abolition on a reciprocal basis with Britain. Thomas Clarkson, visiting France in 1789 to exchange ideas with his opposite numbers in Paris, was at first enthralled and excited by the fervor he found in the capital: 'I should not be surprised,' he wrote to Wilberforce, 'if the French were to do themselves the honour of voting away this diabolical traffic in a night.' Although, he was received with enthusiasm, he was disillusioned to find that the French were reluctant 'to make a moral gesture which could only help their rivals.'

The French view was understandable. With San Domingo at the height of its slave-based prosperity, abolition could threaten France's whole economy. The French Revolutionary ideals of Liberty, Equality and Fraternity which in theory embraced the oppressed slaves, particularly those in San Domingo, would not do so in practice. The slave uprising there, followed by the growth of Napoleon's imperialist ambitions, put an end to any such liberal tendencies. The French did not abolish the slave trade until 1818, and then only under strong pressure from Britain.

The war with France which broke out in 1793 was a disaster for the British abol-

APPEALS TO THE HEART

The British Abolition Committee was established in 1787 to work toward the ending of the slave trade. To aid the policy of achieving Parliamentary legislation to ban the trade, the Committee produced and distributed pamphlets, books, poems and prints dramatizing the fate of slaves. Some of the propaganda prints are reproduced here, along with their accompanying captions and ver-

'Negro Woman, who sittest pining in captivity and weepest over thy sick child; though no one seeth thee, God seeth thee; though no one pitieth thee, God pitieth thee; raise thy voice, forlorn and abandoned one; call upon him from amidst thy bonds for assuredly He will hear thee.'

The much publicized symbol of anti-slavery devised by Wedgwood (see p.138).

ses. Since they were intended for the public at large, the message was generalized and the verse usually bad. Cowper's poem, *The Negro's Complaint,* was one of the best:

'Forc'd from home and all its pleasures,
Afric's coast I left forlorn
To increase a stranger's treasures
O'er the raging billows born.'

But most of the attached verses were pieces of sentimental doggerel designed for mass-market appeal.

'I would not have a Slave to till my ground To carry me, to fan me while I sleep, And tremble when I wake, for all the wealth That sinews bought and sold, have ever earn'd. We have no Slaves at home – why then abroad?' (Cowper)

'The driver's whip unfolds its torturing coil. She only sulks – go, lash her to her toil.'

Erratic idealist: the statesman Charles James Fox lived a dissolute youth – running up gambling debts of £140,000 – but later became a much admired political advocate of libertarianism. The crowning achievement of his career was to carry the bill in 1806 by which Parliament pledged to abolish the slave trade. He died three months later.

itionists. The violent excesses of French egalitarianism alienated the British and made them suspicious of any comparable ideals. The abolitionist cause seemed at best irrelevant and at worst destructive. Many influential backers withdrew financial support, abolitionists were dismissed as 'Jacobins' and Wilberforce himself was subjected to personal abuse – he was challenged to duels, thugs attempted to waylay him and it was even rumored that he had a black mistress.

Undeterred, the society continued its efforts to swing public opinion to its cause. From the library of Battersea Rise, the house in Clapham which Wilberforce shared with Henry Thornton – banker and founder of the South London colony of Evangelicals known as the 'Clapham Sect' – issued a barrage of pamphlets, statistics and illustrations. One famous print was of a drawing by Clarkson showing the methods of stowing slaves aboard the slaveship *Brookes*. These, together with copies of William Cowper's very popular poem, *The Negro's Complaint*, were widely circulated through locally-formed abolitionist societies. Cameos depicting the committee's seal were worn by ladies of fashion and 30,000 housewives were said to have associated themselves with an 'anti-saccarite' movement, refusing sugar in tea.

In 1790 the postponed hearing of trade witnesses began in the House, and in 1791 Wilberforce moved the abolition of the slave trade for the first time. The motion was defeated – despite support from both Fox and Pitt – by 88 votes to 163. As Horace Walpole commented disgustedly: 'commerce had clinked its purse.'

It was to be the first of many such defeats. There was a brief upsurge of optimism in 1792, when, after Wilberforce once again moved for abolition, an amendment was carried in favor of 'gradual abolition,' only to subside when the Lords postponed the bill for a year. The following year, a bill introduced in the Commons to abolish 'the supply by British merchants of slaves to foreign settlements' was passed, only to come to grief once again in the Lords. It seemed to the most dedicated sympathizers that the movement for abolition was doomed to hang in abeyance for ever.

That it did not was largely due to the aftermath of war. Under the 1803 Peace of Amiens, the British gained various French and Dutch sugar islands, acquisitions which at last brought home to the intractable West Indian sector in Parliament the futility of continuing a trade which only served to bolster up the fortunes of others to their own disadvantage. Abolition came back into favor. Abolitionists were no longer derided as 'Jacobins.' The society, having acquired some valuable new members, notably James Stephen and Zachary Macaulay, met again with renewed optimism. And Wilberforce was once again confident enough to move his Abolition Bill, which he had dropped for the past three years.

Although Pitt, in poor health and under pressure from a strong opposition, was for the first time unwilling to give it active support, the bill was passed by the Commons in 1804. Wilberforce once again had to bear the frustration of seeing it held up in the Lords.

After Pitt's death in 1806, Grenville and Fox, always pro-abolitionist, replaced him in a coalition government, and at last the Lords and the Commons were in agreement. The same year a bill was passed ending the foreign supply of slaves and forbidding their 'importation . . . into the colonies won by British arms in the course of the war.' Finally, in 1807, Lord Grenville introduced to the Lords the first clause of a bill which proposed that 'all manner of dealing and trading in slaves' should be 'utterly abolished, prohibited and declared to be unlawful.' It reached the Commons on 23 February and when it became certain that the motion would be carried, the Solicitor-General rose and paid a moving tribute 'of incomparable elegance and beauty' to Wilberforce, the House 'burst out into deafening applause,' and Wilberforce, overcome with emotion, collapsed in tears.

A medal struck in 1807 commemorates Wilberforce and the ending of the British slave trade.

A FORCE TO COMBAT SLAVERS

Although Britain was not the first to ban the slave trade – Denmark had done so in 1803 – and although the US, Sweden and Holland soon followed suit, Britain's campaign against the slave trade was by far the most widespread. From the beginning, the new British law was enforced by ships of the British navy. Penalties were quickly increased, until in 1824 offenders became liable to the death penalty. Diplomatic pressure was brought to bear on European and New World nations to ban the trade and allow British ships the right to board and detain suspected slavers. Spain, Portugal and France all signed so-called reciprocal search treaties by which these nations could stop each others' ships if they were suspected of carrying slaves.

In fact, there was little that was reciprocal in the work involved. Only the British Navy consistently maintained effective anti-slave trade patrols. From 1808 to about 1870 there were up to 30 warships and over a thousand men employed on anti-slave trading patrols. Their captives were taken to Sierre Leone or to ports in America where special courts were established to judge the cases.

The task proved almost hopeless. It was impossible to have a ship watching every mile of coastline. The patrols could stop no more than one in four of the ships trading in slaves illegally. In 1840, the number of slaves exported from West Africa was as high as ever. A million slaves were successfully landed in America between 1825 and 1865, but only 130,000 slaves were released alive from the 1287 slave ships captured – and the cost was high: the average death rate between 1825 and 1845 for British sailors on the West Africa patrol was about one in ten, three times higher than on any other station of the Royal Navy.

It was only the ending of slavery itself, firstly in the United States in 1863 and then in Brazil in the 1880s, that finally killed the trade.

A slaver detained: the boats of HMS *Linnet* – whose captain painted this picture – board a suspected slaver, the *Mellidon*, off the West African coast in April 1854.

Captive: a schooner, the *Pickle* (*front*) seizes a slaving ship, the *Bolodora*, June, 1829, after a 14-hour chase and a battle lasting an hour and 20 minutes.

As of 1 January 1808, the slave trade was outlawed throughout the British Empire. Any Briton caught slave trading was liable to a £100 fine and any ship involved could be forfeit to the Crown – rather light penalties which were made more imposing in 1811, when slave trading became a felony punishable by transportation or death.

The British were not the first to abolish the slave trade – the Danes had done so four years before and many American states had already imposed a ban on overseas slave trading. But the countries still legitimately engaged in the trade – Spain, Portugal, France and Holland – remained as active as ever.

For various reasons, not all of them philanthropic, the British attempted to achieve an international ban on the trade. They wished to 'protect the British West Indies from the competition of slave-produced Cuban and Brazilian sugar' and partly to facilitate the building up of a 'legitimate' trade in oil and cocoa in Africa. In 1818 the French agreed to abolish the trade, as did Holland. Both Portugal and Spain, however, needed financial inducement – Spain in particular being reluctant to relinquish her right to trade with Cuba, her principal slave market. In 1815, Portugal received £750,000 on the understanding she confined 'her share of the traffic to the transport of slaves from south of the Equator to her own colonies.' When Brazil, after attaining independence in 1826, agreed to end the trade, it also became in effect illegal for the Portuguese. In 1817 Spain was paid £400,000 compensation to abandon the trade 'in the northern Hemisphere.'

Had the laws passed by the different powers been respected, the trade would have been extinguished by the 1820s. As it was, the Portuguese and the Spanish flagrantly violated the terms of their agreements, and until 1830 the French continued to carry slaves to Guadeloupe and Martinique. It has been estimated that 1,898,400 slaves crossed the Atlantic between 1811 and 1870, of which some 60 percent went to Brazil, 32 percent to Cuba and Puerto Rico, 5 percent to the French West Indies, nearly 3 percent to the United States and 'an embarrassing trickle' arrived in the British West Indies.

The task of patrolling the West African coast was undertaken by the British Navy. 'Nothing is so bizarre,' wrote Hugh Thomas, 'as this sudden change in the British maritime position from chief slaver to chief policeman.' But, he continued, their ships were 'too few and too old' – in 1808 the task of policing 3000 miles of African coastline was entrusted to a 32-gun frigate and an 18-gun sloop. By 1820 the same stretch of coastline was not much better off, having acquired only four more ships (while it was considered necessary to send 12 ships to guard Napoleon on St Helena). During the 1840s, the number of ships rose to 25–30, but disease undermined the health of the sailors – 1338 officers and men died off the West African coast between 1808 and 1845.

The French maintained a somewhat smaller force of about 20 ships, but wisely 'restricted themselves to looking for abuse of their own flag.' The United States operated a small squadron alongside the British naval patrol, but this soon disintegrated. America's

A Gathering of Idealists

After the end of the slave trade in 1807, both British and American humanitarians turned to the abolition of slavery itself. In Britain, opponents of slavery organized the Anti-Slavery Society in 1823, with Thomas Fowell Buxton as their leader to replace the aging Wilberforce. In 1833, they succeeded: slaves in British territories were freed.

The same year in the United States, William Lloyd Garrison founded the American Anti-Slavery Society, a faction-ridden group which in 1840 split and spawned an organization with a confusingly similar name, the American and Foreign Anti-Slavery Society.

The British in particular were internationalist in their approach. In 1839, to combat the smuggling of slaves from the West African coast to the Americas, a new organization, the British and Foreign Anti-Slavery Society, was formed. The picture at left was painted the following year after a World Anti-Slavery Convention in London. Thomas Clarkson is shown addressing the meeting, Buxton and some former slaves are shown prominently.

Among the delegates were a number of American anti-slavers – some of them women, much to the chagrin of the British abolitionists. They came from local groups and both national organizations, and included one of Garrison's formidable lieutenants, Lucretia Mott.

1 Thomas Clarkson, President of the Convention.
2 James Birney, Vice-President of the Convention, Delegate of the American and Foreign Anti-Slavery Society.
3 George Bradburn, Massachusetts Anti-Slavery Society.
4 Sir Thomas Fowell Buxton, Committee member of the British and Foreign Anti-Slavery Society.
5 L C Lecesne, one of the black members of the British and Foreign Anti-Slavery Society Committee.
6 Henry Beckford, an emancipated slave from Jamaica.
7 Henry Stanton, from the American and Foreign Anti-Slavery Society.
8 M L'Instant, delegate from Haiti.
9 Wendell Phillips, of the American Anti-Slavery Society.
10 James Mott, of the American Anti-Slavery Society.
11 Lucretia Mott, of the American Anti-Slavery Society.

Buxton, Crusader for Human Rights

The idealism that infused the anti-slavery movement was exemplified by – among others – Thomas Fowell Buxton who took over from Wilberforce as the leader of the anti-slavery campaign in the 1820s. For him the abolition of slavery in the British Empire, passed by Parliament in 1833, was merely a step in a wider battle – the eradication of slavery throughout the world.

His arguments seem to foreshadow those of the international Human Rights movement of the present day. Buxton argued that Christian moral responsibility was not limited by the usual dictates of politics and that Britain, as the world's leading imperial power, was in a unique position to lead a humanitarian crusade to enforce an end to slavery, in particular in Africa.

The following extract is taken from the conclusion to his persuasive and well-documented work, *The African Slave Trade and its Remedy:*

‘I am not so sanguine as to suppose that we can at once, by a single effort, solve the problem which lies before us. The deliverance of Africa will put our patience and perseverance to no ordinary trial. We must deliberately make up our minds to large and long-continued expense, to persevering labors, and to serve disappointments. I wish not in any degree to conceal from myself, or from others, these truths.

But the question is, – Shall such an experiment be made? There are two mighty arguments which should prompt us to such an undertaking: the intense miseries of Africa, and the peculiar blessings which have been showered upon this country by the mercy of Divine Providence. With regard to the first, I need not again plunge into the sickening details of the horrors which accompany this bloody trade, and of the sanguinary rites, which there bear the name of religion. Whether we look to the vast space which is there made a theatre of public misery, or calculate how many deeds of cruelty and carnage must be perpetrated every day in the year, in order to make up the surprising total of human distress, which, by indisputable documents, we know to be realized, there is enough to awaken the deepest pity and to arouse the most energetic resolution.

Turning to the second consideration, we cannot fail to see how signally this nation has been preserved, and led forward to an extent of power and prosperity, beyond what almost any other nation has been permitted to reach....

I believe that Great Britain can, if she will, under the favor of the Almighty, confer a blessing on the human race. It may be that at her bidding a thousand nations now steeped in wretchedness, in brutal ignorance, in devouring superstition, possessing but the one trade, and that one the foulest evil that ever blighted public prosperity, or poisoned domestic peace, shall, under British tuition, emerge from their debasement, enjoy a long line of blessings – education, agriculture, commerce, peace, industry, and the wealth that springs from it; and, far above all, shall willingly receive that religion which, while it confers innumerable temporal blessings, opens the way to an eternal futurity of happiness.’

attitude to slave-trading was ambivalent – the need for more and more slaves to till the cotton plantations in the South, and the attractions of trade with Cuba, tempted many American officials to turn a blind eye to the new, fast, slave-clippers (described by one captain as being, 'of racehorse beauty . . . with their arrowy hulls and raking masts'), which put out from Baltimore and New York to serve Cuba and the South. The United States government vigorously opposed persistent pressure from the British for the right to search their ships, with the result that illicit traders from other countries had only to hoist the 'Stars and Stripes' to obtain immunity from inquisitive British naval patrols.

The abolition of the slave trade was a remarkable success for English humanitarianism. But success was a long time coming, and a number of historians have found reason to be criticial of the British for their ambivalent attitude toward something now regarded as a self-evident evil. The British were, in the words of one modern historian, 'regarded by other countries as hypocritical for insisting on abolition after earlier enriching themselves from the trade, for taking no stand against slave-grown sugar or cotton . . . for allowing English manufactured goods still to find their way to Africa to pay for slaves, and for attempting to establish complete command of the sea by trying to negotiate "right to visit" to foreign ships.' And Eric Williams, in *Capitalism and Slavery*, castigates the abolitionists, finding their campaign for emancipation selective, complaining that they were 'boycotting the slave-grown produce of the British West Indies, dyed with the Negro's blood,' while the 'very existence of British capitalism depended upon the slave-grown cotton of the United States.' He finds it reprehensible that it was not until 1823 they made emancipation their 'avowed aim,' berrates them for their 'East Indian Interests' (the Thornton family held East India Stock, and Zachary Macaulay apparently had shares in the East India Company), and finds them blind to the fate of slaves in other parts of the world, notably the plight of those in Brazil and Cuba.

Roger Anstey counters by arguing that Dr Williams fails to show the 'relationship between economic forces and detailed political decisions on abolition.' Anstey also says Williams underestimates the moral force behind abolitionism. The Evangelical view of the 'total depravity of man' and his salvation through conversion was an all-consuming one, penetrating every area of human behavior. 'God Almighty has set before me two great objects,' Wilberforce wrote in his diary in 1787, 'the suppression of the slave trade and the reformation of manners,' – a moral fervor which permeated much of British political life.

Again, it can hardly be seen as a fault in the abolitionists that they limited their aims. They did what they could to condemn slave trading everywhere, but were naturally concerned to concentrate their efforts in those areas where they could hope to exert most influence – on British imperial territories. It is true that their prime intention was to end the trade, rather than slavery itself; but it was generally and sincerely felt that abolition of the trade would, in Wilberforce's words, 'end the worst of slavery' and that amelioration of the slaves' conditions would turn them into 'black equivalents of sturdy yeomen and free peasantry.' His views were based on the assumption that the planters could be educated to treat their slaves properly, and that they would come to see it as a moral duty to do so.

When it became patently obvious that they were prepared to do no such thing, the abolitionists concentrated all their efforts on bringing about emancipation through parliament. The Anti-Slavery Society was founded in 1823, Sir James Stephen went to the West Indies to collect information for a report to use as ammunition against the government, and, Wilberforce being over 60 and in bad health, Thomas Fowell Buxton, a fellow Evangelical, assumed the leadership of the anti-slavery campaign.

As a result, the British government adopted a new policy of reform towards the West Indies. Measures were taken to improve the slaves' lot, such as abolition of the whip, of the Negro Sunday Market, forbidding the flogging of women, giving slaves another day off for religious instruction, the freeing of female children born after 1823, the admission of evidence of slaves in courts, introducing savings banks for slaves and a nine-hour day.

The planters, outraged, protested against such infringements of their 'property rights.' And the slaves themselves, excited by the prospect of sudden change, and overhearing their masters' talk on the subject, became

Let freedom reign: in an abolitionist drawing, West Indians greet Emancipation by gleefully burying the symbols of slavery.

The cost of freedom: while slaves dance around Buxton, England in the form of John Bull (*far right*) is asked to pay the bill – the £20-million compensation to the former slave owners of the West Indies.

restless. Many felt that emancipation was theirs, but was being physically withheld from them by their owners.

Uprisings occurred – in British Guiana in 1808, in Barbados in 1816 and most dramatically in Demerara in 1823. There, some 13,000 slaves locked up their white owners and killed two overseers. Peace was restored partly by military action, which left over a hundred blacks dead, and partly through the moderating counsel of an English missionary, John Smith, who was trusted by the slaves. The Demerarans proclaimed martial law, hanged 47 slaves and sentenced three others to 1000 lashes each. Many others were flogged and imprisoned. Smith himself, in a disastrous error of judgment, was arrested, accused of complicity and sentenced to death. The sentence was accompanied by a recommendation for mercy that was forwarded to London, but before London could act, Smith, a consumptive, died in prison, thus becoming the first abolitionist martyr. His death did more for the abolitionist cause than any petition.

For the next ten years, the abolitionists kept up their campaign. The tide of public opinion was clearly running against slavery, but Parliament proved unwilling to seek the final confrontation with the colonial assemblies and the West Indian lobby at home (although in 1828 'free people of color in the colonies were placed on a footing of legal equality with their fellow citizens').

In 1832, two unrelated events occurred that between them brought a rapid end to slavery in the Empire.

In Jamaica, planters, terrified of their own slaves, of the possibility of abolition and of the hordes of Maroon guerrillas, theatened to secede and join the United States. Fifty thousand slaves rose in rebellion; some 400 blacks died, and another 100 were executed after the rebellion was suppressed.

At home, the Reform Bill extended the vote to all but the poorest men. The newly enfranchised masses elected MPs who owed nothing to the colonies and to entrenched slaving interests. On 26 July 1833 the Bill for the Abolition of Slavery passed its second reading in the Commons and on 29 August it became law. Twenty million pounds was to be paid to the planters in compensation for their loss (about half the market value of their slaves) and the slaves were to become apprentices for seven years, working for their masters for at least three-quarters of the day. All children under six were to be freed at once and 'provision made for their religious and moral instruction.'

When Wilberforce heard the news that the Bill was certain to succeed, he said 'Thank God that I should have lived to witness a day in which England is willing to give twenty millions sterling for the Abolition of Slavery.' On 29 July, just three days after the second reading of the measure to which he had dedicated his life, he died.

CHAPTER VI

THE STATES DIVIDED

THE AMERICAN ABOLITION MOVEMENT
LATE 18th CENTURY-1863

A Union soldier reads the Emancipation Proclamation to a slave household, 1863.

Just before his death, Wilberforce was visited by another reformer who was denounced as a hypocrite for 'his assumption that slavery was the great evil' – the American, William Lloyd Garrison, founder of the anti-slavery magazine *Liberator*, the first number of which appeared in Boston, 'on borrowed paper, with borrowed type,' in January 1831. On the first page Garrison had written: 'I shall strenuously contend for the immediate enfranchisement of our slave population . . . . On this subject I do not wish to think, or speak, or write, with moderation . . . . I am in earnest – I will not equivocate – I will not excuse – I will not retreat a single inch – AND I WILL BE HEARD.' It was a statement of Old Testament ferocity, written by one who was partisan to the point of fanaticism and to whom peaceful attainment of his ends was unthinkable.

Such radical idealism was a more extreme expression of the anti-slavery sentiment which had arisen over the previous four decades in the United States. Apart from the strong anti-slavery tradition among the Quakers, many local abolition societies had been formed since 1794, in both the North and the South. They petitioned State legislatures and Congress, encouraged schools for blacks, published anti-slavery essays, aided free slaves who found themselves in jeopardy from slaveholders under the Fugitive Slave Act of 1793 and protested the slave trade.

Free blacks posed special problems. Neither in the North nor in the South, was the free black regarded with anything but suspicion. 'Free negroes,' as one historian put it, 'were felt to be a nuisance and a menace throughout the United States.' Abolitionists saw the need to provide for the rehabilitation of free blacks and also offer compensation to those slave-holders prepared to manumit their slaves. To these ends, the American Society for Colonizing the Free People of Color of the United States was set up in December, 1816, under the chairmanship of Judge Bushrod Washington (who had not, like his famous uncle, manumitted all his slaves).

The first aim of the society, which consisted mainly of slaveholders from Virginia, Kentucky and Maryland, was to raise enough money to obtain 'a territory on the coast of Africa or at some other place not within any of the states or territorial governments of the United States.' After ten years of private fund-raising, the society had acquired part of Liberia. It then sought Congressional help towards resettling blacks there.

The attitude of free blacks towards these plans for their future was guarded. One man said, 'The Colonizationists want us to go to Liberia if we will; if we won't go there, we may go to hell.' Organizations were formed by blacks to counter such high-handed mea-

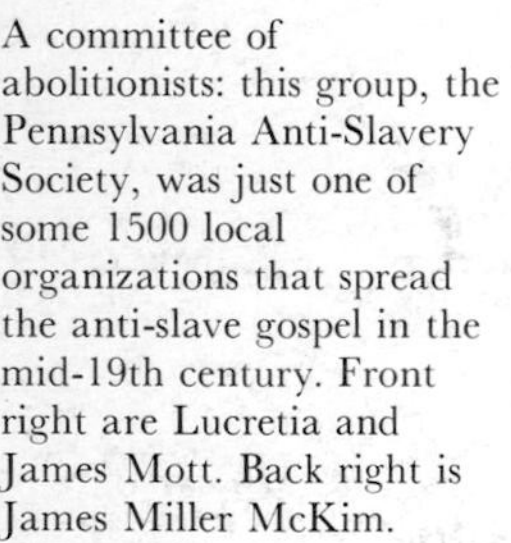

A committee of abolitionists: this group, the Pennsylvania Anti-Slavery Society, was just one of some 1500 local organizations that spread the anti-slave gospel in the mid-19th century. Front right are Lucretia and James Mott. Back right is James Miller McKim.

To slaveholders, William Lloyd Garrison was the 'red under the bed.' He was the most extreme, the most intransigent of the abolitionists. He pursued his ideals with an Old Testament fervor that alienated not only the South but a good deal of the North as well.

Garrison became an abolitionist at the age of 22, after listening to a speech by Benjamin Lundy, a philanthropist who had founded an anti-slavery paper, *The Genius of Universal Emancipation*. Garrison at first favored gradual emancipation and the colonization of freed slaves in Africa. But by the age of 24 he was demanding immediate emancipation. When Garrison joined Lundy in publishing *The Genius*, he rapidly alienated its diminutive readership with his intolerant assaults on slavery.

In 1831, without capital and without a subscriber, he and a partner, Isaac Knapp, began publishing *The Liberator*, avowing their 'determination to print it as long as they could subsist on bread and water.' Garrison's extremism had little practical effect: he did not aid slaves to escape, he did not establish schools, he did not face mobs, he did not write solid treatises, he provided little financial aid to blacks. But he was indisputably a great publicist. In the South, his name was anathema. Georgia offered $5000 reward for his arrest and conviction.

It could be, however, that any positive effect he had was negated by his outspokenness. Although he must take credit for founding the American Anti-Slavery Society in 1833, he was also the cause of its division. He supported the involvement of women in the cause and attacked the churches for not speaking out about slavery. These differences led to the organization of a new, national anti-slavery society in 1840 – The American and Foreign Anti-Slavery Society – and the formation of the Liberty Party in politics. In 1840 many American abolitionists were invited to be present at the World Anti-Slavery Convention in London (see p 149). Garrison too was invited, but refused to attend because America's women abolitionists were at first excluded.

Garrison's fanaticism never waivered. Concluding that the Constitution's pro-slavery clauses were immoral, he denounced it as a 'covenant with death and an agreement with hell,' and advocated a dissolution of the Union. After the Civil War came, he declared that his career as an abolitionist was ended.

William Lloyd Garrison, firebrand, idealist and fighter for black liberation.

LIBERTY, EQUALITY, FRATERNITY,
DEDICATED TO THE SMARTEST NATION IN ALL CREATION.

Hypocrisy in the land of liberty: an English cartoon of 1848 points out the contrast between American democratic ideals and the realities as revealed by the slave system.

sures, to raise money for schools and for speakers to plead their cause. As one American historian wrote, they felt 'they were Americans . . . and their destiny was on this continent, rather than in Africa.'

By 1850, according to one estimate, there were 434,495 free blacks in the United States (compared to 3,204,313 slaves), many of these having 'worked out their own freedom' or been redeemed by the savings of friends and relatives, who had bought them from agreeable slaveholders. Some rose to prominence – the clockmaker, Benjamin Banneker from Maryland became an astronomer, Richard Allen of Philadelphia founded the African Methodist Episcopal Church, James Forten of Philadelphia, 'a wealthy Revolutionary veteran' became active in the anti-slavery movement, as did another rich businessman, Robert Purvis. Some former slaves even had slaves of their own. The vast majority, however, particularly in the South, lived, in squalor; even in Philadelphia, according to a survey by the Quakers of the city's 10,000 blacks, 'they lived in dire need as late as 1838.'

The Colonization Society alienated many anti-slavery societies by its aggressively anti-black bias – William Lloyd Garrison attacked it vigorously in an 1832 pamphlet *Thoughts on African Colonization*, in which he not only showed how little most abolitionists identified with its aims, but also demonstrated how palpably opposed to it most free blacks were. Colonization as such, however, was not ruled out by abolitionists. Benjamin Lundy, the New Jersey Quaker reformer, believed in emancipation and resettlement and, having arranged, in 1825, for some freed South Carolinian blacks to go to Haiti, visited Canada, Texas, Louisiana and Mexico with the object of negotiating land purchases for other such settlements.

There were three main strands in the American abolition movement, which finally came together with the founding of the American Anti-Slavery Society in 1833: a New England faction headed by William Lloyd Garrison and his financial supporter, the New York merchant Arthur Tappan (who had also worked with Benjamin Lundy); in Philadelphia, Isaac T Hopper, a member of the schismatic Quaker sect of Hicksites, was reorganizing the Quaker movement with the active cooperation of black abolitionist leaders, such as James Forten, and assisted by three influential abolitionist women, Lucretia Mott, Abby Kimber and Sarah Pugh; and – after 1830 – in the newly-developed areas, which spread across the mid-West from upstate New York to Illinois. The small bands of fiercely puritanical and revivalist settlers were strongly antipathetic to slavery as an institution (although these 'burned-over districts' were ultimately wary of emancipation and resisted the South during the Civil War more, as Professor Rice put it, to keep the black 'out of the North as a labor competitor . . . than on the grounds of religious or other pity').

The American anti-slavery society could, by 1838, claim over a thousand offshoots, whose members numbered approximately 200,000. All abolitionists, however, faced constant opposition, even north of the Mason and Dixon Line, the Pennsylvania-Maryland border that traditionally divided slave States and free States. Wendell Phillips was 'blackballed from his club,' and a Miss Crondall,

In defense of slavery: a pair of pro-slavery cartoons compare the supposedly happy condition of slaves in the United States with the misery of the badly paid and exploited working classes in England.

The Missouri Compromise

The question of slavery versus freedom was a dominant issue from the time of the Revolution onward. But for a century, the issue was successfully shelved by two great compromises, in 1820 and 1850.

In 1789 North and South, free states and slave states, were approximately equal in numbers. Thereafter, an even balance was maintained in the Senate by the admission of free and slave states alternately. But as settlers pushed west in the early years of the 19th century into the lands of the lower Missouri and the west bank of the Mississippi, the situation changed. Missouri lay almost completely to the north of the dividing line between freedom and slavery. In 1820, by the Missouri Compromise, Missouri was admitted as a slaveholding state, but slavery was prohibited north of lat 36°30′ and Maine, now detached from Massachusetts, was admitted as a free state. The plan was largely that of Henry Clay who thereafter became known as the 'Great Compromiser.'

In the 1840s as a result of acquisitions in the Mexican War, the whole issue re-emerged. Clay, now in his seventies, returned to meet the threat of disunion. The admission of California as an anti-slave state would upset the balance between North and South. Clay suggested a number of compromise bills, among them the admission of California, the creation of New Mexico and Utah without provision for slavery, a strengthened fugitive slave law to reassure the South. The debate on Clay's compromise proposals was one of the great political events of the 19th century. His suggestions were largely accepted. Once more the Union was preserved by compromise, but for the last time.

A precarious balance: the free states (white), slave states (black) and unsettled territories (shaded) after the Compromise of 1850.

Clay addresses the Senate in the debate on the 1850 Compromise.

Mob violence: a mob burns the warehouse of the abolitionist Elijah Lovejoy in Alton, Illinois, on the night of 7 November 1837. Lovejoy was killed as he emerged from the burning house. Northern sentiment was outraged and abolitionism strengthened.

who attempted to introduce a 'pious colored female' into a boarding school for girls in Connecticut in 1832, found herself the victim of a campaign of vilification and hatred, which ended in State legislation banning 'any such school.' Garrison himself was threatened by a mob in Boston and had to seek sanctuary in the local jail. He wrote that he 'found contempt more bitter, opposition more stubborn, and apathy more frozen' in New England than 'among the slave-owners themselves.' The movement also acquired a martyr in the fanatically anti-Catholic form of Elijah P Lovejoy, a newspaper proprietor, who died in Alton, Illinois in November 1837, defending with arms his right to print his controversial anti-slavery views.

Many reformers were, however, becoming increasingly mistrustful of Garrison, whose enthusiasm for 'non-resistance,' an extreme form of pacifism 'which challenged the whole institutional basis of society by disavowing any authority based on the ultimate sanction of force, direct or indirect,' together with his open criticism of the Sabbath and the subjection of women alarmed his most faithful supporters – even Arthur Tappan complained that he wished Garrison had 'more argument and less invective.' The more conservative abolitionists, afraid of jeopardizing their cause as a result of the extremities of their fanatical colleagues, divided against them, and after 1840 the national anti-slavery society disintegrated. As one writer said, 'abolitionist propagandizing fell back into the hands of local societies, who spent as much time arguing against one another as against the South.'

Abolition moved deeper into politics – the Liberty Party (backed by the open-handed Arthur Tappan and his brother Lewis), ran James G Birney, an ex-slaveholder, for the Presidency in 1840. Ex-President John Quincy Adams, although not himself an abolitionist, successfully resisted the 'gag-rule' imposed by Southern Congressmen in 1836 to prevent the reading of the flood of anti-slavery petitions which poured into the House; and after eight years of struggle to obtain support from the Northern States the rule was finally removed.

Ever since the Missouri Compromise in 1820, slavery had been the dominant political issue of the new republic. Both Northern and Southern States were determined to preserve the even balance between pro- and anti-slave States achieved in 1819, when with the admission of Alabama, there were exactly eleven of each. In 1820 the Northern free States had 105 Congressmen representing a population of 5,152,000 and the Southern slave states 81 Congressmen representing 4,485,000 people. Missouri, although technically north of the Ohio and the Mason and Dixon line, was admitted to the Union as a slave state only on condition that slavery would be prohibited in federal territory north of latitude 36° 30′ and that Maine should be admitted as a free state. The power of Congressmen to 'place qualifications upon the admission of new states' was also hotly contested – it being feared by some that the older Eastern states might use it to keep new Western states in subordination.

The problems posed, particularly by the vast territories in the Far West, were immense. Texas, after severing itself from Mexico in 1836 and legalizing slavery, caused a flutter in both North and South by insisting on either annexation, which would give pro-slavers an advantage – or on recognition as a republic. With an eye to the latter, Texas

A peace pledge circulated by abolitionists.

ANTI-SLAVERY PEACE PLEDGE.

WE, the undersigned,

hereby solemnly pledge ourselves not to countenance or aid the United States Government in any war which may be occasioned by the annexation of Texas, or in any other war, foreign or domestic, designed to strengthen or perpetuate slavery.

Name.	Residence.

The 'Underground Railroad'

The underground railroad – a term describing the system by which Northerners helped escaped slaves – was neither underground nor a railroad, but was so called because its activities were conducted in secrecy and because railway terms were used in reference to the conduct of the system. A 'station' for instance was, in modern urban guerrilla terms, a safe house. The system reached northward, in a fork, across Ohio and Indiana and, in the east, to New York and New England. In the North countless philanthropists and escaped slaves raised money and goods to help fugitives of whom some 40,000 moved through Ohio between 1830 and 1860. The most famous of the black guides was Harriet Tubman, called the 'Moses of her people.' She made 19 journeys south and led 300 slaves to freedom. Slaveholders offered a total of $40,000 for her dead or alive.

Escaping slaves fight off whites in Pennsylvania, 1851.

The formidable Harriet Tubman.

Slaves flee northward.

flirted with France and England, both of whom looked covetously at such a welcome foothold in their now lost sphere of influence across the Atlantic. England even went so far as to guarantee a Texan loan 'if the Lone Star Republic would abolish slavery,' but, horrified at the 'prospect of Texas becoming a refuge for fugitive slaves,' Southern statesmen protested furiously and Britain hastily withdrew, denying all such intentions. And at the end of the Mexican War in 1848, bringing as it did formal cession by Mexico to the United States of Texas (with the Rio Grande boundary), New Mexico (including Arizona) and Upper California, it remained, as one historian put it, 'to be seen whether these immense and valuable acquisitions would be added to "Freedom's aerie," or provide "bigger pens to cram with slaves."'

The Southern States, with their visions of a 'great slaveholding republic stretching from the Potomac to the Rio Grande,' were heartened by the reinforcement of the Fugitive Slave Law in 1850, expressly designed to force the North to recognize Southern claims on their slave property. Northerners in response took up an increasingly aggressive stance. The public imagination had been captured by the activities of 'officials,' both black and white, of the 'Underground Railroad' and the deeds of such legendary heroes as the ex-slave Harriet Tubman, who after having escaped herself returned to the South several times and helped more than 300 slaves to reach freedom; the black John Parker, who bought his freedom for $2000 and then joined white abolitionists on the railroad; and Josiah Henderson, a slave who escaped to Canada, taught himself to read and write and then went back to the South to help others to freedom. The abolitionist Frederick Douglass's *Narrative*, an account of his escape from slavery in Maryland, became common reading, and 1851 saw the publication of Harriet Beecher Stowe's *Uncle Tom's Cabin*, said to have been influenced by another black leader, Josiah Henson (who later claimed to be the original 'Uncle Tom').

Orator extraordinary: Frederick Douglass escaped from slavery to become one of the most brilliant campaigners for abolition.

Southerners sprang fiercely to the defense of slavery. Fourteen novels countering the unpleasant picture of Southern slavery painted by Mrs Stowe were written within three years, and other writers fell over themselves to point to the many iniquities of the North, wagging their fingers at 'New England wage-slaves' and the 'hardships of factory labor.'

A PHILANTHROPIC BEST SELLER

Harriet Beecher Stowe.

Uncle Tom's Cabin, the emotive story of a slave by a 'salt-codfish, white-steeple' New Englander, who never lived among slaves, must rank as one of the most successful pieces of propaganda ever written. It was later seen as a major cause of the Civil War. President Lincoln once reportedly addressed the author, Harriet Beecher Stowe, with the words: 'So you're the little woman who made this great war!'

Harriet Beecher was the daughter of a Litchfield, Connecticut, clergyman. In her twenties she moved to Cincinatti, Ohio, where her father was President of the Lane Seminary, a newly founded theological college to promote anti-slavery and black education. There Harriet saw a number of escaping slaves: the 'Underground Railroad ran through Cincinnati. But her only direct experience of slavery was a three-day journey into Kentucky.

In 1850 her husband, Calvin Stowe, moved to Brunswick, Maine, where Harriet wrote *Uncle Tom's Cabin or Life Among the Lowly* for serial publication in the *National Era*, an anti-slavery paper established by the American and Foreign Anti-Slavery Society in Washington, D.C.

When the series appeared as a book in 1852, the easy-to-read, emotional account of slavery from a slave's point of view achieved startling success. Three newspapers in Paris published it simultaneously; 18 publishing houses in London published 40 editions of it; the book was translated into 37 languages, and three times into Welsh.

Immediately after publication, the book was adapted for the stage. The success of the adaptation was equally startling. It was on the stage in numerous versions continuously from 1852 to 1931. Although the stage shows were even more sentimental and melodramatic than the original, they were the only major public entertainment that countered the increasingly popular stereotype of the happy-go-lucky black minstrel.

Understandably, the book now seems less impressive than it did a century ago. At one time Mrs Stowe said *Uncle Tom* was 'living, dramatic, reality' – a view she earnestly propagated with a documentary volume entitled *A Key to Uncle Tom* in which she made much of her minute personal experience of slavery. In fact, the book is, in the words of one critic, of 'a Sunday-school superficiality.' The characters now seem clichéd – a godly, servile slave (whose name has now become an epithet for servility), a sugary-sweet, TB-suffering little girl, an inhumanly brutal owner. The judgments are often vapid: Mrs Stowe writes glibly of 'the African race' as if

A poster for a later, spectacular production of the stage adaptation.

the continent was one small nation. And to modern critics many scenes are of saccharine sentimentality.

Yet it was probably precisely because of her simplicity of approach and the emotional quality of her writing that the book was so popular. She dramatized the woes of slavery without dramatizing the social and political complexities of the institution. She pricked the conscience of the North at a time when it was ready for the pricking. She did not start the war, but she was in no small measure responsible for the optimism with which the North went to war in 1861.

A scene from the first stage adaptation, 1852.

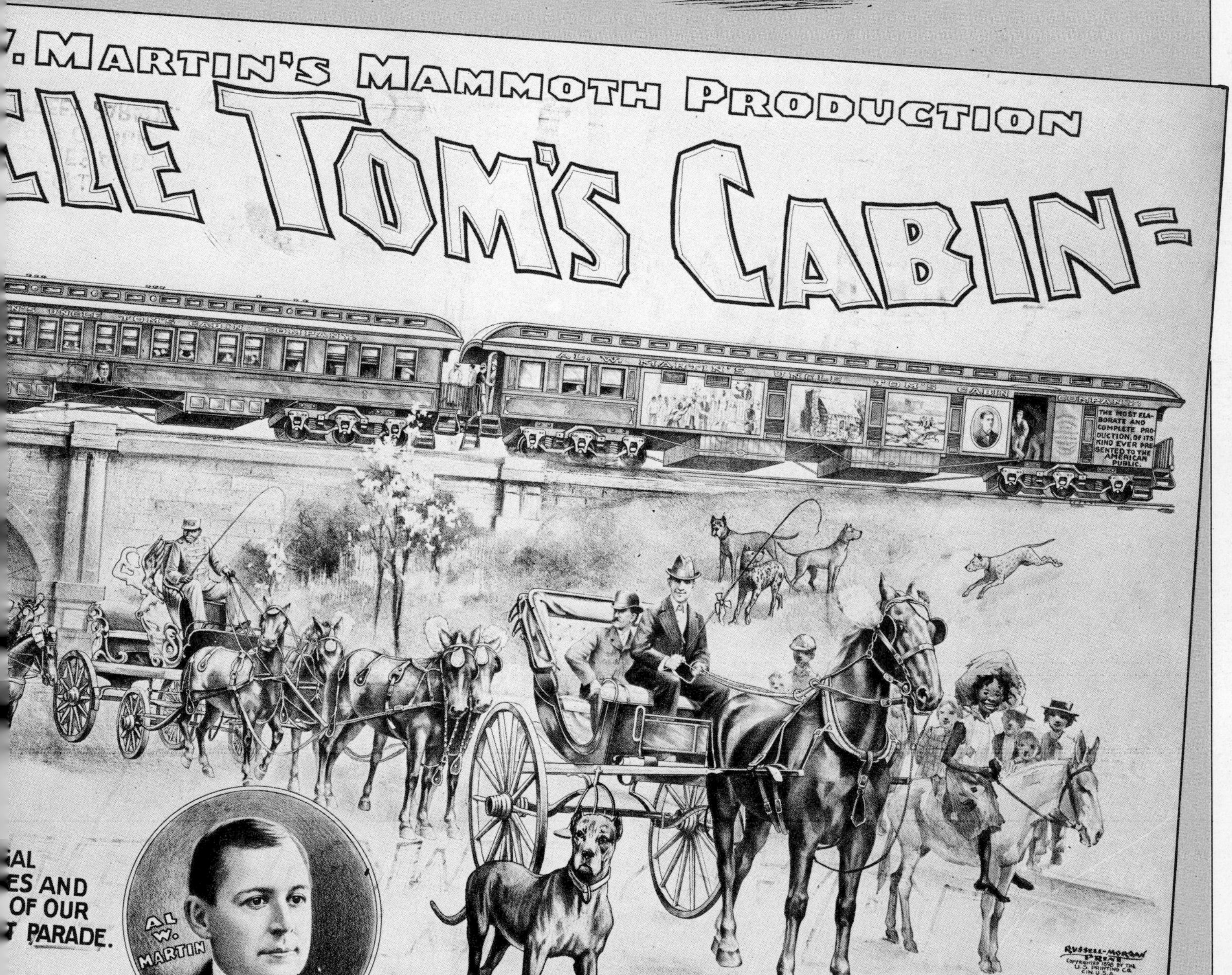

One of the most influential of these propagandists was George Fitzhugh, a lawyer and journalist from Virginia, whose two volumes *Sociology for the South* and *Cannibals All, or Slaves without Masters*, published in 1854 and 1857 created a stir in the South because of the unorthodoxy of many of his opinions. Ardently pro-slavery, he compared the oppressed conditions of the British working class with the sheltered life of plantation slaves. He stressed repeatedly that to remain stable, society needed to be under the domination of a 'master class.' He wanted the South to develop her own industries, protected by a Southern tariff. All this was radical enough, but his most extreme argument – embarrassing even to the most fiercely pro-slavery element in Southern society – was his rejection of the Constitution and the Declaration of Independence on the grounds that he did not 'agree with the authors . . . that governments "derive their just powers from the consent of the governed."'

If George Fitzhugh was an embarrassment to some Southerners, John Brown, whose abolitionism verged on monomania, was equally embarrassing to some Northern abolitionists.

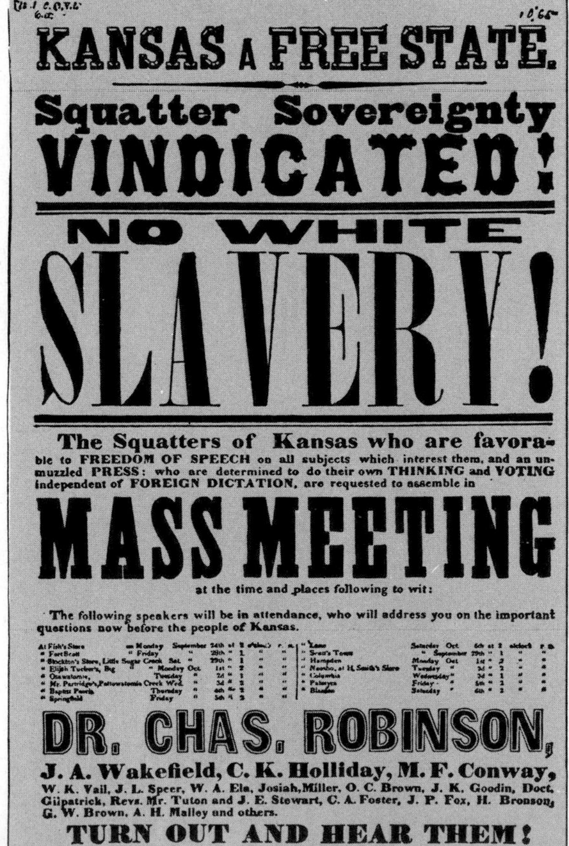

'Bleeding Kansas': an 1855 poster reveals the passion of the pro- and anti-slavery debate that preceeded Kansas' acceptance into the Union as a free state in 1861.

The Ordeal of Henry 'Box' Brown

The decision to attempt to escape to the North was a more conclusive demonstration of resistance than seeking a local hideaway. For the slave, the final outrage was often based on his conviction that the master had broken some unspoken rule of fair dealing. Such was the case of Henry 'Box' Brown, whose master had been unwilling to purchase Brown's wife. Brown's escape was among the most dramatic of all the fugitive experiences. James Miller McKim, a distinguished Unitarian minister and abolitionist (see p 156), declared that he might have been doubtful of this story had he not been present when 'Box' Brown arrived in Philadelphia.

'One day, while I was at work, and my thoughts were eagerly feasting upon the idea of freedom, the idea suddenly flashed across my mind of shutting myself *up in a box*, and getting myself conveyed as dry goods to a free state.

Being now satisfied that this was the plan for me, I went to my friend Dr Smith and having acquainted him with it, we agreed to have it put at once into execution. . . .

My next object was to procure a box, and with the assistance of a carpenter that was very soon accomplished, and taken to the place where the packing was to be performed. In the meantime, the store keeper had written to a friend in Philadelphia. . . . It was deemed necessary that I should get permission to be absent from my work for a few days. . . . I went off directly to the storekeeper who had by this time received an answer from his friend in Philadelphia, and had obtained permission to address the box to him. . . . The box which I had procured was three feet one inch long, two feet six inches high, and two feet wide: and on the morning of the 29th day of March, 1849, I went into the box – having previously bored three gimlet holes opposite my face, for air and provided myself with a bladder of water. . . . Being thus equiped for the battle of liberty, my friends nailed down the lid and had me conveyed to the Express Office. . . .

The next place we arrived at was Potomac Creek, where the baggage had to be removed from the cars, to be put on board the steamer; where I was placed with my head down, and in this dreadful position had to remain nearly an hour and a half. . . . I felt my eyes swelling as if they would burst from their sockets; and the veins on my temples were dreadfully distended with pressure of blood upon my head.... I could hear a man saying to another, that he had traveled a long way and had been standing there two hours, and he would like to get somewhat to sit down; so perceiving my box, standing on end, he threw it down and then the two sat upon it. I was thus relieved from a state of agony which may be more easily imagined than described. I heard one of them asking the other what he supposed *the box contained*; his companion replied he guessed it was "THE MAIL." I too thought it was a mail, but not such a mail as he supposed.

The next place at which we arrived was the city of Washington, where I was taken from the steam-boat, and again placed upon a waggon and carried to the depot right side up with care; but when the driver arrived at the depot I heard him call for some person to help to take the box off the waggon, and some one answered him to the effect that he might throw it off; but, says the driver, it is marked 'this side up with care;' so if I throw it off I might break something. The other answered him that it did not matter if he broke all that was in it, the railway company were able enough to pay for it. No sooner were these words spoken that I began to tumble from the waggon, and falling on the end where my head was, I could hear my neck give a crack, as if it had been snapped asunder and I was knocked completely insensible.... I was then tumbled into the car with my head downward again, but the car had not proceeded far before, more luggage having to be taken in, my box got shifted about and so happened to turn up its right side; and in this position I remained till I got to Philadelphia....

I was then placed on a waggon and conveyed to the house where my friend in Richmond had arranged I should be received. A number of persons soon collected round the box after it was taken in to the house, but as I did not know what was going on I kept myself quiet. I heard a man say 'let us rap on the box and see if he is alive,' and immediately a rap ensued and a voice said, tremblingly, 'Is all right within?' to which I replied – 'all right.' The joy of the friends was very great; when they heard that I was alive they soon managed to break open the box, and then came my resurrection from the grave of slavery. ❜

The release of Henry Brown: second from left is Frederick Douglass. At the right is McKim.

The first *débâcle* associated with him occurred in the newly created territory of Kansas-Nebraska. Controversy arose over the question of whether the settlers should be allowed to decide for themselves if they would have slavery in their territory or not. Nebraska was rapidly won by anti-slavers. But to the south, in Kansas, pro- and anti-slavery passions led to violence. Cities were fortified, men were murdered, the town of Lawrence was sacked by pro-slavers. In May 1854, Brown, convinced he had a divine mission to take vengeance, led four of his sons and three other men to the cabins of suspected pro-slavers along Pottawatomie Creek, dragged out five men and hacked them to death. This was an inexplicably cold-blooded act that not even his followers could justify.

For a 'revolutionary' he had surprisingly few followers. He next dreamed of making war on slavery from an abolitionist republic in the Appalachian mountains, but he attracted only 11 white and 35 black associates. In his final coup, when he seized the federal arsenal at Harpers Ferry, West Virginia on the night of 16 October 1859, his 'army' consisted of 13 whites and only five blacks. He did, however, manage to take some 'leading townspeople' prisoner and defended his position against the state militia and a company of Marines commanded by Colonel Robert E Lee. On 2 December 1859, John Brown died on the scaffold, unrepentant and content 'to die for God's eternal truth.' His attempts to provoke an uprising had caused many Southerners to 'shudder and think of Haiti' and further convinced them that the North was in the grip of fanatical revolutionaries who were prepared to stoop to the ultimate horror of inciting a servile rebellion in order to attain the total destruction of the Southern way of life.

Northerners, meanwhile were still smarting under the Supreme Court's decision over a slave, Dred Scott, who had sued for freedom on the grounds that he had been twice resident on free soil (his owner had twice taken him from Missouri, a slave state to free

'The Disunited States, a black business': an English cartoon of 1856 foresees the coming strife over slavery.

Illinois). Scott received an unfavorable judgment on a number of counts: that a black could not be a citizen of the United States, that being resident in Missouri the laws of Illinois had no bearing on his status, that the Missouri Compromise of 1820 was unconstitutional and that Scott had 'not been emancipated because Congress had no right

Dred Scott: A Blow for Slavery

The Dred Scott case of 1856 was the most famous of all slavery cases; and the judgment that resulted clearly indicated that North and South could not be reconciled.

Dred Scott was an illiterate slave who had been bought in 1833 by a US Army surgeon, John Emerson, then stationed in Missouri. Emerson later took Scott to Illinois, then to the unorganized territory north of lat 36°30′, where slavery had been forbidden by the Missouri Compromise, and finally back to Missouri, where, with the help of anti-slavery lawyers, Scott sued for freedom on the grounds of having twice been a resident on free soil. The lower court and the Missouri Supreme Court ruled against him; and the case went to the US Supreme Court.

Chief Justice Roger Taney – who had so far avoided pronouncing on slavery – and the four Southerners among the associate Supreme Court Justices now hoped to settle the legal question of slavery once and for all.

The case proved horribly contentious. The nine justices filed nine separate opinions which covered 200 pages. Chief Justice Roger Taney, speaking for the court in a final judgment, declared against Scott's claim for freedom on three grounds: (1) as a black he could not be a citizen of the United States, and therefore had no right to sue in a Federal court; (2) as a resident of Missouri the laws of Illinois had no effect on his status; (3) as a resident north of lat 36°30′ he had not been emancipated because Congress had no right to deprive citizens of their property.

The Chief Justice's opinion was disputable and disputed. Blacks had always been considered citizens in most of the Northern states, and Missouri had in seven earlier cases recognized the claim to freedom of a slave who had resided in free territory. But beyond this was a wider issue. Taney also declared that the Missouri Compromise, was unconstitutional and that Congress did not have the power to forbid slavery in the territories. The decision caused a ferment of controversy. Once again, the issue of slavery made war seem inevitable.

Roger Taney.

Dred Scott.

THE EMANCIPATION PROCLAMATION.

WHEREAS, On the twenty-second day of September, in the year of our Lord one thousand eight hundred and sixty-two, a proclamation was issued by the President of the United States, containing, among other things, the following, to wit:

"That on the first day of January, in the year of our Lord one thousand eight hundred and sixty-three, all persons held as slaves within any State, or designated part of a State, the people whereof shall then be in rebellion against the United States, shall be then, thenceforward and forever, free, and the Executive Government of the United States, including the military and naval authority thereof, will recognize and maintain the freedom of such persons, and will do no act or acts to repress such persons, or any of them, in any effort they may make for their active freedom. That the Executive will, on the first day of January aforesaid, by proclamation, designate the States and parts of States, if any, in which the people therein, respectively, shall then be in rebellion against the United States, and the fact that any State, and the people thereof, shall, on that day, be, in good faith, represented in the Congress of the United States, by members chosen thereto at elections, wherein a majority of the qualified voters of such State shall have participated, shall, in the absence of strong countervailing testimony, be deemed conclusive evidence that such State and the people thereof are not then in rebellion against the United States."

Now, therefore, I, ABRAHAM LINCOLN, President of the United States, by virtue of the power in me vested as Commander-in-Chief of the Army and Navy of the United States in time of actual armed rebellion against the authority and Government of the United States, and as a fit and necessary war measure for suppressing the said rebellion, do, on this, the first day of January, in the year of our Lord one thousand eight hundred and sixty-three, and, in accordance with my purpose so do to, publicly proclaim, for the full period of one hundred days from the day first above mentioned, order and designate as the States and parts of States wherein the people thereof respectively are this day in rebellion against the United States, the following, to wit: Arkansas, Texas, Louisiana (except the parishes of St. Bernard, Plaquemines, Jefferson, St. James, Ascension, Assumption, Terrebonne, Lafourche, St. Martin, and Orleans, including the city of New Orleans), Mississippi, Alabama, Florida, Georgia, South Carolina, North Carolina, and Virginia (except the forty-eight counties designated as West Virginia, and also the counties of Berkley, Accomac, Northampton, Elizabeth City, York, Princess Ann, and Norfolk, including the cities of Norfolk and Portsmouth), and which excepted parts are for the present left precisely as if the proclamation were not issued.

And, by virtue of the power and for the purpose aforesaid, I do order and declare that all persons held as slaves within the said designated States and parts of said States, are, and henceforward shall be, free; and that the Executive Government of the United States, including the military and naval authorities thereof, will recognize and maintain the freedom of said persons.

And I hereby enjoin upon the people so declared to be free, to abstain from all violence, unless in necessary self-defence, and I recommend to them that in all cases, when allowed, they labor faithfully for reasonable wages. And I further declare and make known, that such persons, of suitable condition, will be received into the armed service of the United States, to garrison forts, positions, stations and other places, and to man vessels of all sorts in the said service. And upon this act, sincerely believed to be an act of justice, warranted by the constitution, upon military necessity, I invoke the considerate judgment of mankind, and the gracious favor of Almighty God.

In witness whereof I have hereunto set my hand, and caused the seal of the United States to be affixed.

[L. S.] Done at the city of Washington, this, the first day of January, in the year of our Lord one thousand eight hundred and sixty-three, and of the independence of the United States of America the eighty seventh.

A. Lincoln

From slavery to freedom: this drawing by Thomas Nast – the best known cartoonist of his day, whom Lincoln (*center*) called 'our best recruiting sergeant' – shows emancipation dispensing freedom (*left*) and bestowing the blessings of full citizenship (*right*).

to deprive citizens of their property without "due process of Law."' The judgment, though highly disputed (all nine justices filed separate opinions), convinced the North that, as one historian wrote, 'the South now had a judicial loophole to extend slavery (and even worse, blacks) throughout the Union.'

These smoldering resentments north and south of the Mason and Dixon line came to a head in the South after the Republican, Abraham Lincoln, whose anti-slavery views were well known, was elected President in 1860. South Carolina formally seceded from the Union on 20 December of the same year, declaring 'that the Union now subsisting between South Carolina and other states under the name of "The United States of America" is hereby dissolved.' Lincoln, in his inaugural address could cry, 'Physically speaking we cannot separate,' but it was too late – the South saw the North as 'treacherous aggressors' and the North saw the South as intransigent reactionaries, and there was no reconciling them. As Lincoln, in an anti-slavery speech delivered in 1854, put it: 'It is an irrepressible conflict between opposing and enduring forces, and it means that the United States must and will, sooner or later, become entirely a slaveholding nation or entirely a free-labor nation.'

With the firing of the first gun at Fort Sumter on 12 April 1861 the 'crashing, sad, distracted year' began. The bloody conflict of the Civil War was fought to save the Union – Abraham Lincoln wrote in 1862 that his 'paramount object in this struggle is to save the Union and is not either to save or to destroy slavery. If I could save the Union without freeing any slave I would do it; if I could save it by freeing all the slaves I would do it; and if I could do it by freeing some and leaving others alone, I would also do that.' But there was no escaping the issue – there would be no Union without emancipation, and emancipation could not be achieved without bloodshed and violence. 'The grapes of wrath,' as one historian commented, had 'not yet yielded all their bitter vintage.'

THE SAINTLY FANATIC

Of all America's passionate abolitionists, the most passionate – and the most violent – was John Brown. Seeing himself as a sword wielded by the Almighty, he killed – and finally perished himself – for the cause he so fanatically espoused. His plans were ill-judged; he was almost certainly psychotic; yet after the abortive occupation of the armory at Harper's Ferry which led to his death, he became revered by many abolitionists who remembered his ideals and forgot his eccentricities.

Brown was a Connecticut-born Puritan, reared in Ohio. In the words of one historian 'he knew the Bible as Ionian bards knew the *Iliad*.' He adopted his father's intense abolitionism, took his lead from William Lloyd Garrison's *The Liberator* and sought justification in the Old and New Testaments for his dedication to the violent overthrow of slavery. 'Without blood,' he said, quoting St Paul, 'there is no remission of sins.'

In 1856 in Kansas, bitterly divided by free-staters and pro-slavers, he had five pro-

The real John Brown: gaunt, wild, his mouth 'like a crack in a plate.'

slavery men clumsily butchered on Pottawotamie Creek. He dreamed of guerrilla sorties into the South. He gathered round him a gang of anti-slavery marauders, and planned revolution.

The spot Brown chose to begin his uprising was Harper's Ferry, fifty miles north-west of Washington DC, where the Shenandoah and Potomac Rivers join. It had been chosen as the site of a federal arsenal by George Washington because it was near sources of iron ore and charcoal, while the rivers afforded water power. It did not occur to Brown that the town was hemmed in by cliffs and rivers and was impossible to defend.

Top: Harper's Ferry in the 1860s. The Potomac is on the left, the arsenal (detailed, *left*) is boxed.

Lee's troops burst in on a still defiant Brown.

Right. Deification: A saintly Brown casts a sympathetic glance on a mother slave and her child on his way to execution. The figure of Justice (*below left*) stands symbolically blindfolded and broken.

In the fall of 1859, Brown gathered a force of 21 at a rented farm across the Potomac. On the night of 17 October, Brown drove into town in a one-horse wagon, accompanied by 18 men on foot. They cut the telegraph wires and broke into the armory. A train arrived over one of the bridges. A black porter was shot, but the train was later allowed through. At a station up the line, the conductor telegraphed for help. Desultory action, in which two of Brown's sons died continued throughout the day. That evening, Colonel Robert E Lee, soon to become famous as a Confederate general, arrived. Lee's troops battered down the firehouse door and the uprising was over. In all, ten raiders were killed. John Brown was captured with four others. He was hanged, unrepentant, on 2 December 1859.

Brown's glorification came rapidly. It was not long before he was seen by some abolitionists as a Moses figure (an image helped by the heavy beard he grew to disguise his angular jaw). In a way, the attempted apotheosis worked: his soul, in the words of the song, 'goes marching on.'

The end of the road: Brown's execution in a field near Charleston. He died observing that his country was beautiful, that he would serve his cause better as a martyr and that his country could not avoid war.

SIC SE
TYRANNIS
76

The 54th Massachusetts: A regiment of colored troops storms Battery Wagner, a Confederate stronghold by Charleston harbor entrance. The attack failed, but became a symbol among black troops of their dedication to the cause of freedom.

CHAPTER VII

IN THE RANKS OF FREEDOM

BLACKS IN THE CIVIL WAR 1861-1865

By 1863, the Union army had penetrated the South and its troops came face to face for the first time with the slaves they had ostensibly come to liberate. The confrontation was disastrous. The Union army behaved as invading forces have done throughout history. Yankee soldiers murdered slaves who refused to leave the plantations, stripped slave cabins and raped slave women. The Union army appeared to many to be a monster of violence and self-indulgence. Professor Genovese quoted the slave woman who rebuked a soldier for stealing her quilt, 'when he was supposed to be fighting for the freedom of black people.' The soldier shouted at her: 'You're a goddam liar! I'm fighting for $14 a month and the Union!' And an ex-slave from South Carolina wrote sadly that the Yankees seemed to be 'a army dat... more concerned 'bout stealin' than they was 'bout the Holy War for de liberation of de poor African slave people.'

The slaves, for their part, accepted the abuses they suffered at the hands of their liberators in a spirit of dispirited resignation. They were, as Professor Genovese said, 'part of the price to be paid for a freedom they could see coming.' The wanton destruction of the plantations which had hitherto been their only home, saddened and disgusted them, not only because of the homelessness and destitution which resulted, but because it also destroyed their hopes of acquiring land. Most plantation blacks, used as they were to cultivating small plots of their own and raising their own pigs and chickens, saw the acquisition of land as their only means of economic independence.

One immediate result of Union penetration into the South was a flood of slave refugees. From Yorktown, where the Peninsular campaign began, to Memphis, Jackson and Nashville, thousands of freed slaves congregated, waiting patiently for shelter and food. Some of the more enterprising traded with the Yankees. A New York infantryman described the scene at Falmouth on the Rapahannock in April, 1862: 'On the day after our arrival, the Negroes came flocking to the guard line, with baskets of eggs, hoecakes and other luxuries and proved themselves sharp bargainers, doing a lively business.'

Government attitudes towards these new claims on their resources were at first ambivalent. Only gradually did they deal with the

problems. Although abolitionists had long pressed for an end to slavery, the consequences of the sudden emancipation through war of millions of slaves had not been taken into account. Washington was taken by surprise – the government had, as one historian put it, 'failed utterly to foresee the widespread flight of slaves within the Union lines, to assess their needs realistically, and to make considered provision for their future.' A move to create a separate department of Cabinet rank to deal with the special problems of freedmen failed to materialize and the responsibility of setting up refugee camps and finding employment for ex-slaves remained an Army one.

Paradoxically, the Fugitive Slave Act was still valid, and technically it was an offence not to return a runaway slave to any master loyal to the Union cause. Federal Marshals and their deputies were liable to heavy fines if they failed to execute the law. Owners in the Border States in particular went to great lengths to recover their lost 'property,' paying exorbitant 'apprehension' fees to any soldier, sailor or civilian able to restore a contraband fugitive. However, the second Confiscation Act of July 1862 made it an offence for any member of the armed forces to give up a fugitive slave to an owner and established the right of escaped slaves of disloyal masters to 'be forever free.'

In effect, as the Union Army moved further south, all masters were considered to be disloyal, and all refugee slaves could, and often did, become the captured property of the Union forces, entering into Army employ and obtaining, in many cases, 'certificates of liberation.' The Army thus became an instrument both of emancipation and of disruption.

General Ulysses S Grant, in the course of his advance into northern Mississippi, found himself faced with a torrent of black refugees – 7000 poured into Corinth alone. Grant, an enlightened man, set about restoring order, in the teeth of bitter prejudice from his own troops, the majority of whom disliked blacks even more than Southerners, and many of whom were convinced that if 'the dark hordes swamped the advancing columns' the destruction and demoralization of the Union Army would be complete. He assigned some to camp duties, the men building entrenchments, the women working in the hospitals and kitchens. The rest he put to work on the plantations – allowing planters who had

In these two views refugee slaves, ragged, hungry and suffering from exposure, arrive at a Federal camp. The problems posed by the mass of refugees meant that, for most, the road to a better life would be long and hard.

Former slaves, working now as servants of the North, build a road . . .

stayed at home to hire them at the government's rate of pay. Abandoned plantations near the Union lines were leased to white tenants, who could obtain black hands from the government, provided they undertook to 'feed, clothe and kindly supervise them' until 1 February 1864, and to pay them a modest wage ($7 a month for an able-bodied man).

These were the lucky ones – after the occupation of Vicksburg and towns further south some 30,000 contraband blacks were thrown on the mercy of the government. Many died on the streets, in misery and starvation. Many more were taken into refugee camps where, although conscientious efforts were made by the Sanitary Commission and various philanthropists to set up hospitals and to provide enough housing and food, conditions were far from satisfactory. The squalor of one camp, according to one Quaker from Philadelphia gave him a 'feeling that approached despair.'

There was, after 1863, another outlet for the refugee slave – that of service in the Union Army. Black enlistment, strongly supported by abolitionists from the outset of the war, had come up against strenuous opposition,

. . . work a forge . . .

mainly from the Border States, and particularly from Kentucky. Precedents for using black troops, however, had already been set. In Lousiana during 1861 about 1400 free blacks had been enlisted into the militia, and when the Union took New Orleans they showed no compunction about changing sides. They were subsequently enrolled in the volunteer service of the United States, and later served with distinction at Port Hudson – thus doing much to dispel the myth that blacks were unpredictable fighters.

Prejudice against the use of blacks in the armed forces ran deep. General Thomas G Stevenson, sent to the Sea Islands, said in 1863 that 'he would rather have the Union forces defeated than win with Negro troops.' General Stevenson was, in fact, arrested for expressing these sentiments, but he only said openly what many thought privately. William Sherman was, according to Allan Nevins, 'so deeply opposed to the use of black troops to fight white men, and . . . to the placing of Negro garrisons in Southern cities, that his critics accused him of an almost criminal dislike of the race.' Others thought that arming ex-slaves was a step bordering on the suicidally reckless, fearing black regiments might 'touch off bloody slave revolts.'

. . . stand guard. . .

. . . and man trenches.

It was the Emancipation Proclamation of 1863, formally giving ex-slaves the right to be received into the armed forces, combined with the consistent failure to fill Union ranks with white volunteers, which finally broke down official resistance to black troops. In March 1863 General Lorenzo Thomas was authorized to raise and officer black regiments in the Mississippi valley, starting in Cairo, and to establish black commands at Helena, Columbus, Milliken's Bend, Corinth, Memphis and Nashville. In the summer General Grant was able to write expressing his satisfaction with the colored volunteers. They 'stood the climate better than whites,' they 'preserved discipline with less oversight' and 'all that have been tried have fought bravely.' By the autumn the War Department had authorized the enlistment of freedom by General Order and recruiting stations were established in Maryland, Missouri and Tennessee. Loyal slaveholders who freed their slaves and offered them for enlistment were paid $300 a head. By December, over 50,000 had been recruited, with the numbers increasing daily.

The attitude of the South to the sight of armed black opponents was one of fury. As most black recruitment was carried out in the South, the situation was an inflammatory one, and caused persistent violations of the lawful treatment of prisoners-of-war. At-

Emancipated slaves fight with Union troops in the 1864 battle for Milliken's Bend, an important base in the Union campaign focusing on Vicksburg.

rocity stories abounded – Confederate murders of captured black troops were reported at Murfreesboro and Holly Springs and, according to a Confederate witness, a battlefield at Arkansas was left 'a sickening sight, for defying all restraints the Southerners fell on the surviving colored soldiers and butchered them in great heaps.' The South stubbornly refused to exchange black prisoners on the same basis as white ones and, due to the fact that the Union had many more prisoners than the Confederacy, the North was not prepared to compromise. The resultant deadlock left thousands languishing under terrible conditions in prison camps for the duration of the war.

The treatment of blacks within the armed forces varied, but all served for less pay than their white counterparts, receiving $10 a month and one ration, while white volunteers received $13, full rations and a free uniform. While the Army maintained a strict policy of racial segregation, the Navy allowed blacks to serve alongside whites at sea – colored gun crews were singled out for special commendation at Hatteras and Port Royal. In general, however, it was considered that blacks preferred the company of their own kind.

About one hundred black officers obtained commissions, but there was never any shortage of applications from white officers to

command black regiments. Indeed, the standards was high – two out of every five were rejected.

Black troops distinguished themselves throughout the Civil War – in particular during the Vicksburg campaign, when a naval officer wrote: 'the blacks fought like bloodhounds'; and at Fort Wagner, where the 54th Massachusetts Volunteers, the first black troops from a free state to be mustered into federal Service, stormed the ramparts, led by Colonel Robert Gould Shaw, and managed to place their colors inside the fort. Half the black troops died in the attempt, as did Colonel Shaw, whose heroic death 'sent a wave of sorrow over the nation.'

The black troops suffered, as much as, and perhaps more than, white troops. In 1864, at Fort Pillow, an earthwork on the Mississippi River, the Confederate General Nathan Bedford Forrest (a commander whose theory of war was, in his own words, 'Git thar fustest with the mostest') was alleged to have mown down black troops after they had surrendered their arms. It was an accusation he went to some lengths to deny. As Ernest and Trevor Dupuy (authors of *The Compact History of the Civil War*) said, no proof exists 'that any Federal troops, white or colored, were slaughtered after the survivors formally surrendered.' Nevertheless, out of the 560 Union soldiers manning the earthworks, 400 were casualties and more than half were killed. 'Losses,' as the Dupuys remarked, 'among the Negro troops were particularly heavy.'

Perhaps the worst incident involving black troops occurred during the Petersburg campaign. A mine, exploded by Federal troops in the Confederate position, blasted a crater 'about 150 feet long, ninety feet wide, and thirty feet deep.' Lots were drawn as to who should spearhead the attack – the objective being a cemetery on top of an undefended hill behind the mined entrenchments. The task

The Real Meaning of the War

'The privilege of belonging to an admittedly superior race – the deep conviction that there actually were superior and inferior races – could not be wrenched out of human society without a revolutionary convulsion. The convulsion was unthinkable, yet it was beginning to take place, even though hardly anyone had consciously willed it; it was coming down the country roads with the swaggering destructive columns in weathered blue, lying across the landscape behind the haze of smoke that came down from the ridges around Gettysburg and Chattanooga, and there was no stopping it. The bugle that would never call retreat had been heard by people who had not previously been allowed to look upon themselves as persons possessing any rights which other people were bound to respect. To end slavery was to commit the nation permanently to an ideal that might prove humanly unattainable. The inner meaning of the war now was that everything which America had done before – its dreams and its hopes, its sacrifices and its hard-bought victories – was no more than prologue to a new struggle that would go on and on for generations, with a remote ideal lying dim but discernible beyond the dust of the coming years.

Here was the real revolution: here was the fundamental and astounding conclusion, which had been implicit in the first crash of the marsh guns around Fort Sumter, which had followed Old Glory and Palmetto Flag down so many streets amid so many gaily cheering crowds. Here was what was being bought by infinite suffering, tragedy, and loss. Here was the showdown, not to be understood at once, not to be accepted for generations, but nevertheless wholly inexorable . . . down the dusty roads came ten miles of Negroes, bags packed for a journey longer than any man could understand, marching toward a future that could never again be built in the image of the past. . . .

De massa run ha-ha!
De darkey stay, ho-ho!
I tink it must be Kingdom Coming
And de year ob Jubilo!

It would be that sort of year: year of Jubilo, year of overturn . . . hard tramp of marching military feet, endless shuffle of splay-footed refugees . . . the significance of their march being that it led toward the unknown and that all America like it or not, was going to follow.'

Bruce Catton
This Hallowed Ground.

The band of the 107th US Colored Infantry.

fell to a division commanded by Brigadier General James H Ledlie. Ledlie, however, was notorious for being drunk in combat, and almost immediately disappeared into a bomb shelter, accompanied by the commander of the black division, Brigadier General Edward Ferrero, where they settled down to drink themselves into a stupor on medical rum. General Ledlie's division, to whom he had issued the scantiest of instructions, wandered to the edge of the crater, some going to the assistance of Southerners trapped in the debris. Other Confederate soldiers, however, having recovered from the initial shock, moved into the attack, firing on the disoriented Union troops, who tried to shield themselves from the relentless rifle and cannon fire by jumping into the crater. The black division (whose commander was still safe in his bomb shelter) went to their assistance, the majority joining the white soldiers already in the crater. Four thousand out of 20,000 Union troops involved in the resulting fiasco were killed. Most of those left alive surrendered, rather than attempt to clamber out in the face of such an onslaught. Incredibly, although Brigadier General Ledlie was permitted to resign, Brigadier General Ferrero remained in command of the black division 'he had so shockingly betrayed.'

Abraham Lincoln later said, 'There will be some black men who can remember that, with silent tongue and clenched teeth and steady eye, and well-poisoned bayonet, they have helped mankind on to this great consummation; while, I fear, there will be some white ones, unable to forget that, with malignant heart and deceitful speech they have striven to hinder it.' By hindsight, Lincoln's words contain irony: they could have been uttered in another context a century later, when blacks were still struggling against the legacy of slavery.

THE FIGHTING REFUGEES

When war broke out in 1861, slaves from all the border states fled north to Federal camps, seeking safety and a chance to help the cause of their own freedom. Gradually, erratically, the raggle-taggle of refugees were transformed, often against the judgment of Northern generals, and almost always in the face of antagonism from Northern troops, into men and women who took pride in a new beginning. The process is seen in the photographs on this and the following pages. It is also captured by these words taken from Bruce Catton's *This Hallowed Ground*:

‘A Union force came back to its base at Corinth, Mississippi, after some foray deeper into the state, and when it marched in it was followed by hundreds upon hundreds of fugitive slaves. The army command at Corinth did not want these people – had, in fact, very little idea what it could do with or about them – but it could not send them back, and it fenced off a big camp, put the ex-slaves into it, detailed a couple of infantry regiments to guard it, and plucked a chaplain from the 27th Ohio and told him he was in charge. The soldiers objected bitterly to guard duty, declaring that they had come down to Dixie to fight Rebels and not to be policemen for a lot of runaway slaves, and the chaplain came up with an idea. Let him (he urged) form a few infantry companies from among the men in the contraband camp; with a little drill and the proper direction they ought to be able to stand guard....

These contraband camps were not usually very inspiring places to look at. There was a huge one on a levee not far from Vicksburg,

Fugitive slaves ford the Rapahannock River, Virginia, 1862.

crammed with fugitives who huddled without shelter, subsisted on army rations, got no real care from anyone, and died by the dozen from bad sanitation, exposure, overcrowding, and general homesick bewilderment. Yet the faith that had brought them here – a faith that freedom was good and that the road to it somehow led through the camps of the Union army – did not seem to leave them, even when their camp became a shambles. A Wisconsin soldier who was detailed for duty around this camp looked on in silent wonder at the prayer meetings that were held every night. There were no lights; none was needed, he thought, since the leaders of the meeting had no Bibles or hymnals and could not have read from them if they had them; there was just a great crowd of men and women, dimly seen, bowed to the ground, swaying rhythmically as they prayed that God would set His people free and would send His blessing down on Massa Lincoln, Massa Grant, and all of Massa Lincoln's soldiers. ’

A refugee camp for former slaves at Richmond, Virginia, 1865.

Black laborers with the Union Army.

A Union army black soldier and his wife taken about 1865 – a proud record of new status.

Black troops man Union guns.

CHAPTER VIII

CRUSHING THE LAST SLAVERS

AFRICA AND ASIA 1880-1910

A slave trader's end: a slave-carrying Arabian vessel is destroyed by British sailors on the east coast of Africa, 1868.

Black slavery left a bitter legacy to the West Indies. As one colonial official wrote in 1849: 'As the question at present stands, a race has been freed, but a society has not been formed.' The uneasy relationship between master and slave did not slide any more effortlessly into one of employer and employee than it did in the Southern States, and many of the difficulties which faced planters and slaves alike after emancipation have still not entirely been resolved.

Old resentments still simmer beneath the surface, manifesting themselves in sporadic murders and out of violence, in the determination of all classes, and particularly the lower middle class, to avoid the degradation of manual labor by the widespread practice of stealing crops, and in the notoriously casual attitude to marriage in church. 'Around 70 percent of births in the West Indies,' wrote Anthony Richmond, 'are illegitimate,' and legal marriage is 'the mark of middle and upper class status.'

Deeply embedded in the fabric of West Indian society was the desirability of being, if not white, then as near white as possible. The West Indian did not, like the American black, struggle for recognition by attempting to force whites to accept him for what he was, but tried to erase the psychological trauma of his slave status by becoming less black. 'Black' in the West Indies is still synonymous with working class – the lighter the skin color the higher up the social ladder, and the better the job opportunities. Light-skinned women were much in demand as marriage partners for the socially ambitious – as Dr Henriques commented: 'The fact that successful Black men seek out and marry women of a "higher" color in order to improve their social status, has led to the creation of a class of educated, often monied, black spinsters. These women are unable to get married to the type of man they would like to, as such an individual would wish to marry only a woman lighter than himself. . . . A Fair man who marries a Dark or Black woman commits social suicide. A Black man, wishing to be socially successful, who does the same throws away the only opportunity he will have of "raising his color." '

Three West Indians sketched in the late 19th century.

If social disorganization and individual disorientation created a 'fundamental disequilibrium,' both during the after the slave régime, in areas to which slaves had been taken, it also had a correspondingly powerful effect on Africa itself.

Historians differ over the extent to which the West African coastal states were affected by the slave trade. Some feel that there were benefits that, on balance, outweighed the disadvantages. Robin Mallet, in his massive *Africa since 1875*, wrote that 'by providing new commercial opportunities for some African communities through their demand for certain forms of African produce and especially for African slave labor, they [the traders] helped to create conditions favorable for the growth of more elaborate politics, particularly on the Guinea Coast . . . clearly the trade brought impoverishment, desolation, and destruction to some African communities, but for others it provided new opportunities for enrichment and stimulating contacts with a wider world.'

Basil Davidson, on the other hand, felt that during the four centuries of European involvement with West Africa 'the balance of gain was all one way . . . there was no creative marriage of cultures, no passage of ideas, no sharing of wealth or achievement. In enriching themselves, Europeans deprived Africans of the social and political growth necessary for development and change.'

It is, however, by no means certain that these changes would have occurred without a European presence; after abolition, the

The raider's strike: slavers seize blacks for the Arabic slave trade in east Central Africa, 1888.

Ashanti of the Gold Coast, whose slave-raiding activities had been a vehicle for power and self-aggrandizement, began to reassert old feudal rights, to increase the practice of human sacrifice, and to turn their attentions to the inland slave trade.

It was this inland trade, which had its outlets in Egypt and on the East Coast of Africa, in the slave market of Zanzibar that perhaps wreaked the most devastation from the early 19th century on.

While slave trading from the Guinea Coast remained the prerogative of Europeans and raiding its hinterland was the business of native kings, the lakes, rivers and forests of Central Africa had been, for several centuries, dominated by the Arabs, whose search for ivory and slaves had driven them first into the Sudan and then further and further into the interior, in order to satisfy the insatiable demand for these commodities throughout the Muslim world. The slave markets of the Red Sea ports were supplied from the broad belt running across the continent south of the Sahara and north of the rain forests. In the market of Zanzibar slaves from Tanganyika and as far west as the Upper Congo were sold. The lack of roads, the prevalence of the tsetse fly, which carry sleeping sickness and nagana, a wasting disease fatal to horses and cattle, and the prohibitive cost of hired labor – all these factors meant that the transport of ivory to the coast had to be organized with slaves who succumbed in large numbers. Reginald Coupland estimated that between 80,000 and 100,000 died each year, either from enslavement or massacre, and Livingstone (a man not given to exaggeration) put the number at five times that amount. One historian wrote ironically that the use of slaves to transport ivory was a stroke of genius. 'The economic elegance of using one commodity to transport another and then selling both is too obvious to need elaboration.'

Reginald Coupland described the progress of a slave caravan from the coast inland, and back to Zanzibar: 'The composition of a caravan was always much the same – two or three Arab merchants in charge with their half-caste hangers-on, a body of armed slaves, and the long string of porters, slave or free, with the flag of the Sultan at their head –

THE HORRORS OF THE ARABIAN CONNECTION

The slave trade based on Zanzibar – which handled up to 20,000 slaves a year in the 1870s – was fed by the slave trade in the interior of East Africa, which was channeled along caravan routes debouching at Kilwa in the Congo and Bagamoyo, Tanzania. Inland, these routes spread fanlike into the farthest reaches of the eastern Congo, Uganda and the Nyasa area. The following description is of a slave-gang seen by the famous explorer David Livingstone and his companions in the early 1870s.

' In less time than I take to talk about it, these unfortunate creatures – 84 of them – wended their way into the village where we were. Some of them, the eldest, were women from 20 to 22 years of age, and there were youths from 18 to 19, but the large majority was made up of boys and girls from 7 years to 14 or 15 years of age. A more terrible scene than these men, women and children, I do not think I ever came across. To say that they were emaciated would not give you an idea of what human beings can undergo under certain circumstances. . . . Each of them had his neck in a large forked stick, weighing from 30 to 40 pounds, and five or six feet long, cut with a fork at the end of it where the branches of a tree spread out. . . . The women were tethered with bark thongs, which are of all things the most cruel to be tied with. Of course they are soft and supple when first stripped off the trees, but a few hours in the sun make them about as hard as the iron round packing-cases. The little children were fastened by thongs to their mothers. [The travelers released the slaves] As we passed along the path which these slaves had traveled. . . . I was shown a spot in the bushes where a poor woman the day before, unable to keep on the march, and likely to hinder it, was cut down by the axe of one of these slave drivers. . . . We went on further and were shown a place where a child lay. It had been recently born, and its mother was unable to carry it on from debility and exhaustion; so the slave-trader had taken this little infant by its feet and dashed its brains out against one of the trees and thrown it in there. '

This drawing is based on a report of a slave gang seen near Zumbo, some 450 miles up the Zambesi, in Portuguese Mozambique, near the borders of present day Zambia, in 1892.

An Arab slave caravan on its way to the coast.

G. DURAND.

Useless property: exhausted slaves collapse within sight of a water hole (*above*), and a slave-trader prepares to deliver the *coup de grace* to an exhausted slave (*right*).

but its numbers varied from a hundred or so to a thousand or even more. . . . At all points on the way inland and back again the traders were anxious to pick up slaves, if only in twos or threes. . . . But the main sources of supply were the organized slave-raids in the chosen areas, which shifted steadily inland as tract after tract became 'worked out.' The Arabs might conduct a raid themselves, but more usually they incited a chief to attack another tribe, lending him their own armed slaves and guns to ensure his victory. The result, of course, was an increase in inter-tribal warfare till the whole country was in a flame.'

But, sometimes, the Arabs would settle 'in the heart of some quiet community in the remote interior' for a year or two, winning the confidence of local tribesmen by their friendship and honesty and lulling their suspicions by planting vegetables and fruit. Then, as Henry Drummond wrote in *Tropical Africa*, 'one day, suddenly, the inevitable quarrel is picked. And then follows a wholesale massacre. Enough only are spared from the slaughter to carry the ivory to the coast; the grass huts of the village are set on fire; the Arabs strike camp; and the slave march, worse than death, begins.'

Drummond, who traveled extensively in the region toward the end of the 19th century, continued his vivid description of the devastation the Arabs left in their wake as follows: 'It was but yesterday that an explorer crossing from Lake Nyasa to Lake Tanganyika, saw the whole southern end of Tanganyika peopled with large and prosperous villages. The next to follow him found not a solitary human being – nothing but burned houses and bleaching skeletons. It was but yesterday – the close of 1887 – that the Arabs at the north end of Lake Nyasa, after destroying 14 villages with many of their inhabitants, pursued the population of one village into a patch of tall dry grass, set it on

Slaves and ivory: an engraving done in 1889 shows the connection between these two prime types of merchandise for Arab traders in East Africa.

The Tree of Death

The cruelties of the Arab slave trade reflected in part the cruelties of the rulers with whom the traders dealt. This account of an execution in the 1880s was told by a slave in Zinder, Niger.

'The Sarki of Zinder is a cruel man, and much feared by his subjects.... For the least offence he sentences people to death. When a criminal is to be killed he is taken by the executioner to an open place, underneath a lofty tree... called "Itatshe-n-mutua," which means the "Tree of Death"... [It] was bounded by great rocks, wherein the hyenas had their dens, and could eat the bodies of the people executed... its upper branches were covered with innumerable vultures.... There were six men this time to be killed... the last of these men, when the executioner was wrestling with him, bit him several times in the arms, so that he took out pieces of flesh with his teeth, and this so enraged the executioner that... he drew the rope through the man's armpits and then slung him up to the tree.... And when he was thus hung up perpendicularly, and swinging to and fro and turning round, the executioner took his sharp sword, and slowly cut the man to bits in little pieces.'

fire, surrounded it, and slew with the bullet and the spear those who crawled out from the more merciful flames.'

The island of Zanzibar – the destination of the surviving slaves – was under the nominal dominion of Oman. In 1856 it had a population of 60,000 and had grown, within 50 years, from a tiny fishing village to a huge cosmopolitan city, the streets crowded, according to Dr Rushenberger, a surgeon on an American ship, with 'Negroes armed with spears, Arabs bearing swords, dirks and shields, and Banians (East Indians) under high red turbans.' British abolition of the

A portrait of two Arab slave dealers.

slave trade in 1807 had driven many American and Portuguese ships round the Cape of Good Hope in order to load up in Mozambique or Zanzibar with cheaper East Coast slaves. Between March and November, as one captain said, 'Portuguese and Yankee clippers sneak up the Mozambique [Channel] with the last rain of the southwest monsoon without much fear of being captured by our slow men-of-war.' And from December to March the Arab dhows sailed to Zanzibar, returning with their slave cargoes to Arabia, Persia, India and the islands of Mauritius and Réunion from April to December when 'the monsoons conveniently reverse themselves and blow from a southwest direction.'

In 1822, Seyyid Said, Sultan of Oman, moved his court from Muscat to Zanzibar – a tribute to the enormous wealth the Sultanate

Slave mart: the slave market in Zanzibar where purchasers examined and bought some 200–300 slaves a day.

SUPPLYING THE EASTERN HAREMS

Besides supplying labor to the Middle East, the slave traders also sold young girls – mainly from Ethiopia (Abyssinia) and Somalia – as wives and servants to the Sudanese, Egyptians and Turks. The British explorer Samuel Baker in 1861–62 saw the great slave mart at Gallabat on the Sudanese–Ethiopia border:

'The establishments of the various slave merchants were arranged under large tents of

Capture in the Ethiopian highlands.

Slaves in transit.

matting, and contained many young girls of extreme beauty, ranging from nine to seventeen years of age. These lovely captives, of a rich brown tint, with delicately formed features, and eyes like those of the gazelle, were natives of the Galla, on the borders of Abyssinia, from which country they were brought by Abyssinian traders to be sold for the Turkish harems. Although beautiful, these girls were useless for hard labor; they quickly fade away and die unless kindly treated. . . . not only are their faces and figures perfection, but they become extremely attached to those who show them kindness, and they make good and faithful wives. There is something . . . captivating in the natural grace and softness of those young beauties, whose hearts quickly respond to those warmer feelings . . . that are seldom known among the sterner and coarser tribes.'

Going to the sale room.

In the sale room.

Nile slavery: slaves from central Africa turn an Egyptian water wheel.

derived from the shipment of slaves from the mainland of Africa through Zanzibar and the export of cloves (introduced into the island in about 1818) which were cultivated on plantations worked by slave labor. From such rich sources, the Sultan's annual income was said to have risen between 1832 and 1862 from $75,000 to $270,000.

British opposition to the trade was intense. The great missionary and explorer David Livingstone, who cried that 'Africa was bleeding out her life's blood at every pore,' saw his search for the source of the Nile as a way to open the path for commerce and Christianity, to wipe out all tribal evils, in particular the slave trade. The British East Coast Slaving Squadron kept watch at sea. The Anti-Slavery Society protested vehemently. Dedicated missionaries did what they could. One, Arthur West, even went so far as to buy the slave market at Zanzibar for £100,000 – his entire capital.

A view of the church built on the site of the Zanzibar slave market in the 1870s.

Despite these efforts, Arab slavers continued to ply their trade, watched in many cases helplessly by British officers. For although the slave trade from Zanzibar to Arabia was formally abolished by the Hamerton Treaty of 1847, slaves could still be shipped from the African mainland to Zanzibar, and the Arabs found numerous ways of evading the rules to enable them to transport their cargoes northward, relying on speed to outdistance any frigate that might accost them. If, however, it looked as if capture was inevitable, slavers had no hesitation in disposing of their human cargoes – W Cope Devereux apparently saw some Arab pirates 'cut the throats of 240 slaves and throw the corpses overboard,' when a dhow was chased by his ship *The Gorgon*.

In 1876 Sir John Kirk, the Anti-Slavery Commissioner in East Africa, extracted a promise from the Sultan to forbid the export of slaves from Zanzibar, but as late as 1890 it was found that slaves were being sent to the Congo. Also in 1890 the Sultan appealed to the British for protection, in the face of

CUTTING THE ARAB SLAVE ROUTE

The vast extent of waters and shoreline over which the British naval anti-slave trade patrol kept watch, from Mozambique in the south to the Baluchistan coast in the north, posed an impossible challenge for the slender patrol of from three to seven ships assigned to it. The patrols continued until the turn of the century. Their task was made more difficult by the increasing use of the French flag by the Arab slavers, for under it they had immunity from search and capture by British cruisers.

A dhow, the favorite slave-carrying vessel of Arab slave traders.

Arab traders beat their cargo into submission on the run from the African coast to Zanzibar.

This letter was written from Zanzibar in 1865 by a Captain Cornish-Bowden of HMS *Wasp*: 'Last night I heard a vessel was to go with slaves so I sent the pinnace and cutter... The pinnace saw a dhow, fired at her, and boarded her. The dhow, with sail set, ran into her and carried away her mainmast. Lieutenant Theobold at once was thrust through his wrist with a spear, and one poor fellow was killed....

Lieutenant Rising in the cutter boarded aft and after much resistance the Arabs jumped overboard and into a boat and got away except 13 on board. They left three dead. Poor Rising appears to have jumped into the middle very gallantly, but his left hand was chopped nearly off at the knuckles, then he was thrust through the leg with a spear, and... had a sabre cut in the neck.... The first we knew of it was seeing the cutter return "Union down." In it was poor New dead. Rising unable to move covered with blood, but very cheerful....

I steamed out at once and brought back the dhow. On arrival I went on board. She was crammed with slaves, as thick as bees in a hive. No wonder my men fell about on her decks; they had to fight standing as they could on their bodies.... We counted 289 slaves, mostly women and girls. Many are said to have jumped over-board.'

A steam pinnace of HMS *London* puts a warning shot across the bows of a slaving dhow in 1881.

As a British naval vessel approaches, Arabian dealers throw overboard their slaves.

A British cutter boards a heavily laden slave dhow.

Slaves are released aboard a British ship.

increasing German intrusions into East Africa and it was agreed that 'relations with foreign powers should be conducted with the sole advice and through the channels of the British Government.' The new Consul-General, Gerald Portal, felt that the Sultanate was an 'embodiment of all the worst and most barbaric characteristics of primitive Arab despotism' and set himself the task of weeding out corruption. And when in 1896, with an imposing show of strength, the British removed a rival claimant to the Sultanate by the simple expedient of bombarding the palace from British warships (killing 500 people in the process), the British-nominated Sultan – understandably – agreed to 'pass a decree, although in a gradual manner, to abolish the status of slavery.'

'The new crusade': *Punch* trumpets the opening of the 1889 Brussels conference to quell slavery across the world.

The British also exerted themselves to prohibit the traffic of slaves in the Sudan, Egypt and Turkey. Under the Brussels Act of 1890, which was designed to curb slavery world-wide and specifically to protect the aboriginal populations of Africa, positive steps were taken to put an end to the Turkish and Arab slave trades. But although Turkey, Zanzibar and Persia were signatories to the agreement (along with all the major world powers), the Italian Anti-Slavery Society reported in 1893 that 'Turkish vessels carried slaves surreptitiously to various ports in the Levant, the authorities providing the traders with letters of liberation to cover the de-

The British assault a slave-base on the Mozambique coast, 1851.

Breaking the shackles: members of Sir Samuel Baker's anti-slavery expedition of 1869–73, break the shackles from slaves.

ception.' And although the British presence in the Sudan and Egypt effected a nominal understanding with the Khedive, 'continual vigilance was necessary to prevent the smuggling in of . . . slaves from the west and to control the shipment of slaves from the coast.' Progress was also slow in Zanzibar, despite the Sultan's promise.

Nonetheless the Arab slave trade was, at the end of the 19th century, dealt a crushing blow by the ambitious King Leopold II of Belgium, when he acquired the 900,000 square miles of the Congo Free State. His motives were far from altruistic: they exemplified the most vicious kind of imperialist exploitation (although he managed to convince Britain, Germany and the United States at the Berlin Conference of 1884–85 that his aims were 'the moral and material regeneration of the natives' and 'legitimate trade.') Finding, however, that Belgian plans for legitimate trade were obstructed at every turn by ivory-seeking Arabs, who also raided the population for slaves, he was obliged to come to some sort of agreement with the most powerful of all the slavers, Tippo Tib. Leopold made Tippo Governor of the Arab regions (about half the territory) on condition that he not only ceased his own slave-trading, but influenced his fellow Arab leaders to do the same.

It was an uneasy compromise, and with the introduction by the Belgians of high export duties levied on ivory sent to the East Coast and a prohibition on the sale of arms, the Congo-Arabs became increasingly hostile. Armed clashes became frequent, culminating in the Belgian-Arab campaigns of 1892. Leopold waged these wars under the guise of a humanitarian crusade against slavery, having first, in 1889, obtained the full support of the members of the Brussels Anti-Slavery Conference, and also secured a

Black porters carry parts of cannons as a British expedition ventures inland to suppress slavery in northern Nigeria.

loan of 25 million francs from the Belgian State – which provided the means to create and equip a native army.

But for the hapless inhabitants of the Congo, the ensuing Belgian victory was a doubtful blessing. It liberated them from the worst Arab atrocities, only to deliver them to Belgian oppression. Brutally forced to collect ivory and rubber for no pay, the natives were subjected to the rigorous implementation of the 'system' run by State Agents and enforced by the much feared *Force Publique*, or native sentinels. Billeted on villages, these guardians of the 'machinery of force' inflicted hideous punishments on workers who failed to produce the required weekly number of baskets of rubber – whole villages being burned to the ground, women raped and children murdered: as a native proverb went, 'Rubber is death.'

Six years after the institution of slavery was banned in Zanzibar, British assault one of the last of the slavers' stockades.

Traders in the flesh: this rare picture shows three slavers captured in 1892.

Another way of encouraging a reluctant labor force was to confine the lazy, together with their wives and children, in 'hostage houses.' A missionary, the Reverend Somerville Gilchrist, wrote: 'I shall never forget the impression left on my mind by one of these horrible Houses of Detention. It was a small, low-roofed circular building, with the only entrance to it through another building of the same type. The latter was occupied by a number of sentries with Albini rifles. Inside the other were herded a large number of women, girls and boys, a mass of bones held together by black skin . . . the horror of it! Outside the building there was a row of those skeleton women on the chain, followed by a sentry with an Albini and a chicotte, going back and forward from the garden to the river.'

This wholesale subjection of an entire people to the servitude of the State continued, despite vociferous concern from missionaries, and an international campaign for reform which spread as far as the United States, until after King Leopold's death in 1909. Leopold himself, although worried at the extent to which public opinion was against the régime in the Congo, was not prepared to make radical alterations to a system in which his entire personal fortune was sunk, and from which he was receiving such a handsome return. In June 1909, at the Colonial celebrations in Antwerp, he said,

Arab slave traders captured by the British pose after their landing in Zanzibar.

Newly released slaves pose with two British sailors (*background*) in Zanzibar before their return to their homelands.

'Blackbirds' for Australia: Pacific islanders like these (*right*) made up the workforce acquired by traders (lampooned in the cartoon, *far right*) who captured them and transported them (*below*) to work in the Australian sugar plantations around the turn of the century.

'The greatest satisfaction of my life has been to give the Congo to Belgium. The Congo is richer than you think. The duty of a sovereign is to enrich the nation.'

The Belgians were not, however, the only exploiters of native labor. The Portuguese system of contract labor on the islands of St Thomé and Principe was revealed to be based on the fruits of 'slave raiding, slave trading and slave owning,' during the course of a famous case – 'Cadbury v Standard' – in December 1909 (brought to investigate the methods of producing cocoa)

The Australians enticed Polynesian Islanders, known as Kanakas, to work on the cotton and sugar plantations of Queensland. The practice, which existed from 1860, moved the Reverend John Paton, Presbyterian Minister on the Polynesian island of Aniwa, to write in 1870 the following outraged, bitter letter to the Queensland Legislature: 'How can the Queensland Government sanction and protect this horrid trade in human beings with all its crime and bloodshed? The complaints of natives regarding their friends are heartrending. Some are surprised, bound and carried off by force. Others are got on board under every artifice and deception by the agents of the vessels, who are general adepts at deceiving. . . . Some are represented as going ashore in the garb of a missionary, Bible in hand.' The Kanaka labor system was formally abolished in 1890 by the Queensland Government.

The Aborigines Protection Society, however, who had campaigned ceaselessly on behalf of the Polynesians, was, rightly, not convinced that the ban would have much effect. In fact it lingered for 14 years, by which time the islands were so severely depopulated that, as the Society pointed out: 'The difficulties of obtaining fresh recruits from islands deprived of so many of their inhabitants and the rigor with which regulations are enforced as regards both the recruiting and the treatment of the Polynesians while they are in Queensland, appear . . . to have rendered this form of slavery so costly and inconvenient that it is ceasing to be profitable. In this way there is a prospect of the pernicious and disgraceful traffic dying out.' In fact, the practice only finally ended when, in 1904, the federal government agreed to offset any losses sustained by sugar planters.

ATROCITY IN THE CONGO

The Belgian Congo (present day Zaire) owed its existence to the initiative of one man, Leopold II of Belgium. In 1876, Leopold, determined to engineer an African colony for himself, and for his country, commissioned the explorer H M Stanley to sign treaties with the Congolese chiefs. By 1885 Leopold was recognized internationally as the head of the new Congo Free State. By hindsight, the title seems a bad joke. Heavily in debt, Leopold declared that vacant lands – and their products – were to be state property. The Congolese were forced to supply the chief commodity, rubber. The results were so horrific that in 1908 international opinion forced Leopold's retreat and the Congo's annexation by Belgium.

The patriarchal Leopold (*below left*) and a *Punch* cartoon entitled 'In the Rubber Coils' dramatizing the Belgian King's grip on the Congo.

At work in the Congo: Africans under white supervision cut wood and gather rubber – work that for several years led, apparently to few abuses. Only gradually did the system that shocked the international community evolve.

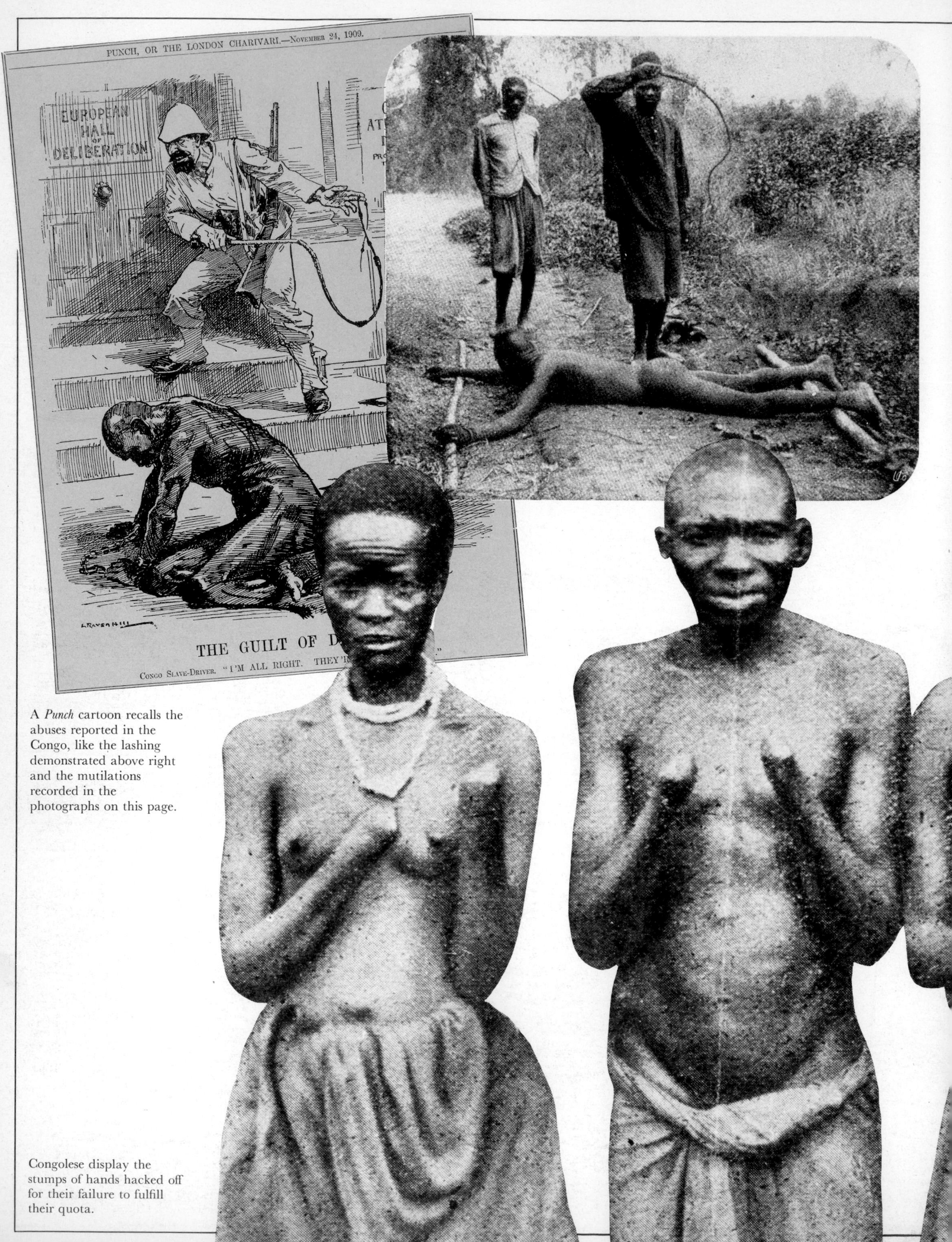

A *Punch* cartoon recalls the abuses reported in the Congo, like the lashing demonstrated above right and the mutilations recorded in the photographs on this page.

Congolese display the stumps of hands hacked off for their failure to fulfill their quota.

In 1911, a Belgian historian described Leopold's system: 'Tax was not paid in money but in work. In the rubber districts in place of work the tax was assessed at so many kilogrammes of rubber. If the stated quantity was not delivered to the "Treasury" there were several methods of enforcing compliance. Chiefs were detained as a punishment until their people furnished their quota of rubber; hostages were taken; women and children imprisoned; the chicotte (a raw hide lash) was used on those who had not brought in to the post their prescribed amount of rubber. Sentinels were posted in centres of population to supervise the work of the natives. Refractory villages received visits from military patrols. At times punitive expeditions were sent to mete out exemplary punishment.'

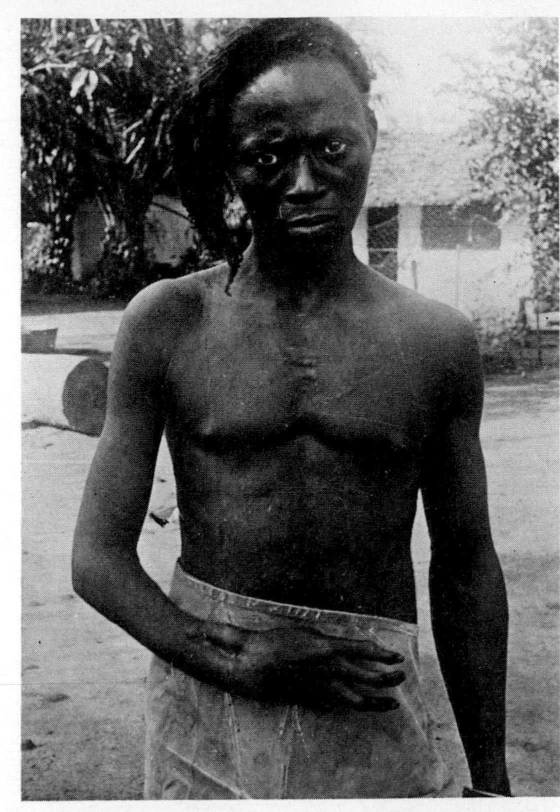

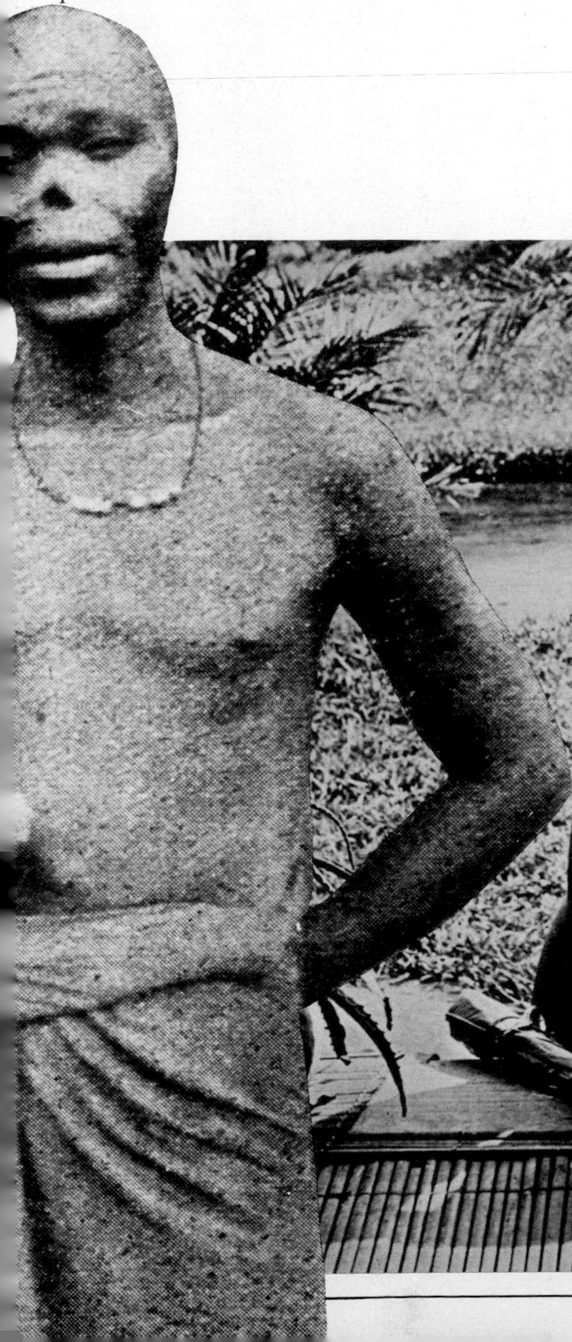

A worker shows a pierced hand to the cameraman (*left*) while below another looks down at a severed hand and foot.

Around the turn of the century, articles began to appear criticising Leopold's rule. In 1903, Britain's Aborigines' Protection Society published *Civilization in Congoland, a Story of Wrongdoing* and the House of Commons advised international action to 'abate the evils prevalent in that state.'

The government commissioned a report on the atrocities from the British Vice-Consul in the Congo, Roger Casement (the Irish patriot who was hanged for treason during World War I). His report confirmed the abuses. In 1904, a shipping agent named A D Morel formed the Congo Reform Association

Sir Roger Casement: his report on the Congo confirmed the atrocities and unleashed an international campaign to have them ended.

Evidence of atrocity: Congolese, accompanied by a white investigator, display severed hands for the camera.

after publishing a book entitled *Red Rubber*. This became something of a rallying cry, and agitation spread to France and the United States. In 1908, the Foreign Secretary, Sir Edward Grey declared that the 'Free State had morally forfeited every right to international recognition.'

It became clear, even to Leopold, that he was becoming an international pariah. Later that year Leopold – who was now 74 and was to die the following year – bowed to pressure at home and abroad.

On 15 November 1908 Belgium annexed the Congo.

After the rule of the lash: British missionaries, who sought to make good the crimes committed in the Congo, hold a prayer meeting on the edge of the jungle.

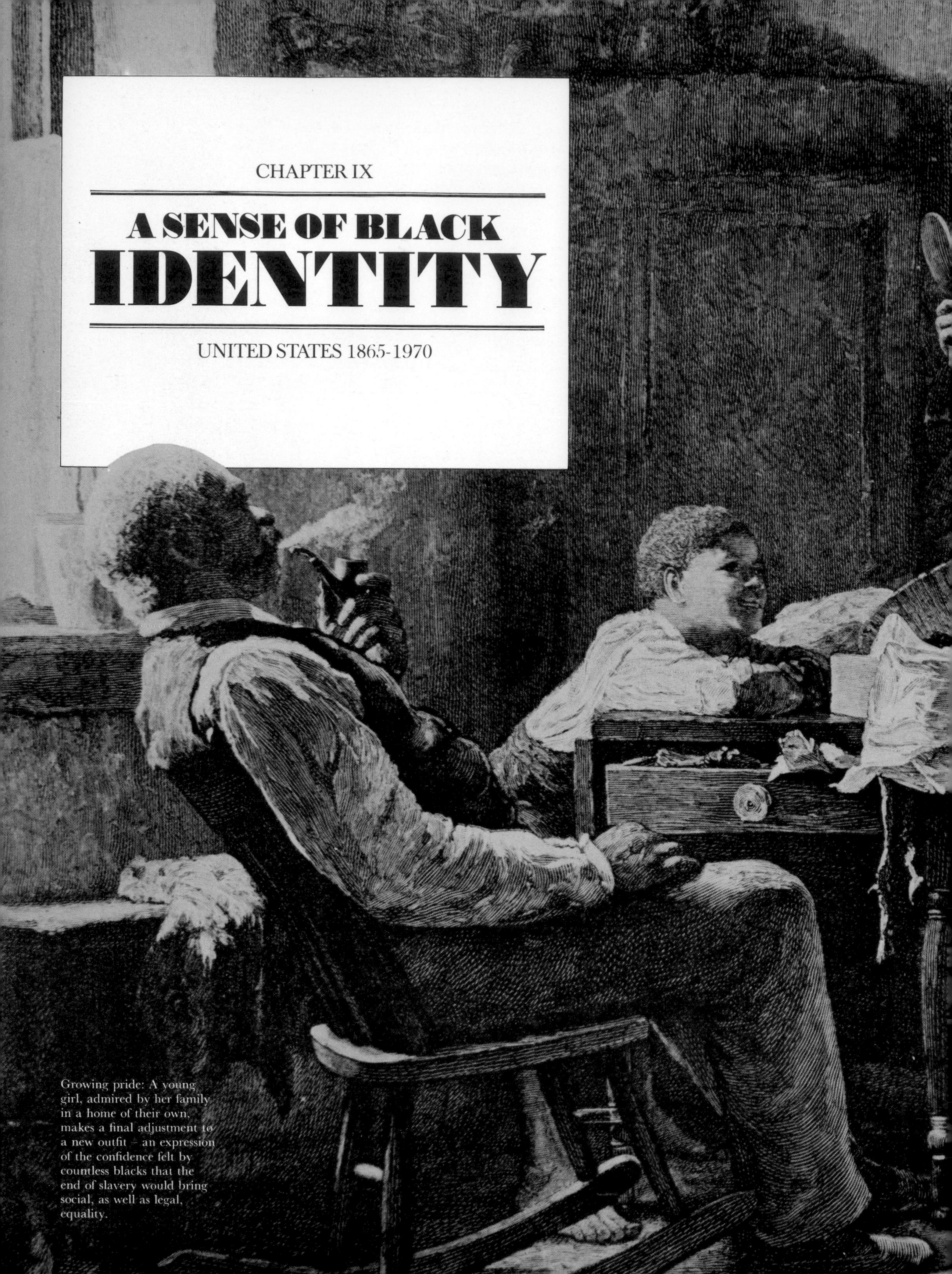

CHAPTER IX

A SENSE OF BLACK IDENTITY

UNITED STATES 1865-1970

Growing pride: A young girl, admired by her family in a home of their own, makes a final adjustment to a new outfit – an expression of the confidence felt by countless blacks that the end of slavery would bring social, as well as legal, equality.

'Freedom is not enough. You do not wipe away the scars of centuries by saying now you're free to go where you want and do as you desire and choose the leaders you please. You do not take a person who for years has been hobbled by chains and liberate him, bring him up to the starting line of a race and then say, you're free to compete with all the others.'
President Lyndon Johnson. June 1965.

The wounds inflicted by the 'peculiar institution' of slavery in the United States have healed slowly; now over one hundred years after emancipation, the scars are still all too visible. There is often little to choose between the emotions blacks expressed then and now.

Charlotte Forten, the highly-educated granddaughter of James Forten, wrote, in the mid-19th century: 'Oh! it is hard to go through life meeting contempt with contempt, hatred with hatred, fearing, with too good reason, to love and trust hardly anyone whose skin is white.... again and again there rises the question "When, oh! when shall this cease."'

James Baldwin, wrote in the mid-20th century, in *Notes of a Native Son*: 'I learned in New Jersey that to be a Negro meant, precisely, that one was never looked at but was simply at the mercy of the reflexes the color of one's skin caused in other people.' And George Jackson wrote from prison in 1970: 'The possibility of us, as persons, misunderstanding each other will always rest on the fact that I am an alien . . . the ordeal of being fair game, hunted, an alien, precludes *for ever* a state of perfect agreement.'

These three quotations reveal the sadness of isolation and the longing for acceptance. For over a century, to be a black has meant separation from the mainstream of society, to be part, as President Johnson also said, of 'another nation, deprived of freedom, crippled by hatred, the doors of opportunity closed to hope.' Black and white Americans together endured the trauma of reconstruction after the Civil War, the Depression, two World Wars and the agony of Vietnam; but the black has in addition fought prejudice, accusations of 'natural inferiority,' the humiliation of segregation, the poverty of exclusion, and the lack of confidence engendered by a heritage of hatred and suspicion.

Looking toward freedom: two emancipated slave children, named simply as Isaac and Rosa, stand dressed in spanking new clothes for this picture taken in 1863, emancipation year.

Emancipation for slaves in the Southern states came in two stages. In 1862, with the war not going well for the Union army, recruitment of blacks became a necessity in order to supplement the Northern troops. Despite itself, the North was, as Professor Genovese said, 'dragged against its will into turning the war into a war against slavery.' Public hostility in the North had, in fact, intensified towards blacks after the outbreak of the war and fear of a vast flood of freed black immigrant labor competitors pouring across the border made the demands of abolitionists for complete and unconditional emancipation a potentially explosive subject. Abraham Lincoln himself reflected this mood when he called for 'compensated and gradual emancipation.'

Despite undoubted instances of coercion, blacks signed up in large numbers in the border states to fight for the Union, and after the refreshed Union army had won its crucial victory over the Confederates at Antietam, Lincoln felt able to issue an Emancipation Proclamation freeing 'all slaves [about a million] held in states still in a state of rebelliousness on 1 January 1863.' Slaves in Union-occupied border areas, however, remained in an anomalous position – Lincoln could not bring himself to antagonize slaveholders in such a sensitive political area until after the war was over. But the boost to morale among slaves at the sight of black soldiers in the 'uniform of their country' was incalculable. As Professor Genovese wrote: 'The slaves marveled at the soldiers' pride in dealing with whites, including their own officers, at their self-control and self-confidence. . . . For the first time they could all see how slavery and freedom shaped men and women differently and yet how much they had in common as black men and women: They could see, that is, a black nation at its genesis.'

But the nation that emerged after the war had to rise from the ashes of a holocaust that stripped the South bare, leaving physical devastation and almost everyone in a state of abject poverty. As one Virginian wrote: 'We had no cattle, hogs, sheep or horses, or anything else. The fences were all gone . . . the barns were all burned; chimneys standing without houses, houses standing without roofs, or doors, or windows . . . bridges all destroyed, roads badly cut up.'

The final emancipation proclamation in 1865 – incorporated in the Constitution as the Thirteenth Amendment – brought freedom to another three million slaves. Four-fifths of former slaves were illiterate, and without land, money or jobs. Many slave owners felt a deep sense of outrage at what they felt was the disloyalty and defection of their slaves – and many slaves felt unable to cope with the unfamiliar problems of personal responsibility and self-reliance in a hostile white environment.

On both sides, however, there were many who felt the struggle to have been worthwhile. Kate Stone, whose mother owned a 1000 acre plantation and 150 slaves in Vicksburg, Mississippi, had to flee from her home in the face of the approaching Union army, returning in 1865 to 'the neglect and defacement of all.' Nevertheless she never regretted the freeing of their slaves: 'Always,' she recorded in her diary, 'I felt the moral guilt of it, felt how impossible it must be for an owner of slaves to win his way into Heaven. Born and raised as we were, what would be our measure of responsibility? . . . The great load of accountability was lifted.' And although there were some who shared the view of one woman when she said, 'If my mistress was living I would rather be back in slavery,' many more felt with Ezra Adams that even if 'freedom ain't nothin' 'less you is got somethin' to live on and a place to call,' it had its compensations; 'it was,' he added, 'sho' worth somethin' to be boss.'

To help ex-slaves come to terms with their new situation, the Freedmen's Aid Bureau was set up in 1865 as a Federal organization under General O O Howard. From 1862 onwards, however, Northern philanthropists had established benevolent societies to 'rehabilitate, evangelize and educate' freed slaves – Lewis Tappan set up the American Missionary Association with the express intention of 'teaching and preaching to the ex-slaves throughout the areas opened by the Northern troops.' Charlotte Forten went as a missionary to the Sea Islands off the United States' southeast coast, and prayed in her diary for all the 'Dear Children! Born in slavery, but free at last!'

All too often, however, it was the children of ex-slaves who suffered most. As one Southern white said, 'the original owners of slaves cannot do without servants, as they have been used to some one and don't want to pay any person for their labor.' Deprived of the services of the parents, ex-masters often forcibly 'apprenticed' their children, invoking old laws 'affecting only free blacks' to substantiate their claims.

The illegal indenture of children and the legalizing of slave marriages were the two most urgent issues dealt with by the Freedmen's Bureau. Others were the setting up of schools for blacks, the distribution of rations, the establishment of hospitals and the settling of freedmen on abandoned and confiscated lands. The activities of the Bureau were hailed by Radical Republicans, whose political machine they rapidly became, as being instruments of, as Carl Schurz put it in a report to President Andrew Johnson in 1865, 'that moral power whose interposition was so necessary to prevent Southern Society from falling . . . into the chaos of a general collision between its different elements'; whereas many Southerners would have agreed with Governor Humphreys of Mississippi, who said bitterly that 'four years of cruel war were scarcely more blighting and destructive on the homes of the white man, and impoverishing, degrading to the Negro . . . than this black incubus.'

The Southern states soon presented other

The Freedmen's Bureau

The Freedmen's Bureau – as the War Department's Bureau of Refugees, Freedmen and Abandoned Lands was popularly known – was established in 1865 to prevent black re-enslavement and to teach blacks how to earn their own keep. It dispensed charity, arranged sharecropping contracts, and established schools. In the seven years of its operation, it also attempted to acquire land for freedmen and ensure their civil rights. In both of these aims it largely failed: pardoned Southerners had their lands restored to them and the whites had no intention of permanently sanctioning racial equality. Here, in a letter of resignation, is one description by a despairing bureau agent in Hawkinsville, Georgia:

'Political excitement is raging here.... I live in continual fear... a col'd man and a white man got into an altercation... up came a large body of whites armed with guns and pistols and commenced firing on him. The col'd man fled, the whites after him. They did not catch him.... This is a sample of doing things in this country. Law, order and justice are things of the past.'

Below: A vicious Southern election poster castigating the Bureau.

Bottom: a bureau in the South: an agent arranges contracts between employers and workers.

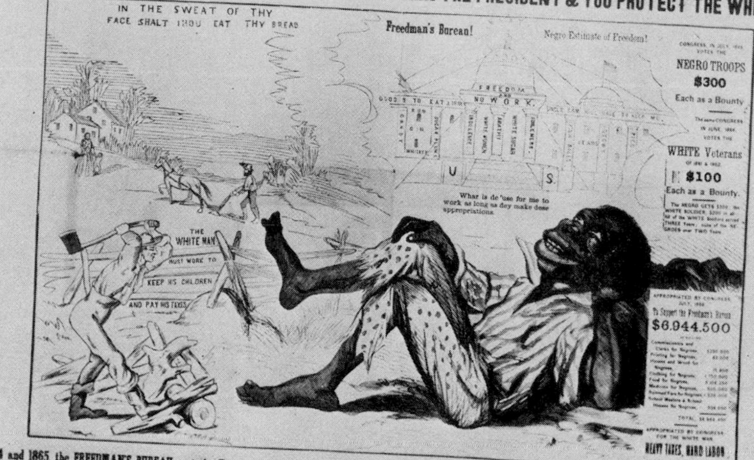

Exercising new rights: Freedmen voting in New Orleans, 1867.

problems infuriating to Northerners. In an attempt to allow former slave owners to retain labor, every Southern State except Tennessee passed 'black codes' – laws which provided for former slaves to be kept as hired help, tenants or sharecroppers. The laws varied in severity from state to state, according to the size of the black population; in South Carolina, for instance, they thinly disguised a system of peonage, but in Virginia and North Carolina they gave blacks the right to own and inherit property, testify in court and to be educated. Nowhere, however, was a black eligible to vote and in some states his occupation was restricted to domestic or agricultural service, which, as one historian commented, 'betrayed a poor-white jealousy of the Negro artisan.'

To appease Northern abolitionist discontent at this turn of events and with an eye to securing the black vote for themselves, the Republican dominated Congress undertook a program of reconstruction in the South, designed to force Southern states to accept the Fourteenth Amendment (a civil rights bill, making it an offence to discriminate against anyone on grounds of race or color), enfranchise blacks, organize state conventions and prolong the life of the Freedmen's Bureau. Failure by any state to put the Fourteenth Amendment into practice would mean exclusion from the Union.

The resentment felt throughout the Southern States by the heavy-handed implementation of Reconstruction legislation was immense. Numerous acts inflamed Southern opinion: the organization in March 1867 of the South into military districts; attempts by Northern military governors to expunge all memories of the 'lost cause' (by suppressing such manifestations of local pride as veterans' associations, or historical societies); the replacement of local officials by 'carpetbaggers' – Northerners seeking rapid fortunes – or blacks; the substitution of civil courts by military tribunals, and the provocative addition of a black militia to the army of occupation.

The final straw was the ratification of the Fifteenth Amendment in 1870, which stated that 'the right of citizens of the United States to vote shall not be denied or abridged . . . on account of race, color, or previous conditions of servitude.' For the first time (and the last until the Voting Rights Act of 1965) blacks had the chance to participate in the political life of the South. Freedmen served on most of the state conventions and 'in almost every one of the reconstructed states there was a Radical Republican majority composed of Negroes and their white allies.'

Although some of these 'allies' turned out to be unscrupulous carpetbaggers or 'scalawags' (white Southern renegades), whose manipulative skills the more innocent black was ill-equipped to resist, and although such uneasy alliances led to embezzlement, election-rigging, and bribery, the contribution made by blacks during the Reconstruction period was by no means an insignificant one. Schools were built, charitable institutions founded, taxation reformed and immigration encouraged. In the decade after the war, the foundations, however tenuous, were laid for the physical rehabilitation of the South.

STEREOTYPES OF RACE AND STATUS

For generations, the public image of the black was a mere stereotype, as these advertisements, drawn from both American and English sources, show. Blacks were portrayed as servants, cooks and entertainers. They were shown as lazy, incompetent, happy-go-lucky and musical. One famous film actor made his living as the archetypical black under the stage name of Steppin Fetchit. In the theater, the dominant image of the black was that of the banjo-strumming minstrel. Such stereotypes, which denied the recognition of individuality and social aspiration, were the counterparts of the 'invisible Negro' syndrome – blacks had little place in history books and little involvement in politics. It took the Civil Rights movement to undermine this heritage of slavery.

Champion's Mustard

LUX
LUX
WONT SHRINK WOOL

The "NUGGET" WATERPROOF POLISHES
THE "NUGGET" POLISHES
Oh de Gemman is "Cutting a Shine."
AS USED IN THE ROYAL HOUSEHOLDS

PEARS' SOAP.
"I have found it Matchless for the Hands and Complexion."

If unable to obtain from your grocer or dealer, send 9d. in stamps to G. F. Sutton, Sons & Co., Brandon Road, King's Cross, London, for a full-sized bottle. Mention name of Magazine.
"Massa uses for de Bath!
Me use for de Cloes and Cabin"
SUTTON'S
CREAM of AMMONIA

GOOD MORNING
GOOD MORNING! Have you used PEARS' SOAP?

Since, however, there had never been any real democracy in the South, the efforts of Northerners to introduce it met with continued resistance. 'When officials came down from the North,' wrote the carpetbagger judge and novelist Albert Tourgée in *Bricks without Straw*, 'to act on their false assumptions, they were taken for rogues or idiots or the mere instruments of Northern malignancy. No wonder, then, that the old class of rulers was driven to restore its authority.'

In the hope of fulfilling Southern dreams of a return to the presumed benevolent despotism of the ante-bellum days, the Ku Klux Klan was born, 'the desperate effort of a proud, brave, and determined people to secure and hold what they *deemed to be their rights*.'

It originated in Tennessee in 1865 as a social *kuklos* (Greek: 'circle') of six Confederate veterans, who found that the long, ghostly Halloween-type robes they adopted terrified superstitious blacks. It rapidly became a secret society for terrorizing blacks and maintaining white supremacy. By the summer of 1868, it was firmly established in every Southern state. The white-sheeted nightriders in their hooded conical hats shot, hanged, burned, and drowned many hundreds of blacks, carpetbaggers and scalawags over the next few years, leaving a heritage which was to bedevil and disgrace the South thereafter.

The activities of the Ku Klux Klan were partially curbed by Enforcement Acts passed by Congress in 1871. By then it had done much to restore Southern morale, assist those Democrats who contested local elections and terrorize those, particularly blacks, who cast Republican votes. As one black writer put it 'Negro voters stayed away from the polls in droves.' Most of the Republican governments were replaced by Southern Democratic ones (Tennessee in 1869, North Carolina and Virginia in 1870, Georgia in 1871, Alabama, Arkansas and Texas in 1874). In the Presidential election of 1876, Southern Democrats guaranteed support for Rutherford B Hayes, the Republican candidate, on condition that federal troops were withdrawn from the South, and when declared President he honored his promise. In 1877 the remaining federal troops left the South, and with Florida, Louisiana, Mississippi and South Carolina in Democratic hands the South was freed from

In this exaggerated view, carpet-baggers and blacks revel in a Southern legislature.

Nast comments on Reconstruction: an unholy white alliance crushes black hopes.

THE RITUAL HATRED OF THE K.K.K.

On a wild Thanksgiving night in 1915, William Simmons and 16 followers climbed Stone Mountain, Georgia, huddled round a flaming cross and vowed to breathe new life into the 'Invisible Empire of the South.' They thus re-established America's most infamous secret society – the Ku Klux Klan. It was the second of the society's three incarnations in the course of a century.

The original Klan began as a friendly club of bored Confederates seeking to recapture wartime comradeship. They chose *Kuklos* (Greek for circle) as the name of their society, adding 'Klan' for alliterative effect. They found their weird robes and rituals struck terror into the local black population, and decided to put that effect to better use. In 1867, the Klan was formally established to assert white supremacy and curb the activities of emancipated blacks by acts of terrorism – burning, whipping and killing. The Klan, and other similar groups, drew the indignation of Congress, which sought to suppress it. Some 7000 were indicted, and 1000 convicted, but the Klan's activities died only as Reconstruction legislation was reversed by Southern states in the 1880s.

Two members of the Ku Klux Klan in their hooded disguises, drawn soon after the Klan's formation in 1867.

The new Knights of the KKK were as committed as their predecessors to white supremacy, but Simmons, as Imperial Wizard, also made the Klan anti-foreign, anti-Jewish and anti-Catholic. He appropriated the original ritual, but added some preposterous touches of his own. The Klansman sang 'klodes,' held 'klonversations,' swore blood oaths, and whispered passwords derived from the initials of the words intended:

'Ayak?' (Are you a Klansman?)

'Akia' (A Klansman I am).

'Capowe' (Countersign and password or written evidence).

By 1921, Simmons could claim some 100,000 members. Then, within two years, two powerful publicity agents and money raisers, Edward Clarke and Elizabeth Tyler, pushed income into the millions and membership up toward 5,000,000. The Klan began to dream of exercising real political power.

It did not last. The Klan's excesses – its killings were detailed by a New York *World* campaign – alienated the public. A Grand Dragon was found guilty of second degree murder when a woman he had attempted to rape died. And the leadership disintegrated in corruption and factionalism: a Dr Hiram Wesley Evans appropriated Simmons' leadership with a payment of $90,000.

By 1930, the Klan's membership had dropped away to a mere 30,000. It disbanded in 1944 when the government tried to collect $685,000 in back taxes, but, tragically, the Civil Rights movement of the 1960s brought it back into existence, and its vindictive racialism is still a factor to be reckoned with in US society.

Klansmen pose for a group photo in Virginia.

A Klan initiation ceremony, complete with burning cross.

Fighter for black power: The uncompromising W E B du Bois was a historian, brilliant author and radical spokesman for black rights until his death at the age of 95 in 1963.

Northern control. As C Vann Woodward wrote, 'the Compromise of 1877 did not restore the old order in the South, nor did it restore the South to parity with other sections. But it did assure the dominant whites political autonomy and non-intervention in matters of race policy and promised them a share in the blessings of the new economic order.'

Towards the end of the 19th century, with the migration of many blacks to the North and a proliferation of small, independent black farmers and businessmen, the white ruling class felt, as Professor W E B du Bois put it, that 'the advance of the freedmen had been too rapid and the South feared it; every effort must be made to "keep the Negro in his place" as a servile caste.'

New laws, drafted between 1890 and 1910, based the right to vote on property and education in such a way as to exclude poor and illiterate blacks and admit all whites. As one black writer commented: 'The result was a maze of voting laws, literacy tests, poll taxes and . . . other ballot box curios that linger until now.' And not content with depriving freedmen of their political rights, the South proceeded to deny them equal educational and social opportunities as well. In 1873, Tennessee passed the first of the so-called Jim Crow laws by which blacks were given 'separate but equal' status. 'All over the South,' wrote one commentator, 'the "white" and "colored" signs went up.' Trains, buses, barbers' shops, schools and all other public places were segregated by law. It was a retrogressive step from which both North and South are still recovering. The old traditions of selective justice and segregation clung to the deep South long after racial integration became law in 1964. The ghosts of racialism are still being exorcised.

Although the origin of the Jim Crow laws could be found in the South's slave-ridden past, their implementation hardened attitudes among whites who had been, albeit forcibly, exposed to change, reduced the possibility of co-operation between black and white, condemned the black to a perpetual struggle to rid himself of the stigma of inferiority and imposed on him the loneliness of isolation within his own country. For, as

Jim Crow: Separate and Unequal

The name of the so-called Jim Crow Laws – which increasingly separated black and white in the South up through the 1920s – had its origin a century earlier.

On a Cincinnati street in the 1820s, Dan Rice, a famous white 'blackface' minstrel, regarded as the father of the minstrel show, saw a ragged little black boy singing a song called 'Jump, Jim Crow.' Rice copied the urchin's lively song-and-dance, which he included in his act in Louisville in 1828. For years, he performed the song with great success, until he became known as 'Jim Crow' Rice.

The title of the song was then applied successively to any minstrel song, to black songs, – as in the cover of an 1847 song album at left –, to the black community as a whole, and finally to the legal segregation of blacks from whites in everyday life.

A minstrel boy dances on a 'Jim Crow' album.

In the corridors of power: The first black representatives in Congress. As a result of Reconstruction legislation, 16 blacks served in Congress between 1869 and 1880. This group includes Hiram Revels, the first black Senator, who served from February, 1870 to March, 1871.

James Baldwin wrote: 'Negroes are Americans and their destiny is the country's destiny. They have no other experience besides their experience on this continent and it is an experience which cannot be rejected.' And to break through the barriers of prejudice and mistrust between black and white required self-knowledge and a consciousness of each other's interlocking destiny.

For nearly a hundred years, these barriers remained impregnable – the Church, schools, universities, the armed forces, all maintained a rigidly discriminatory line. 'The Negro Church,' wrote Louis E Lomax, 'was born because Negro clergymen were denied the right to officiate and otherwise hold forth in "white" . . . churches. The Negro Baptist and Methodist churches are the direct result of overt discrimination.' Springing from the burial and other benevolent societies formed in the 18th century, the black churches were originally a separate part of white-controlled church bodies. Nevertheless the strong folk element, particularly among black Baptists, lent them a distinctiveness all their own, which, Professor Genovese considered, 'saved the slaves from the disaster that some historians erroneously think they suffered – that of being suspended between a lost African culture and a forbidden European one. It enabled them to retain enough of Africa to help them create an appropriate form for the new content they were forging and to contribute to the mainstream of American national culture while shaping an autonomous identity.' It was this spontaneous fusion of African and European cultures, which provided 'the religious foundations of the black nation' from which leaders of the caliber of Booker T Washington, W E B du Bois and later, Martin Luther King could rise.

Booker T Washington, founder of Tuskegee, a black school in Alabama, was an educational philosopher whose views on the educational needs of blacks, provoked criticism from other black academics – notably Professor W E B du Bois. Born in 1859 on a plantation in Franklin County, Virginia, his thirst for knowledge led him, in 1872 at the age of sixteen, by 'walking, begging rides both in wagons and in the cars' to travel 500 miles to Hampton Institute (a Negro college founded by the American Missionary Society) where he obtained his education. It left him, however, a pragmatist, more interested in teaching his fellow blacks how to comport themselves at a prescribed industrial level within a predominantly white world than teaching them any fancy ideals, for, he suggested, 'art and music to people who live

Booker T. Washington, Leader of Non-Militants

Booker T Washington (*below*) was the first black leader of note. Born a slave, he worked his way through school as a janitor and then became a teacher himself. In 1881, he was selected to head a newly established black school at Tuskegee, Alabama. The school occupied two small buildings, had no equipment and very little money, yet at Washington's death 34 years later, Tuskegee Normal and Industrial Institute had over 100 buildings, 1500 students and a faculty of 200. Washington advocated a policy of 'gradualism': he advised blacks to concentrate on economic and educational goals and to stay out of politics – a policy much criticized by the more forthright du Bois.

Washington as a young man.

Classroom learning: Formal, dignified and peaceful.

Learning a trade: In the woodwork shop.

Training for service: Servility abhorent to militant blacks.

in rented houses and with no bank account are not the most important things to which attention should be given. Such education creates wants without a corresponding ability to supply these wants.' With these opinions white Southerners were naturally in entire agreement – many feeling with Mississippi's J K Vardaman that, 'white Northern missionaries who taught Negroes the classics were "ruining our Negroes. They are demanding equality."'

Professor du Bois, then a sociologist at Atlanta University, disagreed with Washington's policy. 'The Negro race, like all races is going to be saved by its exceptional men,' he wrote, 'The problems of education, then, among Negroes must first of all deal with the talented tenth, it is the problem of developing the Best of this race that they may guide the Mass away from the contamination and death of the Worst.' Du Bois's opinions cost him his job – he was forced to resign after various foundations threatened to withdraw financial support from the university as long as he was on the faculty.

In 1900 Booker T Washington founded the Negro Business League – a Utopian dream of a separate black world of black-controlled banks and industries, which foundered largely in the face of competition from white counterparts – although the old-established black enterprises of funeral parlors and insurance companies survived. In 1915 Booker T Washington died 'of overwork.' In the same year the cotton market was hard hit by the boll weevil, wages went down to under seventy-five cents a day and floods left thousands of blacks homeless and penniless. Thousands migrated to the North – Dr John Hope Franklin's conservative estimate was half a million between 1915 and 1918. Professor Herbert Gutman put the black population of Manhattan alone at a quarter of a million by 1930, of which 70 percent lived in Harlem, and Allan H Spear calculated that between 1916 and 1919 the black population of Detroit increased sevenfold.

In 1917 the United States entered World War I. As in other American wars, black troops were among the fighting force (Frederick Douglass once observed caustically that 'in time of trouble the Negro was a citizen and in time of peace he was an alien.') Such, however, was the state of racial prejudice after the turn of the century that, as a Colonel Howard Donovan Queen, a Captain with the 368th Infantry Regiment, 92nd Division during World War I, wrote, 'For Negro America, World War I was a traumatic experience. The treatment of Negro officers was shameful. Negro soldiers were repeatedly humiliated. Both officers and soldiers trained for combat were forced into labor battalions or assigned menial chores. Throughout the war there were ugly conflicts between Negro and white soldiers, and Negro soldiers and white civilians.' Race riots broke out in Texas when whites objected to a black regiment training at Fort des Moisnes and in South Carolina there were white protests over 'black Yankees' in Spartansburg; the 15 officers who passed out of the first black training school at Fort Huachuca, Arizona, in 1917 were informed they would not be commissioned; all black artillery and engineering officers were 'relieved of their commands and made infantry officers. . . . Negro officers could not possibly be intelligent enough to hold these positions, particularly in the engineers.' Strict and humiliating segregation was maintained when in France – no black was allowed to speak to a French woman and French officers were directed not to 'shake hands . . . seek to talk . . . or meet' with black officers, 'outside the requirements of military service,' for fear of offending white American officers.

Similarly shameful behavior by whites towards blacks came to light during World War II. Blacks were excluded from the initial war effort, except in the most lowly capacity. 'It is against company policy,' a statement put out by the North American Aviation Company said bluntly, 'to employ them [Negroes] as aircraft workers or mechanics. . . . There will be some jobs as janitors for Negroes.' Troops fighting overseas were segregated and discriminated against in other ways. For the black soldier 'what rankled most,' as one writer commented, 'was not having to risk his life for a country that disowned him in many ways, but having to *see* that classification by race took precedence over the state of war between Germany and the United States of America.' And significantly, neither world war saw the citation of a black for the Congressional Medal of Honor (although 20 black soldiers won it in the Civil War, 20 in the Indian Wars and eight in the war against the Spanish in 1898).

The sharecroppers fate: share-cropping was originally a device to provide for both impoverished former slaves and impoverished landowners. Both lived by sharing in the product. But both became locked in a cycle of poverty which, for the blacks, was often little more than a new form of slavery. These pictures of sharecroppers in 1937 were taken by Dorothea Lange, whose Depression photographs are classic.

After 1940, conditions for blacks in the United States improved to some extent, but earnings were still lower, jobs still predominantly semi-skilled and the death rate still higher than among the white population. 'In 1949,' wrote Rasi Fein in an essay entitled *An Economic and Social Profile of the Negro American*, 'non-white infant mortality was 70 percent greater than that of whites, and in 1962 it was 90 percent greater . . . even as late as 1952 the chances were barely 50–50 that a Negro baby born in Mississippi was born in a hospital, but the chances were 99 to 100 for white Mississippi-born babies.' Understandably, for many blacks the rate of progress was too slow. In 1954, when the Supreme Court ruled, after various test cases had been brought before it, that 'the segregation of Negro children in public schools . . . was unconstitutional,' and also found the 'separate but equal' doctrine to be a denial 'of the due process of law.' Thereafter various groups were formed to accelerate the enforcement of the social and educational rights which had been withheld from blacks for so long, and to continue to press for the right to vote.

The Supreme Court's judgment was, in

fact, a triumph for the National Association for the Advancement of Colored People (NAACP), an organization founded by the Boston reformer, Moorfield Storey, in 1909, to help blacks obtain their legal and political rights through litigation. But the NAACP, with its emphasis on achieving results through the courts, was considered too slow-moving for many blacks, who were impatient with the way desegregation was obstinately, and often violently, being blocked, particularly in Southern schools.

Two organizations, dedicated to solving the problems of racial equality by peaceful means, arose as a result of more direct action. In 1955, Rosa Parks was arrested in Montgomery, Alabama, for refusing to give up her seat in a bus to a white passenger. The outraged black community of Montgomery called for a boycott of the bus service, the organization of which was undertaken by Martin Luther King, then a 25-year-old local Baptist Minister. Within two years, the Southern Christian Leadership Conference was formed, with Dr King as its leader, which took as its main aim the desegregation of bus services. And on 1 February 1960 in Greensboro, North Carolina, four young black

The march to register: Martin Luther King leads crowds of blacks to Selma, Dallas County, Alabama as part of his drive to have blacks registered to vote. In Dallas County in the early 1960s, 28 whites were registered for every one black. Later that year, President Johnson approved a new law providing for direct Federal intervention to guarantee registration. By this act, blacks were finally included in the democratic process in the way intended by Emancipation a century earlier.

students attempted to have lunch at an all-white lunch counter in the local Woolworth's store, and on being ordered out refused to budge. The storm of sympathetic student protest this action aroused moved its initiators to seek a wider platform, and they contacted CORE (The Congress of Racial Equality) who undertook the organization of other 'sit-ins' throughout the South. By the end of March, similar protests had been made in Alabama, Florida, Georgia, Louisiana, South Carolina, Tennessee, Texas and Virginia, with conspicuously successful results – in August 1960 'it was reported that 28 cities and counties in Florida, Kentucky, North Carolina, Tennessee, Texas and Virginia had abandoned segregation, while on 17 October Woolworth's and three other chain stores announced that their lunch-counters in 112 Southern cities would be integrated.'

It was, however, only a beginning. The Supreme Court could reiterate that segregation was illegal, but it could not legislate against the outbursts of irrational hatred and blind prejudice its judgment provoked throughout the South. For a time between 1957 and 1968, the issue of civil rights seemed about to threaten civil war. The nation divided between young and old, black and white, North and South. Hard-liners cried 'The niggers are in our school,' and, 'We'll lynch them all,' when six black girls and three black boys entered the Central High School at Little Rock, Arkansas in 1957, under the eyes of federal troops. In 1961, 'Freedom Riders,' determined to assert their right to travel by state bus from Washington to New Orleans and use the restaurants and station

Martin Luther King marching in Montgomery, Alabama, 1965: Having done so much to secure legal equality for blacks, he was still struggling for social justice when he was assassinated on 4 April 1968.

waiting-rooms en route without obstruction, found their progress impeded by rioters who assaulted them, beating them with baseball bats, metal bars and knuckledusters, and threatening them with revolvers. In 1963, a bomb planted against a Birmingham, Alabama, church killed four little black girls. The universities of Mississippi and Alabama made extreme efforts to exclude blacks who applied for admission. Governor George Wallace of Alabama's election slogan had been 'Segregation now! Segregation tomorrow! Segregation forever!' The introduction of federal troops into the South together with a revival of the nefarious activities of the Ku Klux Klan, awoke eerie echoes of Reconstruction. And white Southerners maintained a violent dislike for the white Northern liberal supporters who aided and abetted black agitators in the South.

The tide of militancy rose with horrifying speed. Malcolm X (born Malcolm Little), originally a member of the fanatically anti-white and isolationist sect of Black Muslims, founded by Elijah Muhammad in the 1930s with the object of forming a black nation in America, urged his followers in the breakaway Organization of Afro-American Unity to take up arms and 'defend themselves against violence.' Malcom X, however, was himself the victim of violence – on 21 February 1965 he was shot dead while addressing a meeting in New York.

In Selma, Alabama, marches led by Martin Luther King to assert the right of blacks to register as voters provoked unprecedented fury. Three Unitarian ministers were badly beaten up and one, the Reverend James Reeb, died from his injuries. The reaction of Civil Rights sympathizers throughout the country was one of outrage, shock and indignation. As an immediate result, President Johnson pushed through the Voting Rights Bill. This measure banned the complicated literacy tests and the poll tax, and reiterated that it was an offence to obstruct a black in his civic duty.

Yet the flagrant disregard of other civil rights issues throughout the country remained a constant thorn in the flesh of blacks. As Martin Luther King wrote in *Chaos and Community*, 'Let us take a look at the size of the problem through the lens of the Negro's status in 1967. . . . Of the good things in life he has approximately one-half those of white; of the bad he has twice those of whites . . . half of all Negroes live in substandard housing . . . Negroes have half the income of whites. . . . There are twice as many unemployed. The rate of infant mortality . . . among Negroes is double that of whites.' He continued, 'In elementary schools Negroes lag one to three years behind whites and their segregated schools receive substantially less money per student than do the white schools. One-twentieth as many Negroes as whites attend college and half of these are in ill-equipped Southern institutions.'

Out of the frustration and disillusionment created by such deprivations, the Black Power movement was born – itself the child of the biracial Students' Non-Violent Co-ordinating Committee, formed in 1960 under the leadership of James Foreman. Stokely Carmichael, however, elected chairman in 1966, radically changed the organization's image to one of militancy, calling for 'guerrilla warfare in the streets' and complete rejection of integration.

Dr Martin Luther King died on 4 April 1968 in Memphis, Tennessee from an assassin's bullet.

The Swedish economist, Gunnar Myrdal, wrote: 'The Negro problem is not only America's greatest failure but also America's incomparably great opportunity for the future. . . . America can demonstrate that justice, equality and cooperation are possible between white and colored people. . . . America is free to choose whether the Negro shall remain her liability or become her opportunity.'

A measure of how far the United States has gone towards grasping this opportunity can be seen in the progress of integration in Birmingham, Alabama, scene of the dynamiting of a black church in 1963 which killed four young girls. No one had stood trial for this crime. However, in 1970, the new Attorney-General, Bill Baxley, reopened the case, and on 18 November 1977 Robert Chambliss, a former member of the Ku Klux Klan, was found guilty by a predominantly white jury of first degree murder, and sentenced to life imprisonment. Birmingham is now a fully integrated city – that ogre of the 1960s, Governor Wallace, has a black in his cabinet. Martin Luther King wrote 'We still have a choice today; non-violent co-existence or violent co-annihilation.' Alabama, along with many other communities, seems at last to have chosen co-existence.

CHAPTER X

THE END OF THE GREAT EVIL

SLAVERY IN THE MODERN WORLD

An aspect of slavery in the 1970s: Slaves captured on the Nigerian–Niger border.

There was no rapid end to slavery around the world; its control and eradication has demanded repeated international action.

In 1926, the League of Nations estimated that there were between two and five million 'slaves' still in the world. (The Anti-Slavery Convention redefined slavery for the benefit of the League's member states as 'a status or condition of a person over whom any or all the powers attaching to the right of ownership are exercised.') This huge number did not include forced labor. A high percentage of the presumed slaves were girls, sold into domestic slavery in the Far East, particularly China. C H Coates, in his book *The Red Theology in the Far East*, suggested that two million girls from a total population of four hundred million were sold and held in this way. Boys, too, could be sold at an early age – in 1925, the *Central News* reported a raid on a blacksmith's shop in Shanghai, where '31 boys between the ages of 12 and 15 were discovered.' 'The oldest captive,' the report continued, 'had been in slavery for nearly six years, and many of them were in very poor health. Marks on their bodies indicated that they had been burned with rods.' Such abuses were formally ended when the Communists seized power.

In Hong Kong the system of Mui Tsai – child 'adoption,' involving the sale by parents of their children into bondage – caused much embarrassment to the British, whose Crown Colony it was. Pressure from the Colonial Office produced the *Female Domestic Service Ordinance* of 1923, an elaborate four-part document, which studiously avoided the word 'slave' and insisted that 'no . . . payment (of money) can confer any . . . rights whatsoever upon the person making such payment or upon any other person.' Despite these precautions, Mui Tsai has proved difficult to eradicate.

Despite all the Victorian struggles to abolish it, slavery lingered on in Arabia well into the 20th century, supplies coming from Ethiopia and French Somaliland. A Captain Woodward, who commanded a sloop in the

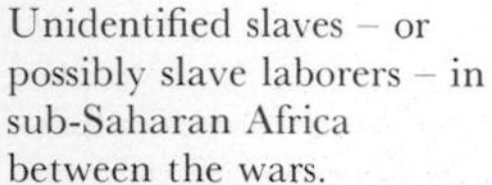

Unidentified slaves – or possibly slave laborers – in sub-Saharan Africa between the wars.

area, wrote of a slave-trader: 'His armed column swoops one night on a village and the entire saleable population, men, women and children, are carried off in chains. For days they are marched towards the coast, through Abyssinia and French Somaliland, right into the streets of Tjoura and Obock, and there shipped in dhows and carried across the Straits of Perim to Southern Arabia.' A communication, dated 10 February 1934 and typical of many such polite notes, from Colonel Reilly, Commissioner in the Yemen, to the Imam, ran: 'I have the honor to refer to my conversations with your Majesty's plenipotentiary relating to the present common desire of all enlightened nations to co-operate in the suppression of the slave trade, and to enquire whether your Majesty will enable me to convey to his Britannic Majesty's Government your Majesty's assurance that you will, by every possible means, assist them in their endeavors to prevent the African slave trade by sea.'

Reilly received the reply: 'In the Name of God the Merciful and Compassionate! After tendering our sincere respects, in reply to your esteemed note . . . wherein you expressed a desire to have assurances from our Government as to the prohibition of the slave trade . . . we agree to the prohibition of the African slave traffic, and we will command all our Amils [Governors] to do their utmost to prevent it in all the Mutawakkili [Yemen] country and ports.'

These sentiments, however sincere, were not put into practice. Slavery persisted throughout the Arabian peninsula for another 36 years – although formally abolished in Saudi Arabia in 1936, in Bahrain in 1937, in Kuwait in 1947, and in Qatar in 1952, it was not finally abolished in the Sultanate of Muscat and Oman until 1970. Professor Gabriel Baer wrote in 1960 that 'slaves are still to be found in the Aden Protectorate, Trucial Oman, Yemen and, most of all, in Saudi Arabia,' continuing that 'slave traffic is mainly from Africa, and there are some private markets. The offspring of slaves and

A slave caravan in Ethiopia after World War II.

Negro couples also contribute to the slave class.'

The United Nations Supplementary Convention of the Abolition of Slavery, the Slave Trade and Institutions and Practices Similar to Slavery, set up in 1956 and to which 84 states were party, bound the member states to eliminate, in addition to slavery, serfdom, debt bondage and 'certain institutions similar to slavery affecting men and women.' But over the last 20 years instances of slavery continued to be reported to the United Nations and the Anti-Slavery Society stated in a pamphlet that slavery, although forbidden by both secular and Islamic law was, until 1967, widespread 'in eight Saharan

countries . . . women fetching (say £150) twice the price of men. Children are saleable separately from their parents.' In 1965 'a public auction of children was witnessed in a Latin American city' and 'West African slaves were being bought by persons on the North African coast, their sons treated as legitimate, their daughters given as presents.' And, according to press reports, 1000 men and boys were said to have been enslaved in 1967 on a government irrigation contract in the Indus, 'some of whom were chained at night.' The 234 officers in the Service for Protection of Indians in Brazil faced charges, in 1968, arising from a government enquiry into reports of the enslavement and murder of

Evidence of a continuing traffic: On the Nigerian–Niger border in 1972, photographer Mauro Colasanti took these shots of the capture of blacks for slave labor. Their subsequent fate was unknown.

Slavery in Pakistan: these pictures were taken in the Thal near Muzaffargarh, Pakistan, in 1966 after police raided a camp at which men and boys – like the 11 year old above and the eight year old in front of the group at right – had been forced to work 20 hours a day for seven days a week on an irrigation canal.

Indian tribes. But, as the Anti-Slavery Society commented, '150 government inquiries into similar reports in 20 years had resulted in no convictions.'

In 1975 a group of experts was appointed at the United Nations to deal only with reports of slavery – the first such body to exist since 1939 to 'implement an international treaty on slavery.' The working group studied reports from, among other places, Fernando Po (now Macias Nguema), where in 1970–71 '95 Nigerian laborers were killed for demanding arrears of wages.' In 1975 the 45,000 Nigerian laborers on the island complained to the Nigerian government of 'brutality and non-payment of wages.' After investigation by the Nigerian authorities, 25,000 workers were repatriated, but a remaining 20,000 Fang tribesmen from Rio Muni work under conditions of forced labor; UN personnel are discouraged from the island and made to purchase a special permit for each visit.

Colonel Patrick Montgomery, the secretary of the Anti-Slavery Society, highlighted the plight of the Paraguayan Indians in a report submitted to the United Nations Commission on Human Rights in 1974 and published in the newspaper *Le Monde*. Commenting on the Ache Indians, he said

that the number 'had been systematically reduced during 1971–73 from 700 to 400' and claimed that the 'Paraguayan Government encouraged the army and private hunters to shoot adult Indians and sell their children into slavery and prostitution.'

It was, fittingly, in Zanzibar in 1964 that the last echoes of the bitterness and loathing of slaves for their masters were reawakened, almost one hundred years after the freeing of slaves in the United States. A bloody revolt overthrew the newly independent Arab-controlled government in a bid by the Afro-Shirazi party to establish racial equality and crush the Arab landowners who had exploited them for so long. The Africans were brutally and overwhelmingly successful. As one historian wrote: 'Within a few weeks at least 10,000 Arabs – more than one fifth of the total Arab population – had been massacred or forcibly expelled. As a ruling class the Zanzibari Arabs ceased to exist: those who remained could be described . . . as a "pariah group" living on "prostitution, beggary and charity."'

It was, perhaps, the last slave uprising the world will see, a suitably dramatic event to symbolize the eradication of a practice, so often declared inhuman, yet so frequently an integral part of human society.

ACKNOWLEDGEMENTS

This book would not have been written but for the help and encouragement of a number of people. The librarian and staff of the Central Library RMA Sandhurst allowed me to borrow an unlimited number of books for an unlimited time. The Staff of the Anti-Slavery Society allowed me to use their premises and pester them with questions over a six-month period. Professor Geoffrey Best of Sussex University proffered excellent advice and Mr Christopher Hibbert kindly lent me some books. Sydney Mayer has been the most tolerant of publishers and John Man the most farsighted of editors. Mrs Jean Fiddian-Green not only gave me moral support but fed my family while I was writing. Mrs Pat Hill typed the manuscript. My husband, John Keegan, read the manuscript and remained, as always, unfailingly helpful and patient. To him, as to the others, I offer my heartfelt thanks.
SIE/RMA Sandhurst/1978

American History Picture Library Back cover, 103, 108, 114–5, 116, 121b, 155, 164b, 165, 173t, 174t
Anti-Slavery Society, London 219–23
Ashmolean Museum 25–7
The British Museum 78–9, 79b, 80
Camera Press Ltd 244t, 246–7, 250, 251t & b, 252–3
Chicago Historical Society 106–7, 190–1
Culver Pictures Inc, New York 112, 162–3t & b, 166, 179, 228t, 230r, 235tr, 236t, 238cr
The Granger Collection 38r, 38b, 38–9, 45b, 68–9, 105tr, 120bl, 121t, 122bl, 126–7, 132, 154–5, 158b, 159b, 163, 164–5, 167b, 168, 169t & b, 170, 171t, 172, 173b, 174b, 175, 176–7, 178, 180t & b, 181t & b, 182–3, 185, 186–7, 188t & b, 189, 224–5, 226, 228, 229, 233t & b, 234, 235b, 236b, 237, 238l
Hirschl & Adler Galleries, New York title page, 118–9
Historical Picture Service 195, 206b
Library of Congress 124–5, 238tr, cr, br, 240–1
Louisiana State Museum 126–7
The Mansell Collection Front cover, 13, 17, 28–9, 40–1, 59b, 73, 88, 90tr, 90b, 91t & b, 92b, 93t & b, 104b, 120–1, 153, 158, 160t, 198–9, 200, 201, 202, 203r, 204–5, 207, 208, 210t & b, 212t, 213, 215t & b, 218l & r, 220tl, 222tl
Mary Evans Picture Library 8–9, 10, 11, 14bl, 20, 33r, 55, 86, 89, 96, 104tc, 132–3, 142–3, 143, 154–5, 192–3, 196, 203, 206tl, 207tr, 211t & b, 216–7b
National Maritime Museum, Greenwich 48–9, 145b
National Portrait Gallery 135, 136, 138, 144t, 148–9, 150
New Haven Colony Historical Society 186–7
The New-York Historical Society 94–5, 128–9, 130, 160b
Peabody Museum, Harvard University 98, 99, 100, 101
A & F Pears Ltd 232tl
Popperfoto 244b
Radio Times Hulton Picture Library 18, 19, 22, 23, 31, 46tl, 60–1, 65b, 74–5b, 104–5b, 104–5t, 141, 152, 161t, 212b, 214, 247, 248
Schlesinger Library, Radcliffe College 164t
Sophia Smith Collection, Smith College 156
US National Archives 128–9
Wedgwood Museum, Barlaston, Staffordshire 139
West India Committee 44–5, 79t, 80t & b

Photographers:
Hillel Burger 99–101
John Goldblatt 35, 45t, 46–7, 62–3, 70t & b, 71t & b, 113, 139tr, 144l, 216tr & tl, 230tl & bl, 231, 232tr & br
James H Karales 242–3
Eileen Tweedy 36, 37, 46–7, 48–9, 52–3, 56, 64, 65tr & cr, 72, 78–9, 81, 82–3, 84, 85, 87, 140, 145, 194

Hand tinting: Susan Wilkes 37
Thanks are also due to the Wilberforce Museum, Hull.

Unless otherwise credited, pictures are courtesy of John Man Books.

BIBLIOGRAPHY

The Ancient World
The First Great Civilizations, Jacquetta Hawkes, Hutchinson 1973.
The Ancient Economy, M.I. Finley, Chatto & Windus 1973.
The Slave Systems of Greek and Roman Antiquity, W.L. Westermann, Philadelphia, 1955.
A History of the Ancient World, M. Rostovtzeff, O.U.P. 1945.
The Mediterranean (Vols. I & II), Ferdinand Braudel, Collins, 1966.
Life and Leisure in Ancient Rome, J.P.V.D. Balsdon, Bodley Head, 1969.
Politics, Aristotle.
The Republic, Plato.

West Africa
The Lost Cities of Africa, Basil Davidson, Atlantic-Little Brown, 1959.
The Portuguese Conquest of Angola, David Birmingham, O.U.P., 1965.
The African Slave Trade, Basil Davidson, Atlantic-Little Brown, 1961.
The Myth of the Negro Past, Melville J. Herskovits, Beacon Press, 1958.
Africa Discovers her Past, ed. J.D. Fage, O.U.P., 1970.

Atlantic Slave Trade
Journal of a Slave Trader, John Newton, ed. B. Martin & M. Spurrell, London, 1962.
The African Slave Trade and its Remedy, Thomas Fowell Buxton, London, 1840.
Black Cargoes, J.P. Mannix with Malcolm Cowley, Longmans Green & Co. Ltd., 1963.
The Sins of the Fathers, James Pope-Hennessy, Weidenfeld & Nicolson, 1967.
The Rise and Fall of Black Slavery, C. Duncan Rice, Macmillan, 1975.
Documents Illustrative of the History of the Slave Trade to America (4 vols.), E. Donnan (ed.), Washington, 1930–5.

The West Indies
Capitalism and Slavery, Eric Williams, André Deutsch, 1964.
The Slavery of the British West India Colonies, James Stephens, Butterworth, 1963.
The Black Jacobins, C.L.R. James, Vintage, 1963.

The Southern States
Roll, Jordan, Roll, Eugene D. Genovese, André Deutsch, 1975.
From Slavery to Freedom, John Hope Franklin, New York, 1956.
The Black Family in Slavery and Freedom, Herbert G. Gutman, Vintage, 1977.
The Story of the Life of John Anderson, the Fugitive Slave, William Tweedie, 1863.
The Cotton Kingdom, Frederick Law Olmsted, Alfred A. Knopf, 1953.
Uncle Tom's Cabin, Harriet Beecher Stowe.
Patriotic Gore, Edmund Wilson, André Deutsch, 1962.

Abolition
The Call to Seriousness, Ian Bradley, Jonathan Cape, 1976.
Views of American Slavery, Anthony Benezet & John Wesley, Philadelphia, 1858.
William Wilberforce, Robin Furneaux, Hamish Hamilton, 1974.
The British Anti-Slavery Movement, Sir Reginald Coupland, Frank Cass & Co. Ltd., 1964.
The Atlantic Slave Trade and British Abolition 1760–1810, Roger Anstey, Macmillan.
The American Slave Trade, John R. Spears, Bickers & Son, 1901.
Documents of American History, Henry Steele Commager, Appleton-Century-Crofts, 1963.

Civil War and After
The War for the Union (Vols. 2 & 3), Allan Nevins, Scribners, 1971.
Patriotic Gore, Edmund Wilson, André Deutsch, 1962.
The Compact History of the Civil War, Dupuy & Dupuy, Hawthorn, 1960.
Federals on the Frontier: The Diary of Benjamin F. McIntyre 1862–64, ed. Nannie M. Tilley, University of Texas Press, 1963.
The Invisible Soldier, ed. Mary Penick Motley, Wayne State University Press, 1975.
Sociology for the South, George Fitzhugh, Richmond, 1854.
Reconstruction after the American Civil War, John White, Longman, 1977
Political and Social Thought in America 1870–1970, ed. Edmund Ions, Weidenfeld & Nicolson, 1970.
The Negro Revolt, Louis E. Lomax, Hamish Hamilton, 1963.
Chaos or Community, Martin Luther King Jr., 1967.
Notes of a Native Son/Nobody Knows My Name/The Fire Next Time, James Baldwin, Michael Joseph
Race Relations in the U.S.A. 1954–1968, Scribners, 1970.
The Negro, W.E. Burghardt du Bois, Henry Holt and Company, 1915.

East African Slave Trade
The Indian Ocean, Alan Villiers, Museum Press Limited, 1952.
David Livingstone, His Life and Letters, George Seaver, Lutterworth Press, 1957.
Zanzibar, Its Society and its Politics, John Middleton & Jane Campbell, London Institute of Race Relations, 1965.
East Africa and its Invaders, R. Coupland, Oxford, 1938.

Slavery after 1865
Heart of Darkness, Joseph Conrad.
Africa since 1875, Robin Hallett, The University of Michigan Press, 1974.
King Leopold's Congo, Ruth Slade, Institute of Race Relations, 1962.
Britain and the Congo in the Nineteenth Century, Roger Anstey, Clarendon Press, 1962.
King Leopold's Legacy, Roger Anstey, O.U.P., 1966.
A Century of Emancipation, John Harris, Dent, 1933.
Australia, A Social and Political History, ed. Gordon Greenwood, Angus & Robertson, 1955.
Aden and the Yemen, Sir Bernard Reilly, H.M.S.O., 1960.
Published reports available from the Anti-Slavery Society, 60, Weymouth Street, London.

INDEX

Illustrations in italics